ONE WORLD MANY ISSUES

NEW EDITION

General editor: Bernard Williams
Lyn Clarke, Mandy Kennick, Graham Langtree

ONE WORLD MANY ISSUES

NEW EDITION

General editor: Bernard Williams

Lyn Clarke, Mandy Kennick,
Graham Langtree

Text © Bernard Williams 2001

Original illustrations © Nelson Thornes Ltd 2001

Published in 2001 by:
Nelson Thornes Ltd
Delta Place
27 Bath Road
CHELTENHAM
GL53 7TH
United Kingdom

01 02 03 04 05 / 10 9 8 7 6 5 4 3 2 1

A catalogue record for this book is available from the British Library

ISBN 0-7487-6257-4

Illustrations by Jane Cope, Linda Jeffrey, Angela Lumley, Peters and Zabransky and Jane Tattersfield

Page make-up by Ann Samuel

Picture research by Sue Sharp

Printed and bound in Italy by Canale

Acknowledgements

With thanks to the following for permission to reproduce photographs and other copyright material in this book:

Advertising Archive: 70 (top); AKG: 197 (middle); Bryan & Cherry Alexander: 120 (bottom), 128; Andes Press Agency: Carlos Reyes-Manzo 6 (middle), 25 (right), 40 (bottom), 72 (bottom), 133; Art Directors & Trip: 16 (bottom), 23 (right), 25 (left), 38 (bottom), 72 (top), 157 (bottom), 169; ASAP: 150 (bottom), 159; Associated Press: Jon Dimis 12 (top left), 12 (bottom), 85 (both), 88, 139 (top), 189; BBC Natural History Unit: 134, Xi Zhinong 135 (top); Bhaktivedanta Archive: 7 (bottom), 38 (top); CAFOD: Jim Holmes 121 (bottom), 124 (bottom); Camera Press: James Pickerell 195; Corbis: Alison Wright 6 (bottom), 21, Chris Lisle 23 (left), 165, Hulton Deutsch Collection 170, 190 (bottom), Bettmann 194 (left), 215, Flip Schulke 205 (top); Daily Telegraph: Brian Smith 113, 182 (middle), 185 (left); Environmental Picture Library: Irene Lengui 124 (top); Martin Godwin: 199; Greenpeace: 127 (logo); The Guardian: 70 (bottom); Martyn Hayhow: 204/205; Helen House Hospice: 76 (middle), 102/103; Michael Holford: 16 (top); Hulton Getty: 216 (top); The Hutchison Library: Isabella Tree 36 (left), Jeremy A. Horner 63, Ian Lloyd 151 (bottom), 178; Impact Photos: Peter Menzel 174, 175; Independent Syndication: David Rose 171, 183 (middle), 203; Islamic Relief: 151 (top), 168; Jewish Aids Trust: 82; Kobal Collection: 162, 163; Magnum Photos: P Jones-Griffiths 164; Mary Evans Picture Library: 31, 32, 35, 186, 192 (both), 202; Murdo McLeod: 77 (bottom), 109; Ahmad Moustafa: 18; Natural History Picture Archive: E A Janes 144 (top); NHS Organ Donor Register: 76 (bottom), 104; Panos Pictures: Morris Carpenter 120 (middle), 122, 126; Ann & Bury Peerless: 36 (right), 121 (middle), 139 (bottom), 196 (right); Peter Sanders Photography: 49 (bottom), 66; Popperfoto: AFP 40 (top), Reuters 12 (top right), 197 (top), 198; Press Association: 84, 100, 127, 129, 182 (bottom), 183 (bottom), 185 (right), 206; Redferns Music Picture Library: Kieran Doherty 158; Rex Features: Bryn Colton 34, 43, 64, 73, Andy Gallagher 77 (middle), 112, Rebecca Cook 94, Andrew Testa 135 (middle), 151 (middle), 176, Larry Burroughs/Time Pix 183 (top), 194 (right), Sipa 188, 196 (left), Today 207, Andrew Dunsmore 216 (bottom); Robert Harding Picture Library: 7 (top), 28 (top right), 51; Science Photo Library: 76 (top), 78, 87, Andrew Leonard 116, Philippe Plailly/Eurelios 144 (bottom), TEK Image 145 (bottom); Still Pictures: Dylan Garcia 121 (top), 135 (bottom) Mark Edwards 125, David Hoffman 185 (top); Topham Picturepoint: 197 (bottom); United Feature Syndicate, Inc. reproduced by permission: 185 (Peanuts Cartoon); The Walking Camera: Alex Keene 48 (top), 50 (bottom), 154, 155, 156 (bottom); The Wellcome Trust Picture Library: Anthea Sieveking 50 (top), T J McMaster 77 (top), 106, 107; Andrew Wiard/reportphotos.com: 145 (top); Bernard Williams: 7 (bottom), 28 (left), 48 (bottom), 55 (bottom left), 211; Jerry Wooldridge: 24.

Dedication

To my family and friends with thanks for their patience, support and love.

Contents

Introduction
One world

Unit aims

In today's world there are many religions. Although each religion is different, they all share similarities and they all confront common problems. People ask many questions about meaning and value but, despite examining the 'evidence' and trying to find out the 'truth', they do not necessarily find answers. The aims of this unit are to introduce students to some of the ways in which the major world religions attempt to answer such questions, recognising that there are some areas on which most of them agree, but that there are also important differences.

Key concepts

Everyone has beliefs of some kind: How do we know what to believe? How do we use evidence to decide what is true? When faced with questions, the impression frequently given by the media is that the 'answers' are to be found exclusively within science. As human beings however, there is another part to our nature – the spiritual aspect, which science cannot easily explain.

What is this unit about?

This unit looks at the ways in which people examine 'evidence' in their search for answers to the many questions that are raised time and time again. Looking for ways of understanding their world leads everyone to have beliefs whether or not they are religious. Some people believe in a Divine Being and state that the 'truth' has been given or revealed by God in a variety of ways: through special people, sacred writings, worship and extraordinary experiences. Some individuals have even put forward arguments 'proving' the existence of God. Others either reject or are unsure about belief in God. They point to the challenges to religious belief raised by astronomy, evolutionary theories and modern cosmology. The question is often raised about the extent to which religious views, concerning the origins of the world and of humanity, can be compatible with scientific theories.

many questions

Despite all the wonderful advances in science and medicine, death is still regarded as a mystery. The one certainty of life is the fact that we all die. Birth and death are the two things we all have in common. So what happens to us at death? What is the purpose of life if death is always threatening? These are probably the most difficult of all the questions that religious traditions set out to answer. In the overall view of things we are unimportant. A bleak (or perhaps realistic) picture is that few of us will be remembered a few years after our death. The major world religions offer a different scenario, one full of hope, of optimism.

One of the greatest mysteries that the world religions have to face is 'Why do people suffer?' Every few months, news reaches us of some disaster and individual cases of suffering are witnessed on a daily basis. People can deliberately act in a very cruel way towards others, accidents can happen and cause unintentional suffering, and there are the devastating results of the force of nature. We constantly witness acts of man-made evil; yet we often see individuals, throughout their lives and despite terrible experiences, acting with courage, sacrifice, understanding and compassion.

Questions and

L ife seems to be full of questions, many of which appear to be easier to answer than others. Some questions can be easily answered by presenting the necessary evidence and establishing what the truth is. It is sometimes very difficult however to determine what the answer to a question is – examining the 'evidence' and finding out what the 'truth' is. For example, evidence for many spiritual or moral truths cannot easily be tested.

There are various types of truth which can be considered (**A**).

A

Scientific truth
This is probably the most established and easily understood type of truth. If a scientist conducts an experiment that achieves certain results and this is repeated time and time again under the same conditions, a truth is established. This type of truth is sometimes called empirical truth.

Moral truth
This is when we might know what is right or wrong but we are not necessarily able to prove it.

Types of
TRUTH

Historical truth
When documentary or archaeological evidence can be used to prove that a particular event took place in the past.

Spiritual truth
This is where people believe in a particular religious authority and follow it. Through their religious faith they discover the 'real truth', a truth that comes from God.

B 'A beautiful world… so how did it come to be like this?'

decisions

It is clear that certain key questions are raised time and time again: *Who am I? What happens when I die? Is there a God? How did life begin?* Questions like these and statements about God and the purpose of life involve a great deal of reflective and critical thinking, but this approach leads us towards an important part of ourselves as human beings, namely the **spiritual** side of our nature.

People believe that being human involves more than just 'flesh and blood'; it is our feelings and emotions that give us our identity as people. Diagram **C** indicates several aspects of our spiritual nature. For some people the spiritual aspect of being human is more important than anything else.

C   What is 'spiritual'?

- searching for meaning in life
- exploring important questions
- exploring and valuing relationships
- feelings of awe, wonder and mystery
- **Spiritual**
- our emotions: love, joy, anger, hurt
- valuing and caring for our environment
- expressing feelings in art, music, drama and literature
- special moments in life, e.g. falling in love, encountering beauty and danger

stop and think!

- **What do you understand by 'spiritual'?**
- **In your life, have you experienced any moments which you would describe as spiritual?**

QUESTIONS

1   What types of 'truth' do most people accept? Why?

2   What idea did you have about the word 'God':

   a   when you were a small child?

   b   last year?

   c   What ideas do you have about 'God' now?

3   Explain why people's views about God may change over the years.

4   If life has a purpose, what do you think this purpose is?

Questions and decisions

D Statements about God

> God is really only another artist – he invented the giraffe, the elephant and the cat. He just goes on trying other things.
>
> *Pablo Picasso*

> When God made man, she was having one of her 'off' days.
>
> *Anon*

> I want to know God's thoughts. The rest are details.
>
> *Albert Einstein*

> God is on everyone's side... And, in the last analysis, he is on the side of those with plenty of money and large armies.
>
> *Jean Anouilh*

> If you talk to God, you are praying; if God talks to you, you have schizophrenia.
>
> *Thomas Szasz*

> If we find the answer to that [why it is that we and the universe exist], it would be the ultimate triumph of human reason – for then we would know the mind of God.
>
> *Stephen Hawking*

E Statements about the purpose of life

> It's not that I'm afraid to die. I just don't want to be there when it happens.
>
> *Woody Allen*

> Life is a gamble at terrible odds – if it was a bet, you wouldn't take it.
>
> *Tom Stoppard*

> If a person hasn't discovered something they would die for, then they're not fit to live.
>
> *Martin Luther King*

> The person who regards their own life and that of their fellow creatures as meaningless is not merely unfortunate but almost disqualified from life.
>
> *Albert Einstein*

> I have come to give you life, life in all its fullness.
>
> *Jesus Christ*

> Life is like a tin of sardines – we're all looking for the key.
>
> *Alan Bennett*

 F Making decisions

In our lives we constantly have to make choices and decisions. Some decisions that we make are fairly easy and straightforward, others are very complicated. Look carefully at the statements in diagram **F** highlighting the factors which influence our decision making. Which statements reflect the way you make decisions about important issues?

All the major world religions have teachings which give guidance for their followers. Although many of the sacred writings were compiled hundreds of years ago, they are still regarded as crucial to the believer's way of life. All have similar themes running through them concerning people's experiences and the ways in which moral guidance can be applied to any age.

Making decisions

- I always weigh up each situation carefully before making up my mind.
- I think about the rights of people involved when making a decision.
- My beliefs determine how I make decisions.
- I base my decision on how I feel about things.
- I'm always guided by my conscience in making decisions.
- I make my decisions according to the rules and laws that apply to the situation.
- In making a decision I always try to think about the possible consequences.

stop and think!

- Read the statements in Figures D and E. Discuss in pairs or small groups what you think each writer is trying to say.

10

Islam

The Muslim way of life focuses on the Ummah, the idea of everyone belonging to one big family. Muslims are concerned about other Muslims throughout the world, no matter where they live. For guidance on all matters, Muslims refer to their holy book, the Qur'an, which is the word of **Allah**. The Qur'an is a full and detailed guide of how a person should live (**G**).

 Muslim teaching

My guidance shall come to you, and whoever follows my guidance. No fear shall be on them, neither shall they grieve.

Surah 2:38

Sikhism

Likewise, Sikhs turn to their holy book for advice, the Guru Granth Sahib (sometimes known as the Adi Granth). Their society is committed to keeping three main commandments – nam japo (worship), kirt karo (work) and vand chako (charity). All Sikhs are instructed to live a useful, active and honest life, caring for others (**H**).

 Sikh teaching

Live amid the hurly burly of life, but remain alert. Do not covet your neighbour's possessions. Without being devoted to God's name we cannot attain inner peace or still our inner hunger... we must be moderate in everything.

Adi Granth 939

Buddhism

The goal of all Buddhist teaching is a right attitude of mind and heart and an appreciation and care for all life (**I**).

How are choices made? How do we decide what is right and wrong? For most religious people there is a clear relationship between what they believe and how they behave. Most Christians, for example, in making moral choices will look for guidance to the Bible, the official teachings of their Church and the advice of other people who are important in their lives.

The choices we make are normally based on our moral values. For some, these values come from religion. For others, a particular course of action will be based on what they consider to be right and wrong behaviour – a moral code. **Morality** is concerned with right and wrong but sometimes there can be a conflict because we know what the 'right' course of action is but it conflicts with what we really want to do. Here our 'conscience', our inner feeling of right and wrong, comes into play. Religious people often claim that our conscience comes from God whereas others believe that the conscience is gradually developed from the many influences that affect us.

The actions we take can be broken down into three broad groups:

- A moral action is one that is thought to be right.

- An immoral action is one that is thought to be wrong.

- An amoral action is one that shows no understanding of the difference between right and wrong, being based only upon what is thought by that individual to be right for that particular situation.

Buddhist teaching

Let one's thoughts of boundless love pervade the whole world – above, below and across – without any obstruction, without hatred, without any enmity. Whether one stands, walks, sits or lies down, as long as one is awake, one should maintain this mindfulness. This, they say, is the sublime state in this life.

Metta Sutra

ONE WORLD
1
MANY QUESTIONS

The American writer Mark Twain (1835–1910), once said that human beings are the only creatures that can blush and are the only ones that ever need to! Our feelings and emotions form an essential part of our humanity. So do our values. The way we regard people, ask questions, make decisions and search for meaning or purpose in life indicates what is important to us.

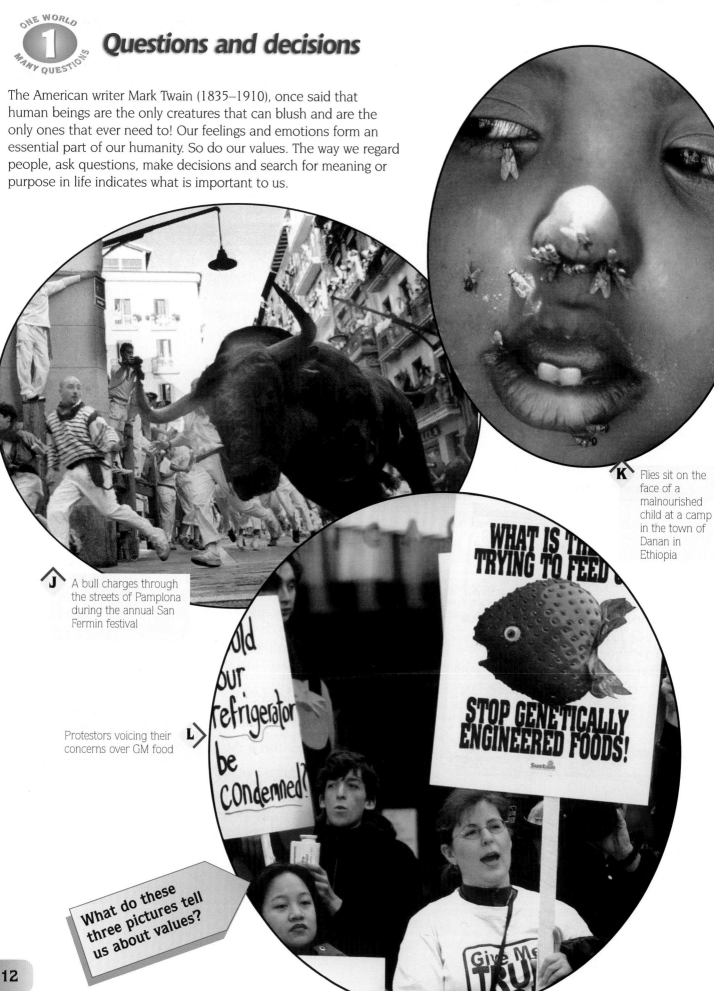

K Flies sit on the face of a malnourished child at a camp in the town of Danan in Ethiopia

J A bull charges through the streets of Pamplona during the annual San Fermin festival

Protestors voicing their concerns over GM food **L**

WHAT IS THE
TRYING TO FEED

STOP GENETICALLY
ENGINEERED FOODS!

old
our
refrigerator
be
condemned?

Give Me

What do these three pictures tell us about values?

It is often thought that people need religion to behave in a moral way, but non-religious people can be very moral just as some religious people can be immoral.

Wherever our moral values come from, there are two main ways of using them to make decisions.

Absolute morality

This is when individuals, regardless of the situation, stick to their values no matter what the consequences are. They believe that there is a right course of action that is true in all situations, regardless of culture, religious tradition, time or age. An example of this would be a person who held the belief that, without exception, it is always wrong to have an abortion.

Relative morality

This is when a person has strong beliefs or principles but is prepared to adopt a different course of action depending on the situation. For example, believing that it is wrong to have an abortion but allowing it if the mother's life is at risk or she is a victim of rape.

Followers from different religious traditions base their moral decision-making on their particular beliefs and the teaching of their faith but, in general, they all share the wish to do what pleases God.

stop and think!

Read the following ideas about life. How many relate to your understanding of life?

a Life is like a present... you never know what to expect.

b Life is hard and then you die.

c Life is love, joy and valuing each other.

d Life is a contrast of happiness and anger; peace and misery; love and hate.

e Life is full of ups and downs.

f You only get out of life what you put into it.

Read through the teachings in Figures G, H and I. Discuss them in pairs or small groups and try to establish how they relate to each other.

QUESTIONS

1 In pairs discuss the following questions:

   a Who do you ask for advice?

   b Do you think 'What would a particular person do in this situation' and try to follow some example?

   c When faced with a problem do you think of different options and choose the one with the best outcome?

   d Is it easy to work out what the outcome to certain choices will be?

2 Consider the following situations (**a**, **b** and **c**) and the quotations. How might someone respond to these situations? Give reasons for your opinions, showing that you have considered the position of someone who holds relative values and someone who holds absolute values on these issues.

 a When a marriage fails:

I tell you that anyone who divorces his wife, except for marital unfaithfulness, and marries another woman commits adultery.

Matthew 19:9

 b Equality:

Men are the protectors and maintainers of women, because Allah has given the one more (strength) than the other, and because they support them from their means.

Surah 4:34

 c Punishment:

But if there is serious injury, you are to take life for life, eye for eye, tooth for tooth, hand for hand, foot for foot, burn for burn, wound for wound, bruise for bruise.

Exodus 21:23–25

Religious beliefs

Everyone has beliefs whether or not they are religious. Some people hold such strong beliefs that it affects their whole attitude and approach to life – the way they act, the way they treat others and their view of the world.

It is quite possible that many of our beliefs are based upon what we think we see and hear. The illustrations set out in Figure **A** are good examples of the way in which our eyes enable us to see yet sometimes our eyes deceive us.

A Not everything is what it seems!

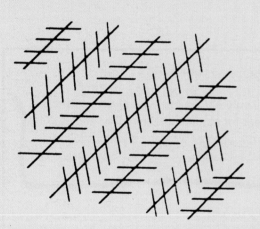

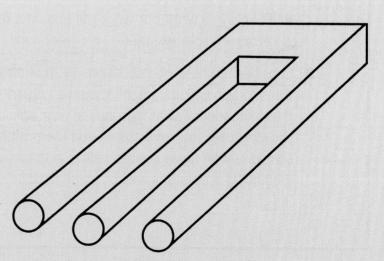

There is no easy or simple definition of 'belief'. One suggestion is that belief means 'being sufficiently convinced of something to act on it, even if we cannot prove it in advance'. If a person has a belief, they accept something as true with or without proof. The word 'faith' is often used to describe religious belief. Faith, however, goes further than belief because it involves putting trust in that belief. For the religious believer faith involves putting trust in a God or force. Faith gives purpose and meaning to the believer's life.

A person may say that they do not believe in religion and that it has no influence on them and yet it still affects many aspects of their life. It has been estimated that, throughout the world, two out of every three people follow a particular religion. For most of these people religion is an ordinary part of their everyday lives.

Without doubt religion is still the most important influence on the lives of most people in the world today. Throughout our communities we find religious buildings and many of us will attend religious ceremonies during our lives. Holidays are nearly always determined by the timing of religious celebrations and our days and months are named after the gods of ancient religions. Learning about the different religions helps us to find out how other people see and understand the world.

Many of the world's main religions talk about a God who is a supreme and divine being who is totally good. These religions are described as monotheistic – belief in only one God. The one religion that does not believe in God, or the immortality of the human soul, is Buddhism. Instead, Buddhists are required to follow the teachings of the Buddha and the idea of enlightenment (**B**). With the exception of Buddhists, believers in the other five main world religions are known as **theists** because they believe in the existence of a God. Those people who are not religious are **atheists** because they do not believe in the existence of a God. People who are unsure whether to believe there is a God or not are classed as **agnostic**.

Clearly, there are many different types of religious belief and it is important to understand the ways in which people arrive at their different religious beliefs. Although the major world religions are separate from one another, they have certain ideas in common with one another, sometimes sharing important links. Jesus, for example, was Jewish even though he is seen as the founder of Christianity. Islam shares links both with Christianity and with Judaism because Jesus and Abraham are respected as important prophets. A Muslim never refers simply to 'Jesus', but always adds the phrase 'upon him be peace'. The Qur'an confirms his virgin birth, and a special surah of the Qur'an is entitled 'Mary' (**C**).

B Statue of Buddha

C Muslim teaching

'Behold!' The angels said: 'O Mary! Allah has chosen you, and purified you – chosen you above the women of all nations... Allah gives you glad tidings of a Word from Him: his name will be Christ Jesus. The son of Mary, held in honour in this world and the Hereafter and of (the company of) those nearest to Allah. He shall speak to the people in childhood and in maturity. And he shall be (of the company) of the righteous.'

Surah 3:42 and 45–46

Whoever believes that there is none worthy of worship but Allah, alone without partner, that Muhammad is His messenger, that Jesus is the servant and messenger of Allah, His word which He bestowed on Mary and a spirit proceeding from Him, and that Paradise and Hell are true, shall be received by Allah into Heaven.

A Hadith from the collections of al Bukhari

Religious beliefs

As well as similarities, however, there are also some important differences. Some followers of Islam, Judaism and Sikhism have difficulty in understanding that Christianity and Hinduism are monotheistic religions. A casual observer of Hinduism could easily assume that followers worship many gods. What they fail to recognise is that although there are lots of gods in Hinduism they are all aspects of one God, Brahman. Basically Brahman has taken three main forms which together are known as the Trimurti – Brahma, the Creator-God, Vishnu, the preserver and maintainer of life, and Shiva, the god of life, death and rebirth (**D**).

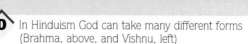
D In Hinduism God can take many different forms (Brahma, above, and Vishnu, left)

Similarly the Christian belief in the Trinity, that God is three persons – the Father, the Son and the Holy Spirit – leads to much confusion. Perhaps it is easier to think of God as having three roles rather than being three different people. (**E**).

E Christian teaching

We believe in the Holy Spirit, the Lord, the giver of life, who proceeds from the Father and the Son. With the Father and the Son he is worshipped and glorified. He has spoken through the Prophets.

The Nicene Creed

So the Father is God, the Son is God: and the Holy Spirit is God. So likewise the Father is Lord, the Son is Lord: and the Holy Spirit is Lord. And yet not three Lords: but one Lord.

The Athanasian Creed

1 What do the following words mean:

   a theist?

   b monotheist?

   c atheist?

   d agnostic?

2 What links Islam with Judaism and Christianity?

3 What phrase do Muslims always add when referring to Jesus or Muhammad?

4 Briefly describe one certain idea that Islam, Sikhism and Judaism have in common.

5 Why would some religious followers have difficulty in describing Hinduism and Christianity as monotheistic religions?

It is impossible to describe God. Some religions talk of God in **impersonal** terms, as mysterious and unknowable, whereas others feel that God is close and **personal**. To describe God as personal, like a human being, is limiting. The attempts to describe a personal God are based on human characteristics and God must be much more than this. Although certain aspects of God can be understood, it is impossible to understand something that is much greater than ourselves. These ideas raise many questions for followers of particular religious traditions. Is God a 'person' like other human beings? If so, how can God be everywhere at the same time, caring for everyone, answering prayers? Others talk of God in impersonal terms but there are problems here too. Is God an impersonal 'spirit'? If so, can humans have a meaningful relationship with God?

Christianity, Judaism and Islam describe God as both **immanent** and **transcendent**. An immanent God is 'present in the universe', a part of human life and acting in human affairs. God is ever-present everywhere within the universe. This means that God can act in the course of human history. Balanced against this idea is a transcendent God – existing 'outside or beyond the created universe', and not bound by the same limits as human beings who live in time and space.

In practice many religious traditions describe God in both ways. Although most emphasise the transcendence of God this does not mean that God is unapproachable or remote. The two concepts may be opposites, but they do not exclude each other.

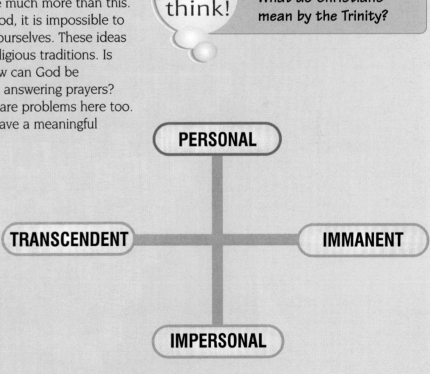

stop and think! • What do Christians mean by the Trinity?

PERSONAL

TRANSCENDENT — IMMANENT

IMPERSONAL

stop and think! • 'I do not believe in religion and it has no influence on me.' How could you explain to this person that, no matter what they believe, religion still affects many aspects of their life?

Religious beliefs

stop and think!

• Many religions forbid drawings or images of God. Why do you think this is?

God is far beyond our thoughts and experiences yet some religions attempt descriptions and there have been many different representations of God in art. The Hindu religion, for example, draws and makes statues of their gods but these images are to help believers to focus on a God who is indescribable. Hindus are allowed to imagine God in any form they might find helpful but these images are not meant to bear a resemblance to God. Followers of Judaism and Islam on the other hand are strictly forbidden to make any images of God (**F**). A Muslim must never draw a picture of Allah. Many different 'names' (sometimes described as 'the ninety nine names'), are used to describe Allah. Not even all of these names can properly describe Allah but they help to describe some of his qualities.

F 'The attributes of divine perfection' is an attempt by Ahmed Moustafa, a Muslim artist, to express the ninety nine names of Allah

One Hindu story describes the difficulty we sometimes face when we look at different religious beliefs. The story about the elephant and five blind people reveals how individuals, even from the same religious faith, can have different views. Everyone approaches life from their own perspective and no one is capable of seeing the whole truth.

There are many versions of this famous story. As each person feels a different part of the elephant they believe that they are feeling the whole object and they each come up with a different idea of what they are touching. The first person thought that the elephant was like a tree trunk because they had found the animal's leg. The second said it was like a rope because they touched the elephant's tail. The third felt a tusk and thought it was a knife. Another felt its body and said it was a wall. The last person laughed at the others. Holding the elephant's trunk they insisted it was a snake. Then a little child walked by and said, 'What are you doing with the elephant?'

Of course they all gave different versions of what the elephant was like because they were unable to recognise the elephant as a whole. They failed to communicate with one another (**G**).

Every religious believer sees God differently, just as people see the same things differently. Each religious tradition has its own distinctive set of practices and beliefs and they often differ in their understanding of God's nature and how one can come to know God.

Each of us comes to understand the world from our own point of view and this understanding will be formed by our experiences, where we live and how we are brought up. Some people are led to a belief in God for a variety of reasons whereas others may believe for one reason. Ultimately the sources of individual faith are a mystery.

G The blind people and the elephant

stop and think!

- 'All religions have beliefs, but not all beliefs belong to a religion.' Do you agree or disagree with this statement? Give clear reasons for your opinion.

QUESTIONS

1 Tell your own modern-day version of the story about the blind people and the elephant in words and pictures. Say what you think the meaning of the story is.

2 The most important prayer in Islam is 'The Opening' (Al-Fatihah) found in the opening chapter of the Qur'an:

In the name of Allah, Most Gracious, Most Merciful.
Praise be to Allah the Cherisher and Sustainer of the worlds;
Most Gracious, Most Merciful; Master of the Day of Judgement.
You do we worship, and Your aid we seek.
Show us the straight way.
The way of those on whom You have bestowed Your Grace,
those whose (portion) is not anger,
and who do not go astray.

Surah 1:1–7

Make a list of the different things that this prayer tells us about Allah.

How God

Long before the major religions started, human beings have looked for ways of understanding their world. They would have wondered why diseases occurred, about what happened to people after they had died, and what caused the sun to rise and fall in the sky. Nature and death were sources of great fear and led to the worship of unseen forces. Beliefs about gods, life after death and special rituals were quite common. Primitive beliefs were often that the world was full of spirits who lived in trees, rocks, rivers, etc. People were worshipping something or some beings that they believed were greater than themselves. This kind of belief is known as animism.

Evidence from the earliest times throughout the world suggests that religious beliefs are as old as human beings themselves. Ancient burial sites were often found to contain weapons, jewellery and tools, suggesting a belief in life after death. Discoveries of huge pyramid structures with inscriptions, statues and wall paintings give us details about ancient Egyptian beliefs in life after death and their mythology – beliefs in many gods and goddesses. The ancient Greeks also had a mythology with certain gods/goddesses controlling parts of nature. One god, in particular, seemed to have control over the others. Zeus was described as the 'father of gods and men'.

With the exception of Buddhism the main world faiths were founded on the belief in one God, who controls everything. At the centre of each religion is the belief that the 'truth' has been given or revealed (revelation) by God in a variety of ways: through special people, sacred writings, worship and supernatural or extraordinary experiences. How important these ways are to believers depends on the tradition they belong to and which different aspects of faith are emphasised. Over time, some find that their beliefs change. Some believers go through periods of doubt, whereas others are very sure of God.

Many religious people believe that God is known through different types of revelation – general revelation and special revelation.

- **General revelation** refers to when God is revealed in an indirect way such as through the natural world or sacred writings.

- **Special revelation** occurs when an individual, or group of people, encounter a direct personal experience of God through a miracle, vision, prophecy or supernatural experience.

In all religions, revelation can provide inspiration and guidance to believers but ultimately the sources of individual faith are a mystery.

stop
and
think!

- **What is the difference between general and special revelation?**

may be known

Special people

Unlike the other major world religions, Buddhism does not rely on supernatural experiences or a belief in one God. The religion was founded by one extraordinary person, Siddatha Gotama, the **Buddha**. He encouraged people to act sensibly and considerately and, in this way, lead a fulfilled and happy life.

Like the other main religions, Buddhism began with the life and teachings of a special person who gathered around him a group of followers. After they had been taught these followers or disciples became believers (**A**).

These Buddhists are praying before the Golden Rock which is believed to have a lock of the Buddha's hair beneath it and was painted gold by monks

Similarly, Christianity began with the teachings of Jesus Christ, Muhammad is Islam's most important prophet and Guru Nanak is recognised as the founder of Sikhism.

Muslims believe that Allah is the 'founder' of Islam. The prophet Muhammad was one of the instruments chosen by Allah through which the religion was developed, completed and perfected and through whom the Qur'an was revealed. He was 40 years old when the beginning of the revelation of the Qur'an started. Over 23 years of his prophethood, verses of the Qur'an were gradually revealed to Muhammad. The guidance of the Qur'an was memorised and written down to make sure that it stayed in its original form (**B**).

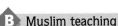
B   Muslim teaching

This day have I perfected your religion for you, completed my favour upon you, and have chosen for you Islam as your religion.

Surah 5:3

Muhammad is no more than a Messenger: many were the Messengers that passed away before him. If he died or were slain, will you then turn back on your heels? If any did turn back on his heels, not the least harm will he do to Allah; But Allah (on the other hand) will swiftly reward those who (serve him) with gratitude.

Surah 3:144

How God may be known

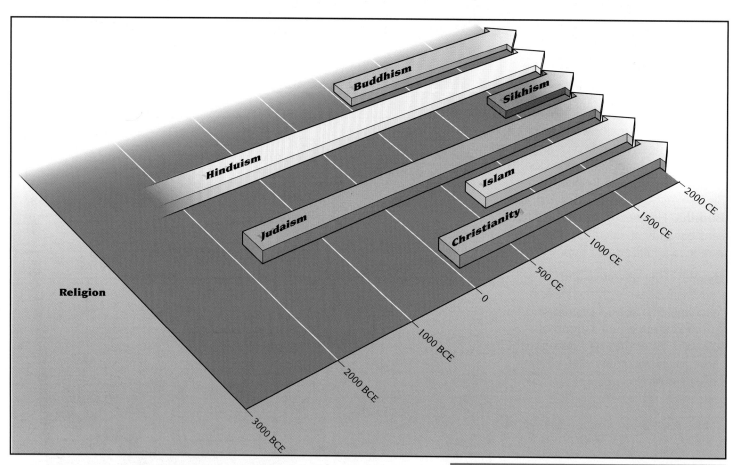

Time-chart showing Religion against dates: Hinduism, Judaism, Buddhism, Christianity, Sikhism, Islam; dates 3000 BCE, 2000 BCE, 1000 BCE, 0, 500 CE, 1000 CE, 1500 CE, 2000 CE.

D Christian teaching

While they were eating, Jesus took bread, gave thanks and broke it, and gave it to his disciples, saying, 'Take and eat; this is my body.' Then he took the cup, gave thanks and offered it to them, saying, 'Drink from it, all of you. This is my blood of the covenant, which is poured out for many for the forgiveness of sins.'

Matthew 26:26–28

When the day of Pentecost came, they were all together in one place. Suddenly a sound like the blowing of a violent wind came from heaven and filled the whole house where they were sitting. They saw what seemed to be tongues of fire that separated and came to rest on each of them. All of them were filled with the Holy Spirit and began to speak in other tongues as the Spirit enabled them.

Acts 2:1–4

Worship

In worship people feel closer to God. All the religions have different forms of formal and informal worship which can include special rituals and ceremonies as well as meditation, prayers, singing, and pilgrimages (**E**, **F**, **I** and **J**).

Although certain Christian denominations celebrate the event in different ways, one of the central acts of formal worship is through the communion service. This is when believers are reminded of the Last Supper that Jesus shared with his disciples before being arrested and executed. Christians believe that after Jesus had been put to death he was resurrected and appeared to his remaining disciples. After he was taken up to heaven his disciples were filled with the Holy Spirit (**D**).

In certain **evangelical** branches of Christianity the outward signs of the Holy Spirit are visible during services. Believers are convinced that God is revealed to them and undoubtedly such events strengthen their faith.

E A **Jain** pilgrim makes an offering to the 17.5 metre high statue of Lord Bahubali. Every 12 years the image is ceremonially bathed in milk, curd and ghee.

Ways to worship

F Orthodox Jews praying at the Wailing Wall that is said to stand on the site of Herod's temple

QUESTIONS

1 What do the following two words mean:
   a animism? **b** mythology?

2 What do you understand by the terms:
   a General revelation?
   b Special revelation?

3 Name the four individuals who are closely associated with:
   a Buddhism? **c** Islam?
   b Christianity? **d** Sikhism?

   Briefly describe the importance of any one of these people.

4 Explain the importance of the communion service in the Christian Church.

23

How God may be known

Sacred writings

All six major world religions have sacred scriptures – holy books which have been carefully preserved and which contain special teachings particular to that faith. As believers read these writings they often feel inspiration or comfort and are given guidance. Some sacred writings such as the Christian Bible, the **Tenakh**, the Guru Granth Sahib and the Qur'an record what God has done but also contain revelations from God.

The sacred writings of Sikhism are contained in two books: the Guru Granth Sahib and the Dasam Granth. All Sikhs are guided by the words of the ten human Gurus (teachers or holy men) which were written down and set out in the Adi Granth or as it is better known today, the Guru Granth Sahib. This holy book is the focal point in a **gurdwara** and it is treated with the greatest possible respect and care. While everyone sits on the ground, it is enthroned with a canopy over it. If it is moved it is carried above the heads of the worshippers (**G**).

The Guru Granth Sahib is consulted for all matters relating to Sikh faith and worship. It is composed of 1,430 pages of poems and hymns which are placed in 31 sections. Each section begins with the Mool Mantra which is sung at both the morning and evening services in the gurdwara. The most important part of the Guru Granth Sahib is the Japji Sahib, a poem written by Guru Nanak, the founder of Sikhism. It is the only hymn that is recited, never sung (**H**).

Sikhs, just like other religious followers, believe that their Holy Scriptures contain important teachings. The sacred texts tell them about the nature of God and give them guidance about how they should live.

G The honoured status of the Guru Granth Sahib – it is carried above the worshippers' heads and a follower waves a chauri (fan) over it. In India, as a sign of respect, chauris are waved over the heads of important individuals.

stop and think!

- What does the treatment of the Guru Granth Sahib suggest about its importance to Sikhs?

- Explain the importance of the Mool Mantra and the Japji Sahib.

H Sikh teaching

There is one God
His name is Truth.
The all-pervading Creator
Without fear and without hatred,
Immortal, unborn, self-existent,
By grace, the Enlightener,
True in the beginning, true throughout the ages,
True even now, Nanak, and forever shall be true.

The Mool Mantra

So pure is God's name,
Whoever obeys God knows the pleasure of it in his own heart.
When the hands are covered in dirt,
You remove it by washing with water.
When the clothes are dirty,
You clean them by washing with soap.
So when the mind is defiled by sin,
It is cleansed by the love of God's Name.

The Japji Sahib

I To bathe in the Ganges at Benares is said to wash away all bad deeds

J The shrine at Lourdes draws over two million Christian pilgrims every year

Extraordinary events

Some people have experiences which they believe make God's power and love very real to them. Experiences such as miracles, visions, and answers to prayers can change an individual's faith and life (**I** and **J**).

Every year millions of Christian pilgrims travel to Lourdes. This French town has become a place of pilgrimage because it is believed that in 1858, a young girl, Bernadette Soubirous, had a series of visions of the Virgin Mary. Over the years, many individuals have claimed to have been healed of illnesses/disabilities by bathing in the spring waters near to where the appearances took place. Some of the 'healings' have been verified by medical experts who cannot explain how they happened. Various explanations have been put forward to explain these events but the individuals concerned are convinced that they experienced a miracle that transformed their life.

In India many rivers are regarded as 'life-giving' and the most holy one is the River Ganges. Hindus believe that by bathing in the sacred waters of the Ganges all bad deeds are washed away. When Hindus die they are cremated and their ashes may be scattered on the Ganges or some other holy river. Hindus will visit places associated with particular gods and make offerings in the hope that their wishes will be fulfilled.

stop and think!
- 'Miracles don't happen nowadays.' Do you agree? Give reasons for your answer, showing that you have considered other points of view.

QUESTIONS

1 What reason would a Hindu give for making a pilgrimage to the Ganges?

2 Describe a religious experience. Explain how it might lead someone to believe in God.

3 Describe two types of religious experience.

4 What makes a place into a centre of religious pilgrimage? Give examples.

The case for God

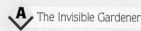

Two people look at a garden. Among the weeds there are lots of flowers and plants growing very well. One person says, 'A gardener must be looking after this plot.' The other disagrees, 'There is no gardener. No one in the area had seen a gardener at work'. The first person dismisses this saying that the gardener must have worked while everybody slept. The other says, 'No, someone would have heard something. Besides, anybody who really cared about the plants would have cleared those weeds'. They examine the garden very carefully. Some things suggest that the garden is looked after but other things suggest the opposite, even that a vandal has been at work.

Still, the first person believes there is a gardener. 'Look at the way it is arranged. There is purpose and a feeling for beauty here. There is an invisible gardener who makes no sound, who secretly looks after the garden.' The other person despairs, 'Just how does your invisible, secretive gardener differ from an imaginary gardener or even from no gardener at all?'

Adapted from John Wisdom, Philosophy and Psychoanalysis *(Blackwell, 1953)*

Throughout history questions have been asked which some religious believers find difficult, perhaps impossible, to answer: 'Who made God?' 'Where did God come from?' 'What proof is there that God exists?' Believers speak of a God who is a supreme spiritual being, far beyond human experience and thoughts. Our five senses – seeing, touching, smelling, hearing and tasting – cannot help us. Believing in God's existence is a matter of trust not proof.

Many decisions that we make are based on trust. Frequently when we make decisions, we cannot prove things in advance. For example, if I decide to catch a train I trust it will arrive on time but I cannot be certain it will. The 'evidence' I use is based on experience that has taught me that it normally does! Religious faith is based on trust and can best be described in the story of the Invisible Gardener (**A**):

The situation facing the two people is the same facing all believers and non-believers. They do not disagree about the 'evidence'; they are, instead, reacting in different ways to the same set of facts. Neither of the rival positions can be properly tested.

One can see from this story that there are those who are willing to trust that God exists and others who refuse to accept this. Any argument put forward to 'prove' the existence of God can only help to reinforce belief, but it will not convince an unbeliever.

Individuals who claim to have had religious experiences are in no doubt that they have strong 'evidence' to show that God exists. The argument based on miracles or religious experiences, however, cannot prove God's existence because such experiences cannot be repeated or tested and it cannot be established whether God was involved or not.

stop and think!

- Consider whether it matters that we cannot test religions in the way we test scientific 'truth'.

Other people suggest that we are born with a sense of right and wrong that comes from God. We can look at the tireless work of individuals like Martin Luther King and Mother Teresa and see how strong their faith was. They, like millions of others, were convinced of God's existence. Does this argument based on morality really prove anything apart from the fact that certain individuals believe in something so strongly that it affects the way they behave and act? Non-believers would say that these people would act in the same way without believing in God.

Despite these problems, several religious writers within the Christian tradition, have attempted to put forward arguments which 'prove' the existence of God.

The design (teleological) argument

In many ways this argument echoes the story of the garden. One person looks at a garden and sees evidence of care and design. The other sees... a disorganised mess! (**B**)

The design argument can be found in the writings of St Thomas Aquinas who lived in the thirteenth century. This argument was developed 500 years later by William Paley in his idea of the 'Divine Watchmaker'. Paley believed that if a person found a watch they would see that its parts had not come together by chance. Even if they had never seen a watch before, and even if it did not work, its mechanism would suggest that someone had designed it. He then applied this analogy to the world, to a designer God.

The design argument appears to be supported by the Anthropic Principle – that certain fundamental features of the universe have enabled it to develop in the particular way it has. If the universe had developed differently, we would not be here. The laws of the universe seem to have been framed in such a way that stars and planets will form and life can emerge. Look at the complexities of nature, for instance, like the human eye or the way in which a fish's gills are perfectly suited to allow it to survive under water. Surely, the odds against these things happening by chance are astronomical. The beauty and order of the universe points to a design rather than simply a matter of chance (**C**).

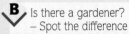

B Is there a gardener? – Spot the difference

The case for God

Design or random?

QUESTIONS

1 Who used the watch as an example of design? Give a brief outline of this 'proof'.

2 Look at the pictures above. The watch shows design but what about the other pictures? Do they show design or are they random? Before you make a decision about the last image turn the picture upside down. Do you see now that this is a designed picture of a Dalmatian dog?

3 'The world is designed so there must be a designer who must be God.' Do you agree? Give reasons for your answer, showing that you have considered other points of view.

The problem is that, just like in the story of the garden, some people will point to the lack of design in the world, to disasters, suffering and evil events. Even if there is a designer who is to say it is God? Despite these obvious criticisms the argument is still popular (**D**).

The cosmological arguments

'Cosmological' is a name given to a group of arguments for God's existence advanced by several great thinkers. One was Aquinas who believed that the fact that the universe actually exists and could not have simply come from nothing was an important piece of evidence. 'Something' cannot come out of 'nothing'. Everything that has a beginning has a cause. Since the universe has a beginning, the universe was caused. Aquinas believed therefore that the universe must have been caused by a nonphysical entity – God.

Aquinas also suggested that every event is caused by some previous event, which is itself caused. There is, therefore, a chain of causes that must have its beginning in a First Cause that is not itself caused – God.

Just like the design argument, it faces criticism. How, for example, can you allow one thing (God) to exist without cause? You appear to contradict your own reasoning. Why should the universe not be the one thing that exists or originates without cause? Why bring God into it?

The ontological argument

This is a difficult argument to understand and was developed in the eleventh century by St Anselm and defended in another form by René Descartes. Unlike the other two arguments it does not start from some feature within the world such as design or cause. It starts by considering the idea of God and states that because we can imagine God, he must therefore exist. Anselm began by defining God as 'that than which nothing greater can be thought'. If this perfect being only exists in the imagination then it cannot be perfect. In other words, to be the 'perfect being' it must exist in the mind and in reality. For the idea of God to make sense, God must exist both in the mind and in reality.

Despite support, all three 'traditional' proofs fail to 'prove' God in a way that would be acceptable to a scientist and they certainly do not succeed in convincing the doubter.

None of the arguments individually can prove that the cause, designer or perfect being were one and the same – they could be three different beings.

In the seventeenth century a brilliant scientist and mathematician, Blaise Pascal, came to exactly the same conclusion – God's existence can be neither proved nor disproved. As far as he was concerned there were only two choices a person could make. Either God exists or he does not – no matter what choice an individual makes, it is a gamble. According to Pascal there was only one sensible choice to make and that is to live in this world as if God exists. You lose nothing if you are wrong and gain everything if you are right.

 The teleological argument even gets support from two of its severest critics!

A purpose, an intention, a design strikes everywhere the most careless, the most stupid thinker.
David Hume, Dialogues Concerning Natural Religion

This proof always deserves to be mentioned with respect. It is the most accordant with the common reason of mankind.
Immanuel Kant, Critique of Pure Reason

QUESTIONS

1 Give three arguments for God's existence.

2 Look at the arguments for the existence of God. Which do you think are the most convincing and unconvincing arguments? Why?

3 How might an intelligent person challenge belief in God?

The case

For Muslims, Jews and Christians there is no question about who is responsible for creating the universe: God is. Followers of these three world faiths believe that:

- **the existence of the universe and human beings is not accidental. Everything was created by God for a purpose.**

- **humanity is unique.**

Islam has always had close links with science. Since Allah is the creator of all knowledge and 'true revelation is scientific', Muslims believe that the Qur'an can withstand the challenges of science. Evolution and cosmology do not create problems for Muslims. Extracts from the Qur'an contain some surprisingly accurate details considering they were written long before many scientific discoveries.

 A Muslim teaching

> It is He who created the Night and the Day, and the sun and the moon: All (the celestial bodies) swim along, each in its rounded course.
>
> *Surah 21:33*

> Do not the unbelievers see that the heavens and the earth were joined together (as one unit of creation) before we clove [tore] them asunder [apart]?
>
> *Surah 21:30*

These extracts show understanding of the sun and moon having separate orbits and suggest that life began in what scientists now describe as the 'primordial soup'.

Without doubt, world religions such as Judaism and Christianity have felt threatened by some scientific discoveries, particularly evolution which appears to undermine the Biblical Creation stories (**B**). It was only in 1996 that the Roman Catholic Church finally accepted evolutionary theories.

 B Christian and Jewish teaching

> In the beginning God created the heavens and the earth.
>
> *Genesis 1:1*

The Biblical account of Creation shows that God created the world in a particular order:

Day one	Day two	Day three	Day four	Day five	Day six
heaven and earth, light and dark.	separation of the sky and the earth.	land and seas, trees and plants.	sun, moon and stars.	birds and fish.	animals and people.

As scientific investigation became more established and more was discovered about the created universe, concerns were expressed about religious authority. Challenges to this 'authority' were seen as dangerous.

against God

The challenge of astronomy – Copernicus and Galileo

The modern age of science is said to have begun in 1543 when a Polish priest, Nicholas Copernicus published *De Revolutionibus Orbium*. The popular view is that he discovered that the earth revolved around the sun. In actual fact, the notion was at least as old as the ancient Greeks. Although Copernicus' work was described as the 'real turning-point' in the history of science it caused very little trouble in Church circles. In fact the Church had openly encouraged Copernicus in his work and he was regarded as a good Roman Catholic.

However, when Galileo burst in on the scene in 1610 with his discoveries, the Church was less willing to embrace his theories. He believed that the earth moved around the sun and observed that Jupiter was orbited by four moons disproving the common held belief that planets revolved exclusively around the earth. Finally, he observed that Venus moved around the sun not the earth. The response to these discoveries ranged from enthusiastic to extremely hostile.

At first the Church was prepared to accept most of Galileo's findings. Unfortunately he became obsessed with trying to change public opinion with his findings and he pushed the Church authorities into a corner with his aggressive tactics and attitude: either they accepted Copernicanism as a fact and reinterpret the Scriptures; or they had to condemn it. The Church offered a third position that was to accept Copernicanism as a theory until further proof could be found. Galileo refused this compromise.

He launched a campaign with a series of pamphlets and letters that circulated around Europe, pointing out how the new science contradicted certain Biblical passages. For example, there was Joshua's command 'Sun, stand still over Gibeon' (Joshua 10:12). Galileo asked why would Joshua say this if the sun did not move at all. Then there were Psalms 93 and 104 stating that the earth was fixed and could not be moved. Not surprisingly the Church had to step in and eventually Galileo was sentenced to keep silent on the subject for the rest of his life. He was placed under house arrest but contrary to popular thought he was still treated very well, living a life of luxury (**C**).

C 'Galileo suffered an honourable detention and a mild reproof, before dying peacefully in his bed' – A N Whitehead

The case against God

The challenge of evolution

The eighteenth and nineteenth centuries witnessed the rapid growth of scientific discovery. Less than 150 years ago, most Christians still obtained their knowledge about the creation of the world from the first two chapters of Genesis. They believed that the account given there was literally true, that is, the words meant exactly what they said. They believed, as the Bible said, that the first man had been formed by God from the dust of the earth, and that the first woman had been created from one of his ribs. A Christian theologian named Archbishop Ussher had even worked out the exact date on which God had started his creation – Sunday, 23 October 4004 BCE! Scientists, however, were beginning to tell a different story.

It was the publication of Charles Darwin's book *The Origin Of Species* in 1859 that was to eventually undermine the argument for a designer God. His ideas were not new but the evidence he put forward for his 'theory of evolution by natural selection' brought the conflict between science and religion to a head. He argued that the many different forms, or species, of life on earth had undergone great changes over millions of years. Some species, such as the dinosaurs, had been unable to survive and had died out. Others had successfully adapted themselves to changing conditions and 'evolved' into different species.

Darwin's theory was supported by the new discoveries of science. Scientists were beginning to find ancient human bones and fossil remains of creatures that no longer lived anywhere on earth. Some Christian leaders claimed that scientists were trying to destroy belief in God. Scientists replied that Christianity was the enemy of progress and that Darwinism made it reasonable to reject theism (**D**).

Darwin's findings posed three particular problems for religious followers. First, the theory of evolution was seen by some Christians as an attack on the historical truth of the Bible. They said it denied the biblical statement that human beings had been directly created by God in his own image. Darwin's suggestion, later reinforced by modern concepts of Biology, that the human body itself could have evolved from the same family as the apes, appeared to treat humans as nothing more than complex animals. Traditionally, Christians had believed the world was created perfect and that humanity was responsible for pain, suffering and death. Science appeared to show that long before humans appeared there was suffering and death.

Second, evolution undermined Paley's design argument. There are just too many faults in the design. Disasters, suffering and evil events all point to a lack of design in the world. No longer could the balance of nature be down to the direct design of God but rather to chance survival.

Finally, when one examines God's traditional attributes – including omniscience (all-knowing), omnipotence (all-powerful) and benevolence (all-good) – one is bound to ask what advantage can there be in the sufferings and disasters throughout time. God appears to have opted for a very cruel way of creating the world (see pages 40–45).

(see pages 40–45)

QUESTIONS

1 What do you understand by:
 a creation?
 b evolution?

2 Have scientific discoveries about evolution damaged religion?

E Life and death in space. The first spectacular image (right) shows a young star, 1,000 light years away, at the beginning of its life. The second image (below) is a dying star with a surface temperature of 200,000°C surrounded by clouds of gas and dust (known as nebulae).

Cosmology

During the twentieth century cosmology (the study of the nature of the universe) produced several theories all of which had implications for religious believers. Scientists revised their understanding of the dimensions and age of the universe. A theory – the Steady State – proposed in the 1950s argued that as the universe expands, new matter is created so that its density remained constant. This has largely given way to a broad acceptance of the standard 'big-bang', theory which implies that the universe does not have an infinite history (**E**).

The theory, that the universe began as one dense concentration of neutrons that exploded and as time went on resulted in the universe, receives a lot of support from scientific research based on observations of the universe.

This scientific 'answer' does not undermine belief in God because one can ask, 'What caused the Big Bang?'

33

The case against God

In recent years, however, some scientists are offering alternative views that could clearly undermine the traditional cosmological arguments. In *A Brief History of Time*, Stephen Hawking has proposed a theory that suggests that the universe has no beginning or end (**F**).

stop and think!

- Look at the arguments against the existence of God. Which do you think are the most convincing and unconvincing arguments? Why?

F 'If the universe is really completely self-contained, having no boundary or edge, it would have neither beginning nor end. What place, then, for a creator?'
Professor Stephen Hawking –
A Brief History of Time, 1988

QUESTIONS

1 What do you understand by:
   a cosmology?
   b the Steady State theory?
   c the Big Bang theory?

2 Explain whether you think there is any real problem in being a scientist and a religious believer.

For centuries, people have asked questions about the origin of the universe. Whilst many people feel that this question is one where science and religion are furthest apart, this is not necessarily true. Admittedly, there are some scientists who believe that when science finally finds the answers, there will be no place for religion. God is used to plug the gap in our current scientific understanding – so called 'God of the Gaps' thinking. There are some religious believers who dismiss scientific theories and insist that God has not left any gaps! Other individuals such as Albert Einstein, however, believe that religion and science have much to offer one another (**G**).

Increasingly today many religions would support the Buddhist view of the world which corresponds closely with Einstein's view (**H**):

G Albert Einstein

 H Buddhist teaching

This view holds that we should not accept any teaching of the Buddha's if we were to find any flaw or inconsistency in the reasoning of that teaching. It is advisable, therefore, to adopt a sceptical attitude and retain a critical mind, even with regard to the Buddha's own words.

Dalai Lama, Beyond Dogma *p181*

'Science without religion is lame

Religion without science is blind'

Albert Einstein

 stop and **think!**

- 'Scientific data is not going to confirm or disprove the existence of God' – *Professor R J Berry.*

  'Science has disproved religion.'

  Which statement do you agree with? Give reasons for your answer, showing that you have considered different points of view.

Life after death

A Mexico – every year on 2 November there is the celebration of the Day of the Dead

China – offerings to the dead in a Chinese temple **B**

Death is the one certainty of life, the one thing we can reliably predict will happen to us. The fact that the medical profession is able to control most diseases and is increasingly 'hi-tech' means that we all tend to view death as a failure. Death is clearly out of our control and we are frightened of the 'unknown'.

Coming to terms with the death of a loved one can be very painful. People in certain countries view death as almost part of everyday routine and they appear to cope with their grief far better than their counterparts in other parts of the world. In Mexico for example there is an annual celebration of the Day of the Dead. To many Westerners this is seen as a rather morbid practice but to Mexicans, it is a positive way of dealing with the loss of loved ones. The dead have not been forgotten and are still loved (**A** and **B**).

The attitude a person adopts to death is often bound up with their particular faith. Most of the world's religions believe in some form of life after death, usually connected with how people have lived on earth and whether they have followed their faith. Generally, the Eastern religions such as Hinduism, Sikhism and Buddhism believe in **reincarnation** in one form or another. The Western religions including many Christians, Jews and Muslims believe in the immortality of the soul and a physical **resurrection**. These beliefs often determine the burial customs. Hindus and Sikhs always cremate dead bodies whereas Jews and Muslims always bury them.

Christians believe that Christ was resurrected from the dead. All four

Gospels record the disciples going to the tomb and finding it empty and then later on meeting the risen Christ. The resurrection of Jesus shows God's total power over death. Many believe that at some time in the future, there will be a Day of Judgement, coinciding with the return of Jesus to the earth – the Second Coming. This belief is clearly stated in Acts 1:6–11 and reiterated every time the **Apostles' Creed** is said.

Salvation is a controversial topic in the Christian faith. Nowadays, some Christians find it difficult to accept the idea of a God punishing people by sending them to hell. Some believe that hell is the knowledge that you will never be in contact with God again whereas heaven is a state of being with God for ever. Other Christians see heaven and hell in more physical terms – the former as a place of pleasure and happiness and the latter as a place of physical torture.

All Christians believe in an afterlife, although they fail to agree what form it might take (**C**). Many Protestants believe in a spiritual resurrection where only the soul (inner self) lives on. Some Evangelical Protestants, however, believe that the body itself will be resurrected after death. The central belief is that after death you are judged by God on how you have lived your life. A life lived according to God's rules will be rewarded with a place in heaven, whereas a life which has ignored God's rules will result in punishment in hell.

The Roman Catholic Church believes in both resurrection and the immortality of the soul. After death the souls of the good and saintly go straight to heaven and the wicked to hell. The majority are those who have sinned but then **repent** and they need to spend time in a stage of preparation called purgatory. Here their souls are 'purged' of their wrong doings and they are prepared before going to heaven.

stop and think!

- What do you understand by:
  heaven?
  hell?
  reincarnation?
  resurrection ?
  immortality?

C Christian teaching

Brothers, we do not want you to be ignorant about those who fall asleep, or to grieve like the rest of men, who have no hope. We believe that Jesus died and rose again and so we believe that God will bring with Jesus those who have fallen asleep in him... For the Lord himself will come down from heaven, with a loud command, with the voice of an archangel and with the trumpet call of God, and the dead in Christ will rise first.

1 Thessalonians 4:13–14, 16

D Muslim teaching

Lost indeed are they who treat it as a falsehood that they must meet Allah – Until on a sudden the hour is on them, and the say: 'Ah! Woe unto us that we took no thought of it'; For they bear their burdens on their backs, and evil indeed are the burdens that they bear. What is the life of this world but play and amusement? But best is the home in the hereafter, for those who are righteous. Will you not then understand?

Surah 6:31–32

Death is not a **taboo** word for Muslims. One of the most important beliefs in Islam is the promise of life after death (Akhirah). Earthly life would be meaningless without life after death. The purpose of Akhirah is to ensure that everyone is responsible for their actions in this life and, after death, accountable to Allah. The Muslim scriptures clearly state that the body must be buried, believing that it will be raised to life again on the Day of Judgement.

According to the teachings of the Qur'an, when a person dies, the soul enters a state of waiting called 'barzakh'. On the Day of Judgement all the people who have ever lived will be resurrected, reunited with their soul and then judged according to the life they have led. Good actions will be rewarded and bad deeds will be punished. The sacred writings describe hell as a place of incredible heat and pain whereas paradise is described as a beautiful garden of perfect peace where there is no suffering or hunger. Every time a Muslim prays they remember that there will be a Day of Judgement and a life after death (**D**).

They know (and understand) all that you do. As for the righteous, they will be in Bliss; and the wicked – they will be in the Fire, which they will enter on the Day of Judgement

Surah 82:10–15

QUESTIONS

1 Explain how the celebration of the Day of the Dead may help to comfort someone who has recently lost a relative or friend.

2 What is the difference between a physical and a spiritual resurrection?

Life after death

The knowledge that Allah knows and sees all things is reassuring to all Muslims. Evil acts will be punished, if not in this world, then in the next. The Qur'an makes clear how easy it is for Allah to resurrect human beings after death: 'Does man think that we cannot assemble his bones? No, we are able to put together in perfect order the very tips of his fingers.' (*Surah* 75:3–4) Interestingly, even though this verse was written over 1,400 years ago it refers to the individuality of finger-prints.

Hindus and Sikhs believe in reincarnation, a continuous cycle of life and death. Hindus believe that death is not the end but merely the separation of the soul (the jiva) from the body, the moment before a new life begins (**E**).

Cremation allows the soul to be released and proceed to its next life. The soul (Atman) is immortal but is continually reborn in a different body, either human or animal.

The law of **karma** states that anything a person does, thinks or says has an impact on others as well as them. Any actions, good or bad, in their previous life can affect an individual in this life or the next. Consequently, the individual is responsible for his/her present condition and future re-birth.

E The Hindu cycle of birth and death

F A funeral pyre is built near the banks of a river in India

Hindus believe that the last stage in a person's life should be spent in preparing for death. At this stage all family responsibilities should be over and a person can concentrate on spiritual matters. The cycle of birth, death and rebirth is eventually broken so the individual is spiritually liberated (Moksha) and can be united with the one great eternal spirit of the universe, Brahman (**G**).

Like the Hindu and Sikh religions, Buddhists believe in the law of karma but take a different view regarding reincarnation or rebirth. The Buddha did not believe that the soul was immortal moving from one life to another. Instead, he thought that all things are constantly re-becoming, they are not fixed. A good example of this is to imagine using a candle to light another candle. The result is two different flames but the second is the result of the first.

Death might be seen, by some, to be a taboo but worldwide, the majority of people do not view it as a tragedy, merely a part of life. Religious beliefs in life after death give meaning and purpose to the present life. Followers of particular faiths believe in a human life on earth and an eternal life that follows. A good life on earth will be rewarded in the after life.

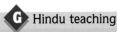 **Hindu teaching**

Atman is not born and never dies. It is eternal, everlasting and ancient. It is not destroyed when the body dies. If a man knows for certain atman is constant and exists eternally, how can that man kill anyone or cause anyone's death? As a person puts on new garments, giving up old ones, the soul similarly accepts new material bodies, giving up the old and useless ones.

Bhagavad Gita 2:21–22

Great souls who have become one with Me have reached the highest good. They do not undergo rebirth, a condition which is impermanent and full of pain and suffering.

Bhagavad Gita 8:15

 stop and think!

- **Why do Hindus think that the way they live will affect what happens to them after death?**
- **Why do you think that most religions emphasise the severe side of God's character as well as the loving and forgiving side?**

1 Can you spot two similarities between the Christian and Muslim ideas about life after death?

2 Match the tops and tails of these sentences and copy them down.

In the Christian faith the emphasis is upon *immortality of the soul and a physical resurrection*

Western religions believe in the *Christ's resurrection from the dead*

Purgatory is *the promise of life after death*

Hindus and Sikhs always *cremate their dead*

Akhirah is *a stage of preparation before going to heaven*

3 State why Hindus almost welcome death and how this affects their funeral customs.

4 What is the main difference between the Hindu and Buddhist views of what happens after death?

5 'Once you're dead, you're dead. There can be no life after death.' How far do you agree with this statement? Give reasons to support your answer and show that you have thought about different points of view.

Evil and

Throughout the course of history countless millions of human beings have been uprooted, enslaved or killed. Today, wars are ongoing, famine and drought continue to take an enormous toll, and human misery can be seen clearly written on the faces of millions of innocent victims (**A** and **B**).

A Image of war

B Scratching in the dust for a grain of food

suffering

Evil and suffering are often linked together because evil always creates suffering. It is important, however, to be clear that suffering is not always evil. A severe toothache causes suffering but is not evil, in fact it can be an early warning of much greater problems like an abscess. When we talk about evil it is also important to consider how much suffering is caused by humans and how much is caused by nature (**C**):

Two categories of
EVIL

C Two categories of evil

Natural evil

The suffering caused by the laws of nature which are out of our control. For example, a volcanic eruption causing destruction of land, property and lives.

Moral evil

The suffering caused by the cruelty, stupidity or carelessness of human beings.

Some events that cause suffering can often be a combination of the two. For example, some natural disasters can cause much physical suffering such as hunger, malnutrition, disease and poverty but these problems can be made far worse because of ignorance or by people refusing to help.

One of the most difficult questions that any religious believer has to cope with is: *Why is there so much suffering and evil in the world?* It would appear that there are three responses to the problem:

- there is a purpose for evil and suffering being in the world;

- God does not exist, or;

- God knows about the suffering and chooses to ignore it or God knows about the problem but is powerless to do anything about it, or God is unaware of all the suffering.

stop and think!
- Can any good come out of emergencies and disasters?

Evil and suffering

The last one hundred years have probably witnessed more of man's inhumanity to man than any previous time. In world history, millions have died in wars – evil on a vast scale. Then there is the untold suffering which happens behind closed doors. All this can be blamed upon mankind. We may ask why God allows us to do this to each other. For many people the responses from the world's religions are clearly inadequate.

In the period 1970 to 1985, over 825 major natural disasters were recorded. To label a disaster as 'natural' often leads people to throw up their hands and declare that there is nothing they can do. Quite often, people are forced to live in situations where they are exposed to more frequent 'natural' hazards. Bangladesh, for example, had 14 major floods in the last century. The most devastating of these occurred in 1988 when 46 per cent of the country was flooded, over 2,000 people died, and over 45 million were made homeless. Such incidents hold people back from belief: if there is a God, he does not make it easy for us.

Followers of Christianity, Judaism and Islam believe in a God who is omnipotent, omniscient, and benevolent. To suggest that God does not exist or is not all-good, all-knowing and all-powerful, would be unacceptable to a Christian, Jew or Muslim.

Therefore, suffering and evil must be serving a purpose.

Muslims believe that evil and suffering, whether caused by human actions or natural disasters, are a test from Allah. According to the Qur'an Allah created the earth and made Adam to look after it. Allah also created angels who did not have free will to act as his messengers and some beings with free will called Jinn. One of the Jinn, called Iblis, refused to obey Allah. He was renamed Shaytan ('rebellious one') and was thrown out of heaven. Allah, however, allowed Shaytan (Satan) and the Jinn who followed him to tempt people away from the true path.

Shaytan has not got the power to make people do evil things because all humans have free will but they can choose to do wrong. Adam and Hawa (Eve) failed the 'test' because they were tempted to disobey Allah. Unlike the Christian faith, Muslims do not believe in original sin, that humans are born with a tendency to evil. Adam's sin did not bring evil into the world. Every person has a choice because they are born with free will. If they do give in to temptation they can be forgiven by Allah if they repent (**D**).

D Muslim teaching

And behold, we said to the angels: 'Bow down to Adam' and they bowed down. Not so Iblis: he refused and was haughty: he was of those who reject Faith.

Surah 2:34

Be sure we shall test you with something of fear and hunger, some loss in goods or lives or the fruits (of your toil), but give glad tidings to those who patiently persevere – who says when afflicted with calamity: 'To Allah we belong, and to Him is our return'.

Surah 2:155–156

stop and think!

- Why is evil a special problem for those people who believe in an all-good and all-powerful God?

Five killed as gunman runs amok

STORMS DEVASTATE VILLAGES

Forests dying because of acid rain

Baby rescued alive from earthquake

Holocaust victims still suffer

HUNTED TO THE BRINK OF EXTINCTION

1 The headlines above highlight different types of suffering. Describe which ones are moral ('man-made') and which are 'natural'.

2 In small groups brainstorm as many other examples of suffering as you can think of. Write each one down on a separate piece of paper and then try to sort them out into categories. First try to sort them out into natural and moral suffering. Then try to work out which ones are both.

3 Describe a recent natural disaster. Could it have been prevented? If so, how? Do you think any good came out of the disaster?

4 Some people regard war as the greatest evil in our world. What do you regard as the greatest evil? Give your reasons.

E Continuous heavy rain caused flooding in South west England in 2000

Evil and suffering

Hinduism

Hindus regard evil and suffering as a natural part of life. Ignorance was the first evil to come about and is often the cause of suffering. Most evil is explained by the law of karma – that all of the actions of life today are the result of the actions of a previous life. Everything that a person does now will shape what happens to them in the future. Doing what is good and right ensures the future well-being of yourself and others. Likewise, if our actions are cruel or evil we build up bad karma and we will suffer for it.

Hindus believe that all suffering results from people's actions, that it is an essential part of samsara (the cycle of birth, death and rebirth) and it has to be endured without questioning. The only way to break away from suffering is to achieve the final stage of existence (moksha), when the soul (atman) is finally freed (**G**).

 F Hindu teaching

For the protection of the good, for the destruction of evildoers, for the setting up of righteousness I come into being age after age.

Bhagavad Gita 4:8

He [Brahman] causes him whom he wishes to lead up from these worlds to perform good action. This one, indeed, also causes him whom he wishes to lead downward, to perform bad action.

Kausitaki Upanishad 3:8

G The cycle of samsara

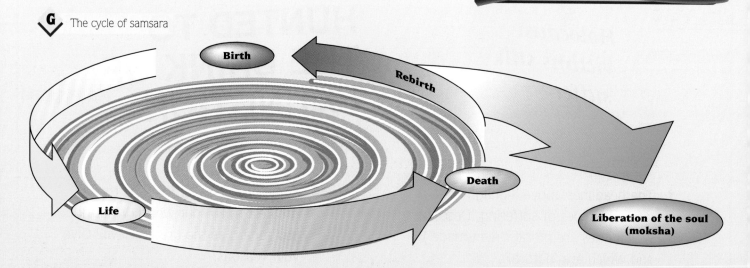

In Hinduism there is no central concern to understand and solve the problem of evil. Through knowledge, it is said that man reaches above good and evil. According to Hindu scriptures some suffering and evil is beyond human control and on some occasions Brahman, in the form of Vishnu, intervenes to restore righteousness on earth (**F**).

The only true substance of the universe is Brahman, so evil cannot be real. Ignoring the one and only reality of Brahman gives rise to karma and brings about suffering. A text in the Kausitaki Upanishad indicates that Brahman himself causes the good and evil done by humans, and so he must be the one responsible for the origin of karma (**F**).

In the Buddhist and Hindu traditions, suffering arises from ignorance and followers are taught a way of living in order to overcome it. In Hinduism the gods are neither all-powerful nor are they depicted as good, that is, personally committed to the well-being and happiness of their worshippers.

stop and think!

- Is the law of karma just? Does the karma law encourage people to live good lives?

- Would you be content to have your life governed by the karma law?

- If someone suffers from ill-health do you think that this is a result of their bad karma?

Christianity

Suffering does not present a problem to the Hindu or Buddhist, but if the religion under scrutiny is Christianity there is no doubt that suffering and evil can appear to be powerful obstacles to faith. Christians – along with Jews and Muslims – believe in a God who is both all-powerful and good. How, then, do they square what their faith teaches about God's nature with what they see in the news and experience in their own lives?

Within Christianity there are two main approaches to the problem. St Augustine of Hippo, writing in the fourth century CE proposed the traditional view held in the Christian Church that suffering was God's punishment for Adam's disobedience and sin. St Irenaeus, writing 200 years earlier, believed that only in a world where there is a struggle for the good, can we freely choose God. Irenaeus did not believe that man was created by God in a perfect state and then deliberately sinned, but rather regarded man as still in the process of creation. God deliberately created a world full of hardships and suffering because this is the only sort of world where we can freely develop faith, where we struggle to become 'children of God'.

More recently, a third approach to the problem has been suggested. 'Process theology' proposes a concept of God that is limited in power, who is not in total control. This view is not easily accepted by the majority of Christians because it limits God's omnipotence. Some thinkers have even suggested that perhaps God is not all-loving – that there is a 'dark side' to God. Again, this view is unacceptable to most Christian believers.

There is no doubt that being a Christian involves sacrifice and suffering. In the end the majority of Christians accept that suffering is a mystery. Although Christians endure many hardships and do not always understand why they are suffering, they should always remember that Jesus promised his help and power in order to conquer evil (**H**).

 Christian teaching

Then Jesus said to his disciples, 'If anyone would come after me, he must deny himself and take up his cross and follow me. For whoever wants to save his life will lose it, but whoever loses his life for me will find it'.

Matthew 16:24–25

I consider that our present sufferings are not worth comparing with the glory that will be revealed in us… For I am convinced that neither death nor life, neither angels nor demons, neither present nor the future, nor any powers, neither height, nor depth, nor anything else in all creation, will be able to separate us from the love of God that is in Christ Jesus our Lord.

Romans 8:18, 38–39

stop and think!

- 'All that is needed for evil to triumph is for good people to do nothing.' Do you agree? Give reasons for your answer, showing that you have considered different points of view.

QUESTIONS

1 Describe one religious response to the problem of evil and suffering.

2 What answers do some Christians give to the problems of suffering?

3 What do you understand by the term 'free will'?

1 Briefly describe what is meant when an action is described as:

a moral

b immoral

c amoral

2 What is the difference between absolute and relative morality?

3 In your own words, explain what religious believers mean when they say God is:

a Immanent

b Transcendent

c Personal

d Impersonal

4 Many religions forbid images or drawings of God. Why do you think this is?

5 'God does not exist.'

'I am not sure if God exists.'

Which of the above statements would be made by:

a an atheist?

b an agnostic?

6 Read the following statements and then answer the questions below.

Statement A: 'I am religious. My holy book and my conscience tell me what is true.'

Statement B: 'The only truth is what science can prove. Belonging to a religion is a waste of time.'

Statement C: 'There is more to life than science can prove. People are more than just machines. I am not religious but I think we all have a spiritual side.'

Look at Statement A.

a Give two examples of a 'holy book'.

b What is meant by 'conscience'?

Look at Statement B.

c How does science prove something is true?

d How would a religious believer argue against the idea that 'belonging to a religion is a waste of time'?

Look at Statement C.

e Explain why it might be said that all people 'have a spiritual side'.

f 'The only truth is what science can prove.' Do you agree? Give reasons for your answer, showing that you have thought about more than one point of view.

7 Give three examples of the way that evolutionary theory has posed problems for Christians.

8 Apart from evil and suffering, what are the main arguments against the existence of God?

9 What conclusion was reached by Blaise Pascal about the case for and against God's existence?

10 Explain why the resurrection is so important to Christians today.

11 In your own words explain the significance to religious believers of the following:
   a purgatory
   b Akhirah
   c Barzakh
   d Atman

12 'If God were good, he would wish to make his creatures perfectly happy and if God were almighty he would be able to do what he wished. But the creatures are not happy. Therefore God lacks either goodness or power, or both.' (*The Problem of Pain* by C S Lewis)

What problems do evil and suffering raise for religious believers?

13 Explain the response of one religion you have studied to the problem of evil and suffering.

14

Cancer victim buried today

BOMBING CAMPAIGN GROWING

RAIL DISASTER – 21 KILLED

Baby abandoned by drug addict mother

Earthquake destroys four villages

All the above are recent newspaper headlines. Describe the different kinds of suffering in each.

15 What are the three main responses to the problems of evil and suffering?

16 What do Muslims believe about Shaytan?

17 When faced with evil and suffering, why is a Buddhist or Hindu less troubled than a Christian?

18 'Suffering can create a better and stronger person.' How far would you agree with this statement?

Introduction
One world

Unit aims

The strong emphasis in all religions is to regard the family as the base from where you learn everything in life. All moral standards, charity and love start from the family. The main aim of this unit is to give you the opportunity to explore the significance of good relationships in life and the challenges people face in their relationships with others. It is important to identify the responsibilities we have and understand the moral and religious principles which influence attitudes and behaviour.

Key concepts

Aspects such as family, marriage and human sexuality are not always easy to understand in our society. One advantage of holding a religious faith is that, normally, very clear guidelines are set out on the ways in which a person should behave. As we shall see, it is not always easy to commit ourselves to putting belief into action, especially when every day we receive many 'mixed messages' about relationships from the media, friends, school and home.

What is this unit about?

The word 'family' can be interpreted in many different ways. To some, 'family' refers to those immediate relatives with whom you live, but it can also include all those people related to you either by birth or marriage. You will find that, for all religious traditions, family life is of utmost importance. This unit illustrates that the exact form it takes sometimes varies, but in almost every society it is evident and seems to suit the needs of most people.

The word 'love' is frequently used to describe a range of experiences but it is important to recognise there is a spiritual as well as a physical dimension to its use. It is this former theme that can be seen in the teachings of all the world faiths. Alongside the virtue of love is the essential concept of forgiveness.

one family?

Although it might take different forms, marriage in every society is always regarded as a special event. Marriage is a relationship based on love between a man and a woman: a commitment which is usually freely given. To some, however, marriage is no longer seen as necessary for children or social stability and divorce appears to be steadily rising.

This unit is also concerned with ageism – the millions of children and elderly people who are exploited and abused. In many societies the younger and more elderly populations are denied their rights because of disasters, wars, poverty and disease. The world religions are increasingly uneasy because the basic needs of millions of people are largely being ignored. Their teachings are quite clear: all children and the elderly must be protected and their rights must be upheld. Many religious traditions also stand accused of promoting the sexism which is so often witnessed throughout the world. It is an accusation that must not be ignored.

ONE WORLD

2

ONE FAMILY?

Family

A

B

What differences do you notice between these two family portraits?

life

Photograph **A** is a family with grandparents, parents and children, whereas photograph **B** depicts just parents and children. We call the former an extended family, the latter a nuclear family. In the last few decades, two additional terms have come into use: 'reconstituted' (step) and 'one-parent' families.

Nuclear

This is the traditional family so frequently depicted in the media today: husband, wife and children living as one unit.

Extended

The extended family consists of several generations possibly living in the same household with other relatives living nearby. This is still very common in some societies, but not so much in Britain.

Reconstituted (step)

When a marriage ends, children often find themselves being brought up in a new situation where at least one parent has re-married.

One-parent

Due to the increasing number of divorces, many children find themselves being brought up by one parent alone, usually the mother.

stop and think!

- What *do* you think are the advantages of an extended family?

- What could be some of the disadvantages of an extended family?

Some couples decide to live together (cohabit) without getting married. Such relationships can be long lasting and very stable. In English law, these are known as 'common law' marriages. Single people, who can be widowed, divorced or unmarried, do not live within a family community but may still be members of a family, normally an extended one.

Family life

It is clear that over the last fifty years our concept of the 'family' has changed a great deal. It is not the size of the family that is of importance but rather what it does (**C**).

The family unit is still seen as having a crucial function. In some societies and religious traditions the structure has not radically altered for centuries, but in the West there has been a huge increase in family break-ups. Some of the world religions have had to accommodate this within their central beliefs.

C The role of the family

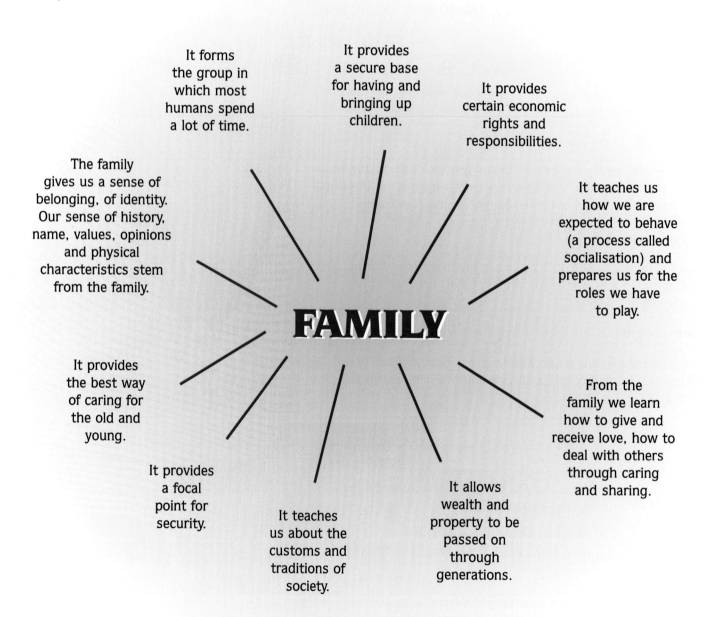

It forms the group in which most humans spend a lot of time.

It provides a secure base for having and bringing up children.

It provides certain economic rights and responsibilities.

The family gives us a sense of belonging, of identity. Our sense of history, name, values, opinions and physical characteristics stem from the family.

It teaches us how we are expected to behave (a process called socialisation) and prepares us for the roles we have to play.

FAMILY

It provides the best way of caring for the old and young.

From the family we learn how to give and receive love, how to deal with others through caring and sharing.

It provides a focal point for security.

It teaches us about the customs and traditions of society.

It allows wealth and property to be passed on through generations.

Many families encounter problems which need to be faced and overcome. Some of these are set out in **D**.

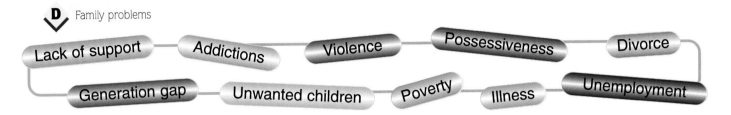

D Family problems

Lack of support — Addictions — Violence — Possessiveness — Divorce

Generation gap — Unwanted children — Poverty — Illness — Unemployment

All the world religions appear to believe that there is a need for mutual respect and tolerance in the family and that there are three main elements necessary for bringing up a family:

love　　　**freedom**　　　**discipline**

Some views of three religious faiths are given in **E**, **F** and **G** below.

E Christian teaching

Children, obey your parents in the Lord, for this is right. 'Honour your father and mother'... Fathers, do not exasperate your children; instead, bring them up in the training and instruction of the Lord.

Ephesians 6:1–2, 4

F Jewish teaching

Listen to your father, who gave you life, and do not despise your mother when she is old... The father of a righteous man has great joy; he who has a wise son delights in him. May your father and mother be glad; may she who gave you birth rejoice!

Proverbs 23:22, 24–25

G Muslim teaching

And We have enjoined on man (to be good) to his parents... show gratitude to Me and to your parents: to Me is (your final) Goal.

Surah 31:14

Do not ask me to be a witness to injustice. Your children have the right to receive equal treatment as you have the right that they should honour you.

Hadith

QUESTIONS

1 Define what you understand by the word 'family'.

2 What is the ideal type of family, in your opinion?

3 Can you think of any advantages and disadvantages of being brought up in a one-parent family?

4 Many people believe that the 'family' is the foundation of society and it is as important today as it has ever been. What do you think? Give reasons.

5 Look at **D**. Can you think of any other family problems?

6 What issues do you think cause the most arguments in a family?

7 Do you think it is possible to discipline someone and, at the same time, love them and give them freedom?

8 Why are love, freedom and discipline all seen as so necessary in bringing up a family?

Love and

We use the word 'love' frequently when we speak, but we do not always mean the same thing by it. The experience of 'loving' our parents is clearly different from 'loving' a pet or a particular food.

The Hindus have twenty different words in Sanskrit which describe love. In the Greek language four different words are used to denote different types of love (**A**).

 A Definitions of four types of love

Agape:

concern for the well-being and dignity of others. Different from all other types of love because it involves charity, tolerance, and respect for all people, even those we do not like. It is a purely selfless love.

Eros:

the love that is based on the physical attraction that people feel for one another. This is the state of 'falling in love'. It is based on sexual affection/passion.

Storge:

the sort of love or affection that we feel towards certain places or things.

Philos:

the kind of love that is expressed in friendships – those close to us, such as relatives and friends.

Christianity

The definition of Christian love (agape) is set out in the famous piece of writing by St Paul in his letter to the Corinthians (**B**). It demands a great deal from people, but it is the ideal which most Christians try to aspire to.

 B Christian teaching

Love is patient, love is kind. It does not envy, it does not boast, it is not proud. It is not rude, it is not self-seeking, it is not easily angered, it keeps no record of wrongs. Love does not delight in evil but rejoices with the truth. It always protects, always trusts, always hopes, always perseveres.

1 Corinthians 13:4–7

However, even amongst the most secure relationships, arguments occur and difficulties can arise. All the world religions, however, recognise the need for forgiveness and would agree with the definition of love as set out in 1 Corinthians 13.

The main aspect of Jesus' teaching was the emphasis he placed on forgiveness both of friends and enemies (**C**).

stop and think!

- How realistic is it to call on people to love their enemies?

- Are there some things which would make you finish a friendship even if you forgave the individual?

 C Christian teaching

You have heard that it was said, 'Love your neighbour and hate your enemy'. But I tell you: 'Love your enemies and pray for those who persecute you'.

Matthew 5:43–45

54

forgiveness

What is love?

Enemies of love

anger

jealousy

pride

disloyalty

flattery

intolerance

selfishness

lying

distrust

dishonesty

QUESTIONS

1 Match the photographs **D** to **G** with the four definitions of love given in **A**.

2 Give examples of four demonstrations of agape in action.

3 The 'Enemies of love' (right) can all cause disagreements. Place them in order of seriousness, and give reasons for your answers.

55

Love and forgiveness

Islam

Islam teaches that all Muslims are equal and should treat each other as members of one community or family, the ummah. Many of the values that Muslims apply to family life such as looking after the young and caring for the elderly are also relevant in the wider Muslim world. The central aims of the ummah are to promote the feelings of care, responsibility, love and respect for others. These can be achieved through the following:

- financially supporting other Muslims (e.g. **Zakah** and Sadaqah – see page 172).
- encouraging people to look after one another.
- encouraging people to act in good ways and reject evil ways.
- working for unity between people.
- da'wah – showing others the example of Islam through good actions and words.

The teachings of the Qur'an and **Sunnah** repeatedly encourage Muslims to help other people. They emphasise key moral values such as humility, modesty, patience, integrity, truthfulness and fulfilling one's promises (**H**).

The teachings of Islam concerning social responsibilities are based on kindness and consideration of others. This involves making an organised effort to turn hatred into friendship through love and forgiveness. In a widening circle of relationships a Muslim's first obligation is to their immediate family, then to other relatives, friends, neighbours, the needy of the community, fellow Muslims and all fellow human beings and animals.

stop and think!

- As Muhammad said:

  'Every good action is a charity and it is a good action to meet a friend with a smiling face.'
  Mushad of Ahmad Hadith 6:6

  Muhammad said:
  'Believers are in relation to one another as parts of one structure. One part strengthens the other.'
  Bukhari Hadith 8:88

- What do these two Hadith tell you about the attitudes Muslims are expected to have towards others?

H Muslim teaching

Do not search for faults in each other, nor yearn after that which others possess, nor envy, nor entertain malice or indifference; be servants of Allah. Visit the sick, feed the hungry and release the suffering.
Hadith

It is not righteousness that you turn your face towards East or West; but it is righteousness to believe in Allah and the Last Day, and the Angels, and the Book, and the Messengers; to spend of your substance, out of love for Him, for your kin, for orphans, for the needy, for the wayfarer, for those who ask, and for the ransom of slaves; to be steadfast in prayer, and practise regular charity, to fulfil the contracts which you have made; and to be firm and patient in pain (or suffering) and adversity.
Surah 2:177

QUESTIONS

Read through **H**.

1 List some of the qualities that Muslims believe individuals should have.

2 What suggestions are made about how these qualities can be expressed practically?

I   Is love always unconditional?

Buddhism

Buddhist teaching corresponds closely with the concept of 'agape'. True love stems not from a need or desire but rather a wish for another's well-being. True love avoids hurting others, it is selfless (**J**).

Central to Buddhist teachings is the idea that the selfless love shown by the mother of the family closely resembles the pure love of a Buddha (**K**).

Buddhists believe that loving kindness must be extended to all the beings in the world not just to parents and relatives.

J Buddhist teaching

There is no need for us to agree philosophically, no need to share a temple or a belief. If we are of good will, our own mind, our own heart, is the temple. Kindness alone is enough. This is my own religion.

Voices of Survival in the Nuclear Age, *by the Dalai Lama*

K Buddhist teaching

My mother's kindness is responsible for all the opportunities I have… My mother always took care of me, feeding me properly, protecting me from dangers, directing my life… From the time of my conception she has been worried and concerned about me.

The Wishfulfilling Golden Sun, *by Lama Zopa Rinpoche*

stop and think!

- Can you think of a person who is giving their life for others?

- According to the teachings of the Buddha, there are four friends who are good hearted: the friend who will always help; the friend who is always the same in happiness and disaster; the friend who gives good advice; the friend who sympathises with your problems. What sort of qualities would you expect from a good friend? Do you think that we are attracted to people like ourselves?

QUESTIONS

Look at **K**.

1 a Do Buddhists value a mother's love more than that of the father?

   b Why might this be?

2 a Is a mother's love different from a father's?

   b Why is it used as a model for true love?

57

Marriage and divorce

A

I know I've got to find,
some kind of peace of mind,
I've been looking everywhere,
just to find someone who'll care.

Jimmy Ruffin, soul singer, What becomes of the broken-hearted?

When Jimmy Ruffin sang these lyrics in **A** in the 1960s, he was expressing what many individuals seek in marriage. Nowadays, it often seems that marriage no longer provides 'some kind of peace of mind' for very long. With a rising divorce rate showing little sign of slowing down, some Christian churches and other world religions have had to reassess their stances on marriage and divorce.

B Christian teaching

[Marriage] … is a way of life that all should honour; and it must not be undertaken lightly, carelessly or selfishly, but reverently, responsibly and after serious thought.
[The couple promise to love and cherish one another] … for better, for worse, for richer, for poorer, in sickness and in health… till death us do part, according to God's holy law.
Church of England marriage ceremony

C Hindu teaching

In a Hindu wedding, the couple take seven steps towards a sacred fire. Each step is believed to have special significance.

Step 1 – food

Step 2 – strength

Step 3 – increasing wealth

Step 4 – good fortune

Step 5 – children

Step 6 – the seasons

Step 7 – everlasting friendship

Marriage

Most religious faiths believe that sexual relationships should only take place within a permanent relationship; in other words, marriage. All the major religions view marriage as a very serious lifelong commitment (**B**).

Many of the forms of marriage service used by different Christian groups are quite distinctive, but all of them contain certain details which appear to be in common:

- a statement of what marriage is
- questions ensuring that the couple are free to marry and that they understand their responsibilities
- the taking of vows (promises)
- the exchange of rings
- the declaration that the couple are husband and wife
- blessings and prayers
- the signing of the state register in front of witnesses.

In Britain, the legal age requirement for marriage is 18, or 16 with parental permission. In Islamic and Hindu communities the age can be lower and many marriages are **assisted** or **arranged**. Unlike many western marriages, where the emphasis is often on love, successful marriages within these traditions are based on a shared set of values. Of course, love is seen as important, but this is something which may develop after marriage, not necessarily before. It is important to remember, as well, that arranged marriages were quite normal in Britain in past centuries. Even today, some people in western society view marriage as a 'convenience' – a way of continuing the family line, and of sharing property and money.

Being married as opposed to living together means that it is harder to just walk out on one's partner. In marriage services, whether **civil** or religious there are vows, a publicly sworn commitment to one another.

Every religious tradition approaches the marriage ceremony in a unique way but certain themes are common throughout all of them (**D**).

Normally both partners are unmarried at the time of marrying, and may only be married to one person at any one time (**monogamy**) although some religions, such as Islam, allow the man to have more than one wife (**polygamy**). Generally, however, most Muslim men marry only one.

Polygamy was more common in the past than it is today, particularly in times of war, when large numbers of men would be killed in battle. Consequently, there would be many women without husbands, and widows often faced difficulties in bringing up their children. By allowing limited polygamy, Islam ensured that these women would not struggle as one-parent families, but instead, could be offered the chance of a secure home with the full rights of a wife.

The teachings of Islam, set out clearly in the Hadith, state clearly what is important in a marriage (**E**).

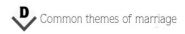

D Common themes of marriage

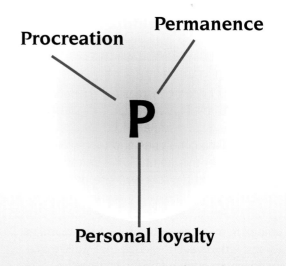

Procreation

Permanence

P

Personal loyalty

E Muslim teaching

Do not marry only for a person's looks; their beauty might become the cause of moral decline. Do not marry for wealth, since this may become the cause for disobedience. Marry rather on the grounds of religious devotion… make it a relationship of mutual love, peace, faithfulness and co-operation.

Hadith

QUESTIONS

1 Look through the following qualities of a marriage partner and decide the order of importance.

2 Why do you think many marriages break down?

3 Describe some of the ways in which both parents and children might suffer or even benefit if a marriage breaks up.

intelligence	common interest	physical looks	generosity
patience	forgiveness	trust	sexual compatibility
faithfulness	sense of humour	practical abilities	

Marriage and divorce

Divorce

During the last few decades, divorce in every society has become increasingly common. The main world religions have had to face up to the problem and seek some kind of compromise. Some Christian churches find themselves in a dilemma over this point. Some denominations, such as Roman Catholicism, interpret particular biblical passages about divorce in certain ways, and refuse to accept any second unions in an attempt to protect the marriage values. Others acknowledge that we live in a world where human failures can poison relationships, and accept that staying together is sometimes the worst of all possible solutions.

There are many reasons why marriages in all societies break down and why there is such an increase in the divorce rate:

- People may expect too much from marriage. When hardships occur, such as lack of money or illness, couples find it difficult to cope.
- Children (or lack of them) can cause a great amount of strain.
- Women are more likely to continue working and are often financially free from their husbands.
- Pressure from the media – extra-marital sex in films, television and magazines is presented as the 'norm'.
- Divorce is now far easier to obtain and is no longer seen as a **stigma**.
- Individuals often get married very young and change as they grow older.
- People tend to live longer and healthier lives. In the past, second marriages often took place after a partner's death.
- Women's roles have changed – they do not necessarily want to give up work and look after children or the household.

F The breakdown of marriage

ROYAL DIVORCE WILL GO AHEAD

No wisdom of Solomon in courts of last resort

THREE RUNAWAY SISTERS TRY TO MEND THEIR PARENTS' BROKEN MARRIAGE

The law can't save marriages

MEDIATION COULD SAVE MARRIAGES

The real problem is not how hard divorce is, but how easy it is to get married

COUPLES REFLECT ON DIVORCE

Breakdown rate

LAW AND CHURCH WELCOME END TO QUICKIE DIVORCES

How children are damaged by divorce

£50 MILLION DIVORCE

Although divorce is allowed in most religions, it is clear that it should not be taken lightly and should only be carried out after all attempts at **reconciliation** have been tried and have failed.

Islam

Islam allows a man to divorce his wife but such an action is not really approved of. Before divorcing, three things must be done:

- The couple must attempt to sort out their problems.
- If this fails, then two relatives or friends should try to mediate.
- If this does not work, then the couple must wait for four months before the marriage is ended.

Neither partner can marry for a period of time after the divorce – usually three months. This is in case the woman finds that she is pregnant.

Christianity

Most Christians accept divorce, but Roman Catholics believe that a marriage cannot be broken. Instead, they allow an **annulment**. If a marriage did not take place properly then it can be cancelled (for example, if one partner was forced into the marriage, or was insane).

Different branches of the Christian Church interpret the biblical passages about divorce in different ways. All Christians agree on the importance of marriage and that all attempts at reconciliation should be made but, with the exception of the Roman Catholic Church, they all allow remarriage. However, this remarriage may not always be allowed in a church.

Hinduism

Hinduism disapproves of divorce, but it is allowed if the husband is cruel or, after fifteen years of marriage, there are no children. However, divorce is not common in Hindu society, and it can be seen as a social stigma. The more traditional Hindus still refuse to accept divorce or remarriage.

Buddhism

Buddhists accept that some marriages will fail and that, in such cases, divorce is the most sensible course of action. The divorce must go ahead as smoothly and as sensitively as possible. The Buddhist scriptures clearly state that hurting others can never bring satisfaction, but accept that divorce will involve pain for everyone concerned.

stop and think!

- In your opinion, which of the following should be grounds for a divorce?

  - cruelty
  - adultery
  - desertion
  - inability to have children
  - insanity
  - physical disability
  - one partner sent to prison
  - no longer in love with the partner
  - unreasonable behaviour

- What do you think 'unreasonable behaviour' might include?

- What matters have to be sorted out if a couple decide to get a divorce?

Ageism – youth

A Christian teaching

People were bringing little children to Jesus to have him touch them, but the disciples rebuked them. When Jesus saw this, he was indignant. He said to them, 'Let the little children come to me, and do not hinder them, for the kingdom of God belongs to such as these. I tell you the truth, anyone who will not receive the kingdom of God like a little child will never enter it.' And he took the children in his arms, put his hands on them and blessed them.

Mark 10:13–16

Children, obey your parents in everything, for this pleases the Lord. Fathers, do not embitter your children, or they will become discouraged.

Colossians 3:20–1

B Muslim teaching

May his nose be rubbed in dust who found his parents approaching old age and lost his right to enter Paradise because he did not look after them.

Hadith

Your children are not your children.
They are the sons and daughters of Life's longing for itself.
They came through you but not from you,
And though they are with you yet they belong not to you.
You may give them your love but not your thoughts,
For they have their own thoughts.
You may house their bodies but not their souls,
For their souls dwell in the house of tomorrow, which you cannot visit, not even in your dreams.

Kahlil Gibran, The Prophet, *Mandarin Paperback, 1994*

With regard to children, society considers that the role of the family is to:

- **avoid the end of society by ensuring the creation of new lives**

- **provide a safe and secure environment for children**

- **educate children by passing on skills and knowledge.**

In all the world religions, children are regarded as very important and all the faiths have teachings concerning parent/child relationships (**A**, **B** and **C**). Parents and children have responsibilities towards one another. Parents must accept that children have rights that should be acknowledged. Parents are clearly expected to raise their children with moral guidance.

C Jewish teaching

Children understand their parents very well. When they see their parents consistently leading moral lives, and not out simply to satisfy their personal pleasure, they respect them and try to be like them.

Rabbi Moses Chaim Luzzato

Honour your father and your mother, so that you may live long in the land the Lord your God is giving you.

Exodus 20:12

Making sure that children all over the world have basic rights is the reason UNICEF (United Nations International Children's Emergency Fund) was set up in 1946. The main work of UNICEF is in developing countries where it tries to ensure that all children have access to proper health care, a balanced diet, education, clean drinking water and other basic essentials.

The rights which determine UNICEF's work were set out in the Declaration of the Rights of the Child, and accepted by the United Nations in 1959.

The basis of the Declaration is that 'mankind owes the child the best it has to give'.

The problem with 'Declarations' is that they are considered 'soft' laws because, although governments may agree to accept them, if the Declaration is broken in any way, there is very little the United Nations, or any other organisation, can do about it. This is why, in 1989, the United Nations adopted The Convention of the Rights of the Child. Countries which accept a 'Convention' are taking on a commitment which is binding and which has specific penalties for breaking any part of it.

QUESTIONS

1 Read **A**.

   a What qualities might Jesus have seen in children that are needed by all Christians?

   b What kind of relationship do these teachings encourage between parents and children?

   c Do you agree with these teachings?

2 How has the role of the family changed in recent years?

3 What are the main difficulties for parents and children today?

stop and think!

The Declaration of the Rights of the Child was published in 1959 by the United Nations. The six key points were:

Children have the right to

a protection, allowing them to grow and develop

b a name and nationality

c adequate food, medical treatment and education

d love and care from parents or guardians

e protection from neglect, cruelty and danger

f protection from discrimination.

In what order of importance do you think these points should be? Try to explain why you made your choices.

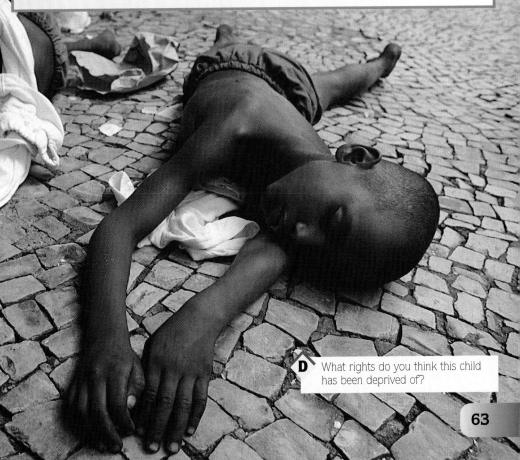

D What rights do you think this child has been deprived of?

ONE WORLD ONE FAMILY?

2 Ageism – old age

In the 1960s, one line from a song called 'My Generation', seemed to typify the younger generations' attitude to the older members of society – 'Hope I die before I get old'. Today, not much has changed. Western societies still seem preoccupied with youth, beauty and material possessions and many people fear growing old and losing their independence.

In the last 20 years the main emphasis has been on promoting the rights of children and now many people believe that the other end of the life span – considering the rights of older people – has been largely ignored. Life expectancy has risen as medical technology, better diets and working conditions have improved. Survival into old age will now become normal, rather than exceptional. Whether people age well or badly depends on how elderly people cope with problems associated with old age (**B**), the way others relate to them and on how they relate to those near to them. Often, younger people display negative attitudes towards the older generation which are based on false generalisations that must be challenged.

A Defying ageist attitudes – John Glenn was an astronaut again at the age of 77!

B The main problems associated with old age

MONEY

HEALTH

OLD AGE

LONELINESS

IMAGE

Many of the negative images people have about older people are promoted by the media. Too often, they are portrayed as frail and helpless, victims of poverty, crime, neglect or as figures of fun or ridicule. Rather than being seen as experienced and resilient the impression is given that all older people are vulnerable and weak. Television programmes and advertising in particular are often irresponsible in stereotyping older characters.

By stereotyping and often ignoring the increasing population of over 60s the media has been accused of reinforcing widespread gerontophobia (fear of ageing). Instead of emphasising negative images of dependency, illness and isolation, The Centre for Policy on Ageing believes that people should be described by four sociological stages (**C**).

The four stages of life

- Childhood and upbringing
- Full-time employment and family life
- Active independence
- Decline and dependence

 C The four stages of life

In Islamic countries it is expected, wherever possible, that the old and sick should be cared for at home in the family setting. Support for the elderly is important and all Muslims are taught to respect and care for the older members of their families (**D**). The Qur'an contains about a dozen passages that make significant reference to elders and old age. The attitude towards old age suggested by these passages takes for granted the relatively weak and limited character of human life in contrast to the absolute majesty and power of Allah. With the onset of old age the loss of certain capacities is the inevitable condition of all humans.

Care or retirement homes for the elderly are virtually unknown in the Muslim world. In Islam parents have a right to expect to be looked after by their children. No one should express any anger or frustration when, through no fault of their own, the old become difficult to handle. The strain of caring for one's parents is considered an honour and a blessing.

In general Eastern societies tend to treat old people with great respect and life goes on for older people as it always has. Although changes are taking place, the extended family structure ensures that older relatives are valued and play an important role in family life. By tradition, no important decisions are made without first consulting the senior members of the community who still hold the most power and influence within their families.

D Muslim teaching

It is He who has created you from dust, then a drop of semen, then the embryo; afterwards He brings you forth as a child; then you attain the age of manhood, and then reach old age. But some of you die before you reach the appointed term that you may haply understand. It is He who gives you life and death.

Surah 40:67–68

Your Lord has commanded that you worship none but Him, and be kind to your parents. Whether one or both of them attain old age in your life, say not to them a word of contempt, nor repel them, but address them in terms of honour and kindness. Treat them with humility, and say, 'My Lord! Have mercy on them, for they did care for me when I was little'.

Surah 17:23–24

QUESTIONS

1 List four ways in which elderly people are often stereotyped in our society.

2 What are the main problems associated with old age? In your opinion, what is the greatest difficulty a person faces as they get old?

3 What is the Muslim attitude about caring for the elderly?

4 Why are care or retirement homes virtually unknown in the Muslim world?

5 In what ways can respect for parents be shown? Does it change as the children get older? In your answer refer to a range of suggestions.

Ageism – old age

Compared with Eastern societies, societies in the West tend to treat old people with far less respect. In many European countries the image of the elderly means that old people often feel that there is little sense of caring or regard for their worth. The traditional family structure has been eroded in many developed countries. Where once several generations would live in close proximity, now families are split up as individuals have moved away looking for work or better opportunities. Historically older people have played an important role within their families and communities. These traditional institutions have come under pressure and broken down, undermining the influence of the elderly.

 Most religious traditions promote the view that the young are nurtured and the older members are cared for

Once you become aware of it, ageism is apparent in many walks of life. Older people are described in **derogatory** ways as 'old fogies' or 'wrinklies'. Hospitals and doctors have been criticised for neglecting elderly patients whose need of treatment is regarded as too expensive for limited national Health budgets. The embarrassment so often expressed when older people continue to have an interest in sex or if they dress inappropriately is again a sad reflection on the rest of society.

In October 1999 Pope John Paul II addressed these problems in a Letter to the Elderly. In it he pointed out that life expectancy has increased significantly in many parts of the world and he reflected upon fundamental Christian teachings regarding old age (**F**).

There is a growing awareness that the prejudice of ageism needs to be confronted as ruthlessly as does that of sexism and racism. It is important to remember that there is a strong likelihood that many of us will live to an old age. We should, therefore, want to challenge ageist attitudes. If we do not we will, in turn, become victims of ageism.

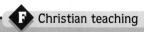
F Christian teaching

Still, it remains true that the years pass quickly, and the gift of life, for all the effort and pain it involves, is too beautiful and precious for us ever to grow tired of it... each stage of life has its own beauty and its own tasks. Indeed, in the word of God, old age is so highly esteemed that long life is seen as a sign of divine favour.

And what of today? If we stop to consider the current situation, we see that among some peoples old age is esteemed and valued, while among others this is much less the case, due to a mentality which gives priority to immediate human usefulness and productivity. Such an attitude frequently leads to contempt for the later years of life, while older people themselves are led to wonder whether their lives are still worthwhile.

Letter of Pope John Paul II to the Elderly

QUESTIONS

1 What do you understand by the words 'ageism' and 'gerontophobia'?

2 To what extent do you think families should be responsible for their elderly relatives?

3 What do you think is the best way of looking after elderly people?

4 What concerns did Pope John Paul II express in his Letter to the Elderly?

5 'The United Nations have drawn up lists of "rights" for children, the mentally and physically disabled and women. It is about time they drew up a list for the Elderly.' Do you agree? Give reasons for your answer, showing that you have considered other points of view.

Sexism

Sexism is best described as prejudice and discrimination against members of one sex, especially women. For thousands of years men have dominated societies, having the power and wealth, and forming the ideas which have left women as second-class citizens. It is difficult to examine the status of women during this time because generally they have had none!

We are now supposed to be living in a world where women are treated equally and with respect. Unfortunately, some things appear to take a great deal of time to get used to especially when both women and men are conditioned by society to accept their roles of **'subordinate'** and **'dominant'** respectively. Despite the changes that have taken place throughout the world regarding the status of women in society, relatively few play an influential part in decision making. Inequality between the sexes is apparent in several areas and until these are put right sexism will never be abolished (**A**):

 A Sexism throughout the world

- **In most societies throughout the world, women's opportunities to develop as individuals are not as clear-cut as men's. Men have better educational prospects, better pay and consequently greater freedom and independence.**

- **Religious beliefs can be seen to promote old fashioned ideas about inequality.**

Sexism throughout the world

- **Most of the influential and powerful people in society are men and major policy decisions tend to favour them.**

- **Old attitudes still persist even in the face of new laws for equal opportunity.**

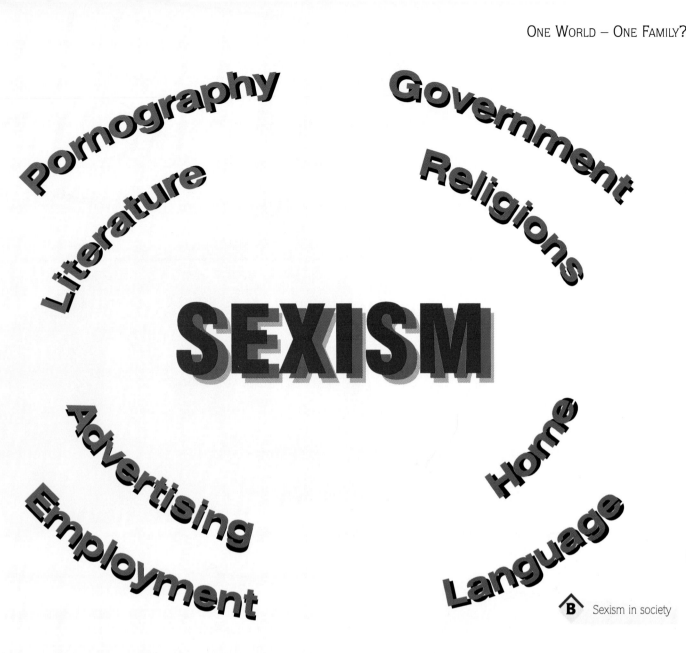

Pornography

Government

Religions

Literature

SEXISM

Home

Advertising

Language

Employment

B Sexism in society

...rly some of the roles of the sexes have changed and continue to evolve in many ...es. Attitudes towards recognising the proper role of women in society are ... to change but there is still a long way to go before true equality is achieved. ...rs there has been a greater awareness of sexist issues. Towards the end of ...rtrayal of women in advertising began to reverse the usual exploitation ...biects' or in 'washing-up' and 'cleaning' roles. We now see ...emales. Certain workplaces now ... of women but this practice has almost

... place and sexism can be seen in the ways in ...exploited for the benefit of men (**B**). Statistics ...the lower paid jobs and poorer pensions, are ...and are less likely to attain the top positions in ...few exceptions, women receive lower wages and fewer ...oughout their working lives. Over half of Britain's population ...t reflected in government circles. Our language is often sexist ...sing exploits the female form. **Pornography**, almost inevitably targets ...is one of the biggest growth industries in the world.

Sexism

Islam

Generally the world faiths are accused of accepting the way some societies are run and the way in which their many values reinforce the belief that men see themselves as the dominant sex. The Islamic faith, for example, has often been accused of being a patriarchal society where men dominate and women are exploited and yet nothing could be further from the truth. Ironically many people in Western society see nothing wrong with the image of scantily clad women being used in a sexist way to advertise anything from cars to mineral water (**C**) and yet are quick to protest about the Islamic 'treatment' of women.

Contrary to the 'stereotypical' image portrayed in the Western media, woman have a very important role to play in Islamic society. The notion that Muslim women are prisoners in the home without any rights, having to obey their husbands and fathers is based on ignorance of Islam (**D**).

The teachings of the Prophet Muhammad helped to improve women's status and position. The Qur'an places equal religious duties on men and women (**E**).

C Sexism – controversial images!

D How does Islam elevate the status of women?

HOW DOES ISLAM ELEVATE THE STATUS OF WOMEN?

According to the Qur'an, men and women are equal before God; women are not blamed for violating the "forbidden tree," nor is their suffering in pregnancy and childbirth a punishment for that act.

Islam sees a woman, whether single or married, as an individual in her own right, with the right to own and dispose of her property and earnings. A marital gift is given by the groom to the bride for her own personal use, and she may keep her own family name rather than adopting her husband's. Roles of men and women are complementary and collaborative. Rights and responsibilities of both sexes are equitable and balanced in their totality.

Both men and women are expected to dress in a way that is simple, modest and dignified; specific traditions of female dress found in some Muslim countries are often the expression of local customs rather than religious principle. Likewise, treatment of women in some areas of the Muslim world sometimes reflects cultural practices which may be inconsistent, if not contrary, to authentic Islamic teachings.

Prophet Muhammad said:
"The most perfect in faith amongst believers is he who is best in manner and kindest to his wife."

Discover Islam

E Muslim teaching

For Muslim men and women – For believing men and women, for devout men and women, for true men and women, for men and women who are patient and constant, for men and women who humble themselves, for men and women who give in charity, for men and women who fast (and deny themselves), for men and women who guard their chastity, and for men and women who engage much in Allah's praise – For them has Allah prepared forgiveness and great reward.

Surah 33:35

Say to the believing men that they should lower their gaze and guard their modesty... And say to the believing women that they should lower their gaze and guard their modesty; that they should not display the beauty and ornaments except what (must ordinarily) appear thereof; that they should draw their veils over their bosoms and not display their beauty except to their husbands and [close family members].

Surah 24:30, 31

Muslims point out that it is only over the last 100 years that women have been accepted as citizens in Britain, gaining the right to vote and able to own property in their own name. Islam granted these rights over 1,400 years ago! Islam recognises that although women are 'equal' to men, they are not the 'same'. Within society both have their own roles with the relevant rights and responsibilities. Little attention is paid to the Islamic countries where women participate fully in public life, holding positions in parliament and even state leadership. Increasing numbers of women hold professional posts in science, medicine, education and the **judiciary**. Rather, as can be seen in figure **F** the Western media prefers to focus attention and **stereotype** the acceptance of the 'traditional' roles adopted by Muslim men and women.

F Stereotyping and reality

Women are forced to accept arranged marriages and cannot get divorced.

Women cannot be forced into marriage against their will and have the right to choose their husbands. They also have the right to divorce their husbands if they wish.

Little attention is given to educating females – it is seen as a waste of time and money.

To be educated and given the opportunity to study at the highest levels is a right for women as well as men.

Muslim women are forced to dress modestly by wearing veiled clothing (hijab) and are not allowed to mix freely with strangers.

It is true that the Islamic guidance on dress and mixing with strangers is expected to be observed. The principle of Islamic dress is modesty. By covering their bodies women cannot be seen as 'sex objects'. In this way, they are appreciated because of their intelligence and personality rather than appearance. Interestingly, similar sentiments are expressed in the writings of St Paul (1 Timothy 2:9–10) and the other world religions but Islam is the one singled out for media attention.

The place of Muslim women is in the home looking after the children.

The traditional role of Muslim women is to care for the home and bring up any children in the marriage but this does not stop them earning their own money by going out to work if they wish.

QUESTIONS

1 Give four examples of sexism in society today. Which, in your opinion, is the most damaging?

2 Outline a number of adverts which could be described as sexist.

3 Discuss in small groups the areas where women do not receive equal treatment and note down whether boys and girls have different views on this.

4 Examine the role of women in Islamic societies.

5 Outline the responses that Muslim leaders make to the following charges:
'Women are forced into arranged marriages.'
'Muslim women must always dress modestly.'

Sexism

G Notice the difference in the seating arrangements in an Orthodox (above) and Reform synagogue (below)

H Christian teaching

A woman should learn in quietness and full submission. I do not permit a woman to teach or to have authority over a man; she must be silent. For Adam was formed first, then Eve. And Adam was not the one deceived; it was the woman who was deceived and became a sinner.

1 Timothy 2:11–14

Every woman should be overwhelmed with shame at the thought that she is a woman.

Clement of Alexandria

Judaism

Like Islam, Judaism recognises men and women as complete equals with shared responsibilities but women have fewer religious duties than men. Within the Jewish faith women have always played a prominent role in the home bringing up the family. The reasons for this were twofold: First, in Jewish society women rarely took part in public activities or assumed leadership roles. Second, Judaism taught that being a wife and mother were important for the development of a woman's personality.

In the last century there were many far reaching changes especially in women's educational and career opportunities. In recent years, many women have also begun to take a more active part in worshipping in the synagogue (**G**). In the Orthodox tradition women sit apart from men in the synagogue and take no part in conducting the service. The men are obliged to pray at certain set times whereas the women are free to pray when they want. In many **Reform** and some Masorti synagogues, however, men and women sit together. Women may carry the Torah scrolls, can recite blessings before and after the reading and in some cases may help to make up a minyan – the ten worshippers (usually men) needed for communal prayer. Some Reform synagogues allow women to be rabbis.

Christianity

Despite fairly recent moves in the Church of England, most Christian denominations do not allow women to hold any positions of power. Sexism goes back a long way in Christian history. In the Old Testament men were dominant in society and this role was carried over in the teachings of the early Christian Church. The teachings of St Paul and other leaders were often used to justify this position (**H**). In 584 CE there was a Council of Church leaders in Mâcon, France, where there was a debate on the question, 'Are women human?' The vote was 32 votes for women being human and 31 against! Through the centuries examples of inequality and sexism can easily be seen.

For almost 2,000 years the Christian Church has maintained a male priesthood. During the twentieth century increasing numbers of different Churches began to admit women to the priesthood. At the beginning of the twenty first century women began to play an increasingly important role in the Christian Church. Most Protestant churches allow women to become priests and to hold positions of leadership. In the Church of England the first women were ordained in 1994 (**I**).

The Roman Catholic Church, however, continues to refuse to allow women priests and is unlikely to change its stance in the near future. In worship, a woman may lead the prayers and singing, act as stewards, collect money and read from the Bible in Church, except for the gospels. Facing heavy criticism the Church continues to oppose the ordination of women on three grounds (**J**).

J Roman Catholic opposition to the ordination of women

> ▶ **At the central act of worship (Mass) the priest represents Christ. This role can only be performed by a man.**
>
> ▶ **Jesus only chose men to be his apostles.**
>
> ▶ **Tradition and the Holy Scriptures state that only men should be priests. The ordination of women would undermine the authority of the Church.**

I Since 1994, the Church of England has admitted women to the priesthood

Within the world religions customs are changing but it would be fair to say that in many religious traditions women are still struggling to achieve the rights that men have. Although women today are less submissive and restricted than they were in previous generations, there are still many customs that prevent women from playing an equal role in religious duties and worship.

stop and think!

• 'Religion is completely sexist. Just look at the relative positions of men and women in the various religions... it is unfair.' Do you agree?

QUESTIONS

1 Within Judaism, what are the two reasons that are given to explain why women have fewer religious duties than men?

2 Describe one change that has taken place in Judaism regarding women worshipping in the synagogue.

3 Give an outline of the main reasons why the Roman Catholic Church opposes the ordination of women.

Question bank

1 What has brought about changes in the structure of the family in Britain?

2 Describe the structure of a particular type of family and the advantages and disadvantages of living within it.

3 Describe a number of advertisements in which the nuclear family is regarded as the 'normal' family.

4 What are the three elements that all the world religions believe are necessary to bring up a family?

5 Explain the main problems that face a Christian family in today's society. How do Christians respond to these problems?

6 Which four words did the Greeks use for love? What did they mean by them?

7 Read 1 Corinthians 13 and make a list of the ten qualities of love described in the passage.

8 What did Jesus teach about the way in which Christians should treat their enemies?

9 What modern examples can you give of people who come close to carrying out the Christian ideals of love and forgiveness?

10 What qualities would you expect to find in a friend? Do you think it is difficult to be friends with someone who has more money than you, or is of a different religion or has different coloured skin?

11 Describe occasions when, acting out of love, you might be offending others or even breaking the law.

12 Discuss how the Buddhist view of love differs from other views.

13 Give a brief account of the main elements of a Christian marriage ceremony.

14 In some traditions, marriages are 'arranged'. Do you think this is a good idea?

15 Which three themes are common in the marriage ceremonies of most religious traditions?

16 What do the following terms mean:
a monogamy?
b polygamy?

Within a Muslim marriage, the husband and wife have separate, but equally important, roles.

'The best of treasures is a good wife. She is pleasing to her husband's eyes, obedient to his word and watchful over his possessions in his absence: and the best of you are those who treat their wives best.' *Hadith*

Use this quotation to describe the desired qualities of:

a a Muslim wife

b a Muslim husband

 Why do Muslims have to wait for three months after their divorce before marrying again?

 'The real problem isn't how hard divorce is, but how easy it is to get married.' Do you agree with this statement? Give reasons for your answer.

 In which four main areas is inequality between the sexes apparent?

 Do you think that men and women are equal in the following areas? Give reasons to support your views.

a the workplace

b relationships

c the home

 What tasks can women perform in a Reform synagogue which they are not allowed to do in the Orthodox tradition?

 'All the people in the world are equal and should be treated the same.'

Do you agree? Give reasons to support your answer and show that you have thought about different points of view.

Introduction
One world

Unit aims

The main aim of this unit is to introduce you to the 'medical **ethics** debate' through an examination of some of the key issues stemming from medical advances. You should be aware of legal facts and moral factors concerning these issues, and recognise the influence of religious teachings and ideas, including differences of viewpoint within the same religious tradition.

Key concepts

Many religions have difficulty in adapting and coping with change. The developments in medical technology over the past twenty-five years have forced the world faiths to re-examine their teachings about life and death, in particular the traditional sanctity of life principle. Religious leaders, in the face of rapid advances in medical ethics, are now trying to offer guidelines to their followers, while at the same time making sure that there are safeguards against abuse.

What is this unit about?

Religious believers can find themselves in a very difficult position when confronted with issues raised by advances in medicine. In the last twenty-five years alone, medical research has created techniques which allow us to live without our own lungs, kidneys or heart. Even the brain can be 'replaced' by machinery which allows all our organs to function. Many religious traditions will argue that 'God gives life and only God can take it away'. Some doctors seem to be 'playing God' and we can become confused over where precisely life begins and when it ends.

Medical technology can now predict potential problems in pregnancy with far greater accuracy than ever before but the issue of abortion remains largely the same as in years past.

NHS Organ Donor Register

donorcard

to help others to live in the event of m...

many choices

New 'halfway technologies' – those that do not cure, but merely delay death – are on a steady increase and have brought about a total reshaping of the euthanasia issue. The definition of the 'natural dying process' has had to be revised. Now individuals in a persistent vegetative state (PVS) can easily be kept 'alive'.

In recent years, developments in contraception, embryology and genetic engineering have prompted many uncomfortable questions not just for religious people but also for medical authorities, the courts and governments. Science is clearly going into uncharted moral territory and there is no one body helping us to decide how to act. Decisions in such matters should never be taken lightly nor can they be taken in isolation.

Medical

A Is a foetus a human being?

There is always a lot of discussion about medical ethics as people's beliefs about life and death are different. People have different opinions, too, about what quality of life to expect and the rights of the individual to determine this. Religious groups play a large part in influencing people's opinions in these matters.

What is the nature of life?

According to the Oxford dictionary, life is 'the state of ceaseless change and functional activity peculiar to organised matter'.

The exact moment that life begins is very important when dealing with issues like abortion or experimentation on embryos. Some people refer to 'the primitive streak', the period from conception to the fifteenth day when it is possible for a fertilised ovum to split several times or even rejoin. Most religions consider that God determines the moment of conception.

The medical terms for the different stages of development are:

Pre-embryo conception to 2 weeks	Embryo 2 weeks to 8 weeks	Foetus 8 weeks onwards

stop and think!

- When do you think life begins?

- What do you base your opinion on?

- In what ways has medical technology changed people's understanding of what 'life' is?

The advances in medical technology witnessed over the last two decades have re-focused the debate on the 'mystery of life'. We can now see potential medical problems in foetuses; we can keep people alive on life support machines who would otherwise die; 'designer' animals and even humans are now within our grasp; hundreds of new treatments are now possible. The mystery of life appears to be increasingly explained as every month brings fresh discoveries. In the face of such advances, the major world faiths accept that there are profound religious and spiritual questions to face, one of which is: *When does life begin and when does it end?*

ethics

When is the moment of death?

In order to sustain independent life, without any artificial means of support, the heart, the lungs and the brain must be fully functional.

This raises questions about life support systems, and will influence the decision to withdraw that support if it appears that one major organ in a patient will never fully function without it.

One really important question to consider is: *Who should make the decisions in life and death situations?*

- The medical profession?
- Scientists?
- Legal experts?
- The government of a country?
- Representatives of religious groups?
- The patient?
- The patient's family?
- Some combination of all these?

Another question to consider is: *When should a person be declared dead, and who decides?*

B Hindu teaching

Hindus feel profoundly the sanctity of every life, and bringing one into [being] is for them a sacred act. Even before the parents unite, they pray to be entrusted with the type of child they believe they could best love and help. Thus the first step is taken when the life has not yet entered the womb. For the second and third steps, during the mother's pregnancy, selected foods are given to her, and meditation is practised to create the right atmosphere for the coming child.

Yorke Crompton, Hinduism, *Ward Lock Educational, 1980*

C Christian teaching

In the Church's tradition, that the principle of respect for human life from conception has been constant since its early days is well documented by recent historical studies.

Dr Teresa Iglesias, Essays in Medical Ethics, *from Christian Theology Trust*

D Jewish teaching

You created my inmost being; you knit me together in my mother's womb... My frame was not hidden from you when I was made in the secret place. When I was woven together in the depths of the earth, your eyes saw my unformed body...

Psalm 139:13,15,16

stop and think!

- **What do you think are the most important factors to consider when deciding whether to switch off a person's life support machine?**
- **Is all life sacred?**

QUESTIONS

1 Reference is often made to 'clinical' death. What is the difference between 'clinical' death and 'real' or 'actual' death?

2 Should doctors always maintain life if there is the technology available?

3 People with pacemakers can lead a virtually normal life, but without them they would die. Where should dependence on technology end?

Contraception

With advances in medical technology and the widespread access to contraceptive advice, there should be fewer instances of unwanted pregnancies and yet every day we read stories of young, single mothers – some facing hopeless situations. On a global scale, the world faces an escalating population problem and, sooner or later, it will not be able feed or support its citizens (**A**).

A The population boom

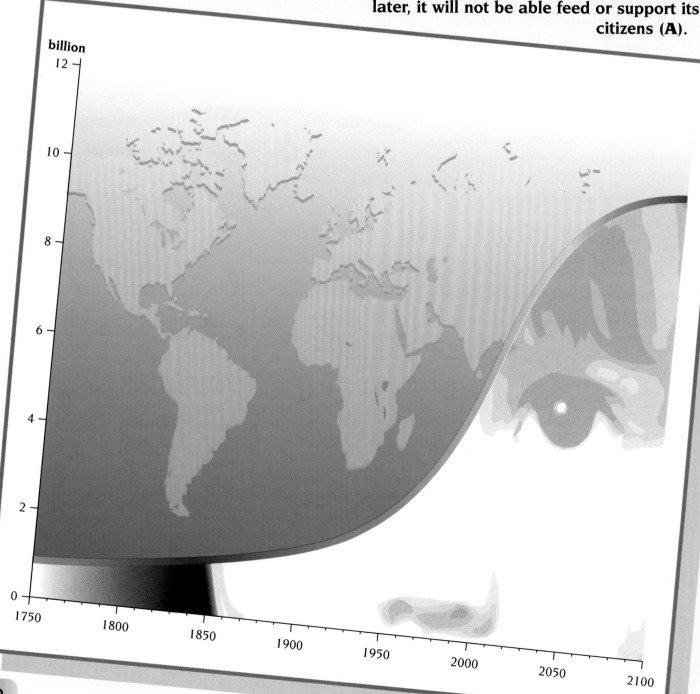

B Methods of contraception

Artificial methods of contraception

Devices and/or chemicals to stop the sperm from reaching the ovum:

- Condom
- Cervical cap
- Contraceptive sponge
- Diaphragm
- Spermicide

Hormonal (or 'synthetic'): **progestogens** and **oestrogens**: These work by suppressing ovulation as well as acting on the cervical mucus:

- The contraceptive pill
- Injection
- Implants

Postcoital: prevents pregnancy after unprotected sex. Only used in very exceptional circumstances:

- 'Morning after' pill

Intrauterine device (IUD): inserted in the uterus to inhibit implanting of the fertilised egg.

Sterilisation/vasectomy: a reliable form of birth control but only used as a last resort as it is normally irreversible.

Natural methods of contraception

- Calendar method (prediction of a woman's **fertile** period during her menstrual cycle)
- Temperature method (the temperature of a woman's body is higher after ovulation has taken place)
- Cervical mucus (around the time of ovulation, mucus turns thin and flows more easily)
- Symptothermal (this combines the temperature and cervical mucus methods)
- Withdrawal (the male partner withdraws before ejaculation occurs – not reliable as sperm are often released before orgasm)

Modern medical technology has produced reliable and comfortable methods of **contraception** (**B**) which may be used for a variety of reasons:

- when the physical or mental condition of the mother might be harmed by pregnancy or childbirth.

- to limit the number of children a couple has in order not to damage their living standards and perhaps affect other children.

- by couples who have sexual relationships but have no wish to have children at a particular stage of their lives.

Some countries, such as India and China, with population explosions, offer incentives to have fewer children. Family planning clinics are established throughout the world, but certain poorer areas with a very high infant mortality rate tend to make little use of them. Instead of encouraging couples to make use of these clinics or to use contraception many of the world religions are accused of being irresponsible in their teachings. Yet this accusation is largely unfounded. In many religious traditions, family planning and birth control appear acceptable as long as they are used to restrict the size of the family and not simply to stop having children altogether.

Birth control is the term used for controlling the number of babies a couple has. Contraception is the method used to control the timing and number of babies a couple has. This is known as family planning.

Contraception

Judaism

Despite the constant warnings given about overpopulation, the teachings of the world religions do not seem opposed to large families. In fact, some see this as fulfilling God's will (**C**).

Like many other religions, Judaism appears to be divided about the use of contraception. Many Orthodox Jews believe that contraceptives interfere with the physical union between a man and a woman. Reform Jews, on the other hand believe that artificial forms of contraception are allowable.

 D The Jewish AIDS Trust tries to promote safe sex in order to prevent HIV transmission

 C Jewish teaching

God blessed them and said to them, 'Be fruitful and increase in number; fill the earth...'

Genesis 1:28

For this is what the Lord says – he who created the heavens, he is God; he who fashioned and made the earth, he founded it; he did not create it to be empty, but formed it to be inhabited.

Isaiah 45:18

The generally accepted view within Judaism is that neither couples who do not want children nor unmarried people should be allowed to use contraception. Views regarding the use of contraception appear to be more relaxed if a couple has already had children. If a woman's life were to be endangered if she became pregnant, then the use of contraception would, in most cases, be accepted. Similarly, if a further pregnancy would cause hardship within the existing family or if there was a risk of a future child having a genetic disease then the use of certain types of contraceptives would be permitted. The responsibility for using the contraceptive is normally the woman's.

In the past, sterilisation or vasectomies were not permitted because they 'mutilated' the body. Similarly, condoms were not approved of because they interfered with complete bodily contact between couples. Nowadays, attitudes seem to have relaxed. Some **rabbinic** authorities have permitted vasectomies for sound medical reasons and the use of condoms appears to be encouraged as a positive and responsible way of helping prevent the spread of **AIDS** (**D**).

Islam

The Islamic position is that, unlike abortion, contraception is not directed against a living human being. But to have children is a great blessing so pregnancy should not be prevented. As with abortion, contraception can be used within marriage if it is established that pregnancy would threaten the wife's life but it should not be continually used to prevent children. If it is used, it must be with the consent of both husband and wife.

The evidence that the use of temporary or reversible methods of contraception are not religiously forbidden derives from various reports since the time of Muhammad (**E**).

 Muslim teaching

Allah intends every facility for you: He does not want to put you to difficulties...
No soul shall have a burden laid on it greater than it can bear.
No mother shall be treated unfairly on account of her child.
Nor father on account of his child.

Surah 2:185 and 233

We practised contraception by withdrawal (coitus interruptus) at the time of the Prophet peace be upon him, at the time the Qur'an kept being revealed to him, and when he knew he did not forbid us.

Jabir – a companion of Muhammad

stop and think!

- What is the difference between birth control and contraception?

- What is the difference between natural and artificial methods of contraception?

Some Muslims do not agree with the use of contraception because they insist that it interferes with Allah's plans. Many Muslims, however, accept the use of contraception as long as it does not totally prevent the procreative function of marriage. In Islam the emphasis is mainly on the quality of life the parents want for their children and that the required standards of raising the children and looking after the whole family might not be possible with a large number of children. In recent years, the Conference on Islam and Family Planning has agreed that contraception can be used if the family does not have the money to bring up a child.

In addition, contraception can be used if:

- the mother's health would be threatened by pregnancy.

- there is a chance of a child being born mentally or physically handicapped.

At all times, the Islamic rule of 'No harm and no harming' should be carefully observed. Unless the safety of the contraceptive method is proven, it should not be used. Muslim scholars point out that although the contraceptive pill has been available since the 1950s it continues to be modified and this creates media health scares about the safety of it. In addition, the use of certain contraceptives such as the 'morning after pill' and some IUDs, which cause the abortion of a fertilised egg, are strictly forbidden by Islam.

QUESTIONS

1 Give brief accounts of the generally accepted Muslim and Jewish attitudes to contraception.

2 Choose one of these religions and make a list of the religious reasons on which these attitudes are based.

3 Explain why some Jews/Muslims disagree with this attitude.

Contraception

Christianity

Of all the world faiths, Christianity is probably the most divided over the use of contraception. Within the Christian tradition, having children is a central part of marriage and for many centuries all forms of birth control were opposed because they were regarded as interfering with God's plans.

The largest Christian denomination, the Roman Catholic Church remains opposed to all forms of artificial contraception stating that their use is against Natural Law (not in keeping with human nature). Since the 1960s it has, however, allowed the use of certain natural birth control methods such as the rhythm method.

The teachings of the Roman Catholic Church are very clear. Sexual partners should always accept that new life may result from intercourse and therefore this should not be prevented. In 1930 Pope Pius XI condemned the use of artificial contraception. In 1951 Pope Pius XII said that Catholics could use the rhythm method. In 1968 this view was restated by Pope Paul VI (**F**) in Humanae Vitae. Later Catholic documents such as Veritatis Splendor (1993) and Evangelium Vitae (1995) reinforced and defended this point (**G**).

F In Humanae Vitae Pope Paul VI declared that 'each and every marriage act must remain open to the transmission of life'. Today this remains the official teaching of the Roman Catholic Church but how many Catholics support it?

G Roman Catholic teaching

It is frequently asserted that contraception, if made safe and available to all, is the most effective remedy against abortion. The Catholic Church is then accused of actually promoting abortion, because she obstinately continues to teach the moral unlawfulness of contraception. When looked at carefully this objection is clearly unfounded... It is morally unacceptable to encourage, let alone impose, the use of methods such as contraception, sterilisation and abortion in order to regulate births.

Pope John Paul II – Evangelium Vitae

A special commitment is needed with regard to certain aspects of the Gospel's radical message which are often less well understood, even to the point of making the Church's presence unpopular, but which nevertheless must be a part of her mission of charity. I am speaking of the duty to be committed to respect for the life of every human being, from conception until natural death.

Apostolic Letter of his Holiness Pope John Paul II to the Bishops, Clergy and Lay Faithful (Novo Millenio Ineunte)
6 January 2001

 stop and think!

- The world's population is growing at a staggering rate. Some countries actively encourage population increase, but others believe there must be a control.

  a What do you think are the reasons for these different attitudes?

  b Is it realistic to expect people from developing countries to limit the size of their families when it is traditional to have a large number of children?

Not all Roman Catholics find the views set out by successive Popes acceptable. Referring to Humanae Vitae, Jack Dominian observed that 'at the heart of this view is an instinctual, biological view of sexual intercourse which... is inconsistent with reality'. Another writer described the Roman Catholic Church's insistence that intercourse 'has conception as its only natural purpose, and that the rhythm method is the only proper means of birth control' as a tragedy.

The majority of Christian denominations do not draw a distinction between 'artificial' and 'natural' means of birth control. Instead they leave the question of birth control to be decided by the conscience of individual couples. Provided that both partners agree, the Orthodox and the majority of other Protestant denominations including the Church of England and Methodists, support the use of contraception as a responsible way of arranging a family. Some Christians argue that contraception helps a marriage by allowing more opportunity for relationships to develop (**H**).

In the face of rising populations some governments have set up massive family planning programmes. In addition, the rise of AIDS has led to a worldwide campaign to prevent the transmission of **HIV** by encouraging safe sex. It is argued that by adopting very strict guidelines on the use of contraceptives and opposing these initiatives, certain religious groups are being irresponsible.

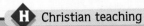

H Christian teaching

With the use of contraception, the unitive and creative aspects of intercourse can play their full part in the healing and development of a marriage.

Statement by the Methodist Church – What the Churches Say

I Marking World AIDS Day – high profile campaigns help to turn the tide in the treatment of AIDS sufferers.

QUESTIONS

1 What are the different Christian attitudes to contraception?

2 Give a brief outline of the arguments concerning contraception put forward by Roman Catholics.

3 'God intended sex to be enjoyed by a married couple not to make hardships.' Do you agree? Give reasons for your opinion, showing you have considered another point of view.

Abortion

The word 'abortion' comes from the Latin word 'aboriri', meaning 'to fail to be born'. Medically the term describes the destruction of life after conception and before birth. Abortion is not a new issue, but it has only been legal in Britain since 1967. Abortion is a very high profile moral issue and something which cannot be debated without feelings being involved. A person's opinions are determined by their beliefs, attitudes, experiences and circumstances. For example, there are those who would argue that abortion is permissible in the case of rape, but debatable when the woman has chosen to be in a sexual relationship.

Arguments often focus on when life begins and the various stages of human development (**A**).

> Life begins at the exact moment when the sperm fuses with the egg (ovum).

> Life begins at the moment when the fertilised egg is safely lodged in the womb.

> Life begins at the moment when the baby, if born prematurely, could sustain life outside the womb.

> Life begins at the moment of birth.

A When does life begin?

In 1861 The Offences Against the Person Act was passed to reduce the number of deaths from '**backstreet**' (illegal) abortions. The Act made it illegal to 'procure a miscarriage'.

These dangerous 'back-street' operations continued however and in the 1930s a campaign began to legalise abortion. In 1938 Dr Aleck Bourne invited police to prosecute him for carrying out an abortion on a 14 year-old rape victim. He was let off on the grounds that he acted to save her life. By the 1960s, legal abortion could be obtained by those who could afford to pay a surgeon and two psychiatrists to testify that the pregnant woman's mental health would be in danger if she went through with the pregnancy. Another alternative was to travel to a country where abortion was legal and pay to have the operation. However, those seeking reform of the abortion law accepted that these two options were not available to very poor people. It is estimated that over 100,000 illegal operations were performed each year in the early 1960s. There were at least 12 reported deaths and many women suffered infertility or illness as a result.

A further important factor which influenced the law on abortion was the Thalidomide drug, originally prescribed to women early on in pregnancy to avoid sickness. In the early 1960s the public began to witness the terrible side-effects of the drug as babies were born with awful physical deformities. Steadfast campaigning by groups such as the Abortion Law Reform Society ensured that there was a public demand for change in the abortion laws.

B

Human development

6 weeks (length 2cm)

Human embryo. Limbs start to form. All internal organs, such as liver and stomach, have begun to form. The heart has been beating for 3 weeks.

9 weeks (2.5cm)

The embryo has now become a foetus. The liver, kidneys, stomach and brain all function, and brain waves can be detected. Arms and legs are distinct and fingers, toes and teeth buds are beginning to form. It is starting to move.

18 weeks (20cm)

Fingernails and eyelashes have formed. The foetus is developing rapidly and is very active.

16 weeks (16cm)

The foetus is growing rapidly and is able to move vigorously, although these movements are still not felt by the mother. Its head has distinct human features and may have hair. Sexual organs and vocal chords have formed and the bones are closing to form joints.

12 weeks (7.5cm)

The heartbeat can be detected. The foetus can suck its thumb and fingers, eyelids and ears are developed. Tiny nails are growing on its fingers and toes.

24 weeks (33cm)

Eyes may now open. All systems are formed – 25 per cent or more babies survive outside the womb, provided they are given sufficient medical care.

Abortion

The continuing
war of words c⟩

The legal position

In the 1960s concerns about the number of so-called 'backstreet' or illegal abortions began to make headline news. The 1967 Abortion Act, introduced by David Steel as a private members bill, permitted abortions to be carried out.

The Abortion Act (1967)

An abortion may be performed legally if two or more doctors certify that:

1 The mental or physical health of the woman or her existing children will suffer if the pregnancy continues, or

2 The child, if born, would be seriously physically or mentally handicapped.

Contrary to popular belief, no time limit was set but under normal circumstances the pregnancy should not have passed the 28th week.

From April 1991 **The Human Fertilisation and Embryology Act** became law. The conditions for an abortion remained the same but the time limit was reduced to 24 weeks. The operation is still permitted after 24 weeks if the pregnancy involves risk to the life of the woman or in the case of the foetus being seriously handicapped.

As well as for the situations covered in the Abortion Act, there are many other reasons why a woman may seek an abortion, although in some cases the foetus may be perfectly healthy. Some reasons might be:

● to continue with the pregnancy would destroy or totally change the woman's plans for the future.

● the woman would be unable to support the child financially and/or care for the child emotionally – she may be very young.

● the woman may be afraid of rejecting the child, particularly in the case of rape.

Opinions remain divided over abortion. Some people believe that the choice should rest solely with the pregnant woman but is she the only one with rights in this case? Some people feel that the father should have a voice in the matter. Others argue that the deliberate killing of unborn human life is always wrong.

A number of organisations offer advice and support for different situations. Some will help with abortions others are actively against them.

QUESTIONS

Look through the information above on the Abortion Act, then read the statements below. Try and determine whether an abortion would be allowed under the 1991 law for the following:

a An amniocentesis test showing that the baby has a serious deformity.

b The baby is a result of rape.

c The parents are extremely poor and cannot afford a child.

d Through scanning, the baby has been established as female and the parents want a boy.

e The mother's life would be put at risk if the pregnancy went to full term.

f The parents are both in their late forties.

A pro-life organisation: Life

Life is a voluntary organisation made up of people of all beliefs and political persuasions. They are opposed to abortion because they believe that human life begins at conception (fertilisation) and that every human being should be protected from that moment until death from natural causes. They maintain that the deliberate killing of unborn human life is always wrong, and that the unborn child, whether 'wanted' or not, should have the full protection of the law, like any other human being. They believe that abortion is bad for women and men. Their nationwide pregnancy care service provides the positive alternative to what they see as the negative violence of abortion. They say they are truly pro-women people.

A pro-choice organisation: BPAS

The British Pregnancy Advisory Service is a non-profit making charitable organisation founded in 1967 to help women faced with unplanned pregnancies. As an organisation BPAS believes that the right choice is the woman's personal choice. It does not campaign for or against but believes that it is essential that abortion remains legal because women who feel unable to continue with a pregnancy will often risk their health or life to end it.

Without doubt the arguments for and against abortion are powerful and persuasive (**D**).

 D   Abortion – life in the balance

For abortion (pro-choice)

- Women should have the right to choose what happens to their bodies.
- The mother's life or her physical/mental health is at risk.
- It is irresponsible to have an unwanted child.
- Tests reveal an abnormality of the foetus.
- The mother is HIV positive.
- The pregnancy is a result of a sexual crime.
- The mother is very young or physically or emotionally immature.
- The quality of life for the rest of the family will be reduced.
- Prevents 'backstreet' abortions.

Against abortion (pro-life)

- No one has the right to take a life and the foetus is a potential human being.
- The rights of the unborn child are equal to those of the mother.
- If abortions are allowed the 'sanctity of life' principle could become increasingly weakened.
- Late abortion operations can be dangerous and use up hospital resources that could help others.
- The effects of abortion can cause the mother emotional distress and create health problems in the future.
- Doctors and nurses feel that the saving of human life is more satisfying than destroying it.
- When there are contraceptives freely available, abortion should not be used as a 'last resort' birth control.
- Many couples would adopt if babies were available.
- Physically or mentally handicapped individuals can lead full and rewarding lives.

 stop and think!

- **Should the father have any rights in the matter of abortion, or is it solely the woman's decision?**

QUESTIONS

1   Why do you think the 1967 Abortion Act was seen as necessary?

2   Look through the arguments for and against abortion. Draw up your own list of what you think are the three main arguments for and against abortion.

Islam

The official Muslim view on abortion is clear: it is a crime against a living human being and is therefore forbidden. If, though, it is reliably established that the continuance of the pregnancy will result in the mother's death, then an abortion is allowable. In the Muslim faith, the mother's life takes precedence over the baby's. The reasons for this are clear. The mother has many responsibilities and duties and, although regrettable, an abortion will be less disruptive to the family than the mother's death.

Generally life is seen as a gift from God and should only be regarded as a loan to humanity and not as a possession. As life is only on loan, it is not ours to do with as we like, but must be cared for and protected (**E**).

 Muslim teaching

Kill not your children for fear of want: We shall provide sustenance for them as well as for you. Verily the killing of them is a great sin.

Surah 17:31

Then we made the sperm into a clot of congealed blood; then of that clot we made a (foetus) lump; then we made out of that lump bones and clothed the bones with flesh; then we developed out of it another creature. So blessed be Allah, the best to create!

Surah 23:14

 Hindu teaching

His being is the source of all being, the seed of all things that in this life have their life... He is God, hidden in all beings... He watches the works of Creation, lives in all things, watches all things.

Svetasvatara Upanishad

In Him all things exist, from Him all things originate. He has become all.

Mahabharata Shanti Parva 47–56

Hinduism

Hindus believe that all life is sacred, so there should be no interference with the natural processes. All life forms have their source in God. Abortion would not normally be acceptable (**F**), however, it might be considered if the mother's life is at risk.

Judaism

Jews believe that all life comes from God, and that human beings are born in his image.

Human beings have a special place in God's creation, having been given the responsibility to care for all life in the natural world. Jews have tried to explain the special relationship between God and human beings by suggesting that human life has been **sanctified** (**G**).

 Jewish teaching

So God created man in his own image, in the image of God he created him; male and female he created them.

Genesis 1:27

You shall not murder.

Exodus 20:13

The word of the Lord came to me, saying, 'Before I formed you in the womb I knew you, before you were born I set you apart...'

Jeremiah 1:4–5

Christianity

There is no single Christian view on abortion and individual Christians may not even totally agree with their denomination's official stance.

The Roman Catholic and Orthodox Churches forbid abortion (**H**). The official Canon Law of the Roman Catholic Church states that anyone who commits the sin of abortion automatically **excommunicates** themselves from the Church. However, the Roman Catholic Church does preach an attitude of love and support, not condemnation, for those who have had an abortion.

The Church of England and most Protestant Churches agree with the Roman Catholic and Orthodox stance in principle, but are prepared to allow abortion in certain circumstances and leave more to the conscience of the individual (**I**). Such circumstances would be in the case of rape, risk to the mother's life, or serious risk of disability.

H Christian teaching

The human being is to be respected and treated as a person from the moment of conception; therefore, from the same moment, his rights as a person must be recognised among which in the first place is the inviolable right of every innocent human being to life.

Donum Vitae – The Congregation for the Doctrine of the Faith 1987

I Christian teaching

We affirm that every human life, created in the divine image, is unique... and that holds for each of us, born or yet to be born... Although the foetus is to be specially respected and protected, nonetheless the life of the foetus is not absolutely paramount.

Church of England Report, 1984

Circumstances which may often justify an abortion are direct threats to the life of the mother, or the probable birth of a severely abnormal child. The woman's other children, bad housing and family should also be considered.

Methodist Synod, 1976

We have been created by Almighty God in His image and likeness. No pregnancy is unplanned, because no baby can be conceived unless Almighty God intends that conception and has willed that particular and completely unique person into existence. The merciless slaughter of unborn babies is never justified.

Based on Catechism of the Catholic Church, Catholic Truth Society, 1990

QUESTIONS

1 Is abortion the deliberate taking of life?

2 Might there be occasions when abortion is acceptable?

3 What are the effects of abortion on society?

4 What is the key idea underlying religious objections to abortion?

5 a Why do you think that there is no agreed view of abortion among Christians?

   b Would it be a help or a hindrance to have just one agreed view?

6 Has your opinion on abortion changed since studying this unit? If so, in what way? Give reasons for your opinion, showing that you have considered other points of view.

stop and think!

- Jesus asked his followers to love one another. In what circumstances might a Christian feel that allowing an abortion might be an act of love?

Adoption

Although abortion may be a sensible decision for a woman to take when faced with an unwanted baby, some other people strongly disagree, saying that there is always the alternative of adoption. There are thousands of couples in Britain who cannot have a baby of their own and who are desperate to adopt. However, the increasing number of abortions has made adoption much more difficult.

In favour of adoption

● The child will be given the chance of life.

● The mother will not have to live with the physical and mental after-effects of abortion.

● The child will be received into a loving home knowing that he or she is wanted.

Against adoption

● The mother may find it hard to give the child away. There might be many guilty feelings.

● The child might not have a true sense of identity. He or she may feel rejected.

● The mother might always wonder and worry about her child.

● The mother might change her mind and want the child back.

Quite clearly, there is a constant theme running through all the teachings of the world faiths regarding care for children and the needy. If children have lost their parents, other families are expected to show compassion and to rally around and take care of them. At the same time, these children must never be misled about their background and parentage.

Judaism

In Judaism, the positive attitude towards adoption is seen in the story of Esther. She was adopted at a young age, and became a heroine in Jewish history when she saved her people from being killed (**A**).

Islam

Although Muslims are encouraged to foster children who have been orphaned or abandoned, certain difficulties arise over official adoption because such procedures, in the eyes of civil law, would give the adopted child the same status as a natural child born to the couple.

This legal recognition would create problems in the light of some Islamic beliefs. When an adopted son reached puberty, for example, he would not be able to mix socially with the women of his household, because he was not related to them by blood. The women would have to wear full Islamic dress in front of him, but not in front of their own sons or nephews (**B**).

Hinduism

For Hindus, in particular, the question of adoption is slightly more problematic because of the caste system. Although the system was officially abolished in 1950, it still governs many aspects of Hindu life. Hindus have no worries about adopting from relatives because this takes away any doubts about the child's ancestry and inheritance. The religious teachings remind Hindus of their duty to respect all people, regardless of their background (**C**).

The organisation Life clearly believes the decision to give a child up for adoption is not an easy one, but it is an unselfish and caring decision to give the unborn child the chance of life. As such, it is a responsible and caring choice. In its research on adoption procedures, Life has praised the number of adoption agencies that take tremendous care over the vetting of prospective parents and the matching of children to families.

 A Jewish teaching

This girl... known as Esther, was lovely in form and features, and Mordecai had taken her as his own daughter when her father and mother died.

Esther 2:7

B Muslim teaching

Nor has He made your adopted sons your sons... Call them by (the names of) their fathers: that is juster in the sight of Allah.

Surah 33:4 and 5

C Hindu teaching

Children are loved not for their own sake, but because the Self lives in them... Everything is loved not for its own sake, but because the Self lives in it ...

Brihadaranyaka Upanishad 4:6

 stop and think!

As an adopted child gets older, what difficulties do you think could arise for:
- **the adopted child?**
- **the adoptive parents?**
- **the natural parents?**

QUESTIONS

1 Do you agree with Life that adoption is a 'responsible and caring choice'?

2 Read **D**.

 a Is it possible to guarantee that all adopted children will be happy?

 b Is it realistic to think that all adoptive parents would be this open? Is such openness necessarily a good thing?

 D An adopted child's view

My adoptive parents were really open with me and I grew up knowing that I had natural parents, but that the people I called Mum and Dad had chosen me specially.

93

Euthanasia

Today, advances in medical technology enable very sick or injured people, who would otherwise have died, to live on, possibly for years, sometimes with no meaningful quality of life. This has led to debate about the medical profession's commitment to continuing life whatever the quality of that life is.

The term 'euthanasia' comes from the Greek language: eu meaning 'good' and thanatos meaning 'death'. It now refers to the act of ending another person's life, at their request, by painless means in order to minimise suffering, in other words 'mercy killing'.

Euthanasia can take three forms: voluntary, involuntary and non-voluntary. Voluntary euthanasia (sometimes called assisted **suicide**) is carried out at the request of the person killed. This is when people wanting to die may be physically incapable of killing themselves. Involuntary euthanasia is when the person killed is capable of consenting to their own death but does not do so. In virtually all such cases this amounts to murder. Non-voluntary euthanasia occurs when the subject is unable to consent: for instance, when an individual is in a coma from which they will not recover and so cannot express an opinion. These people are described by doctors as being in a Persistent Vegetative State (PVS).

A Dr Jack Kervorkian became known as 'Dr Death' as he repeatedly challenged the US courts by admitting that he was helping terminally ill patients to die. Eventually he was imprisoned for his actions.

All three kinds of euthanasia can be either passive or active. Legally the former is acceptable whereas the latter is regarded as murder.

- **Passive** Allowing a patient to die by withholding medical treatment.
- **Active** Deliberately taking action designed to end a patient's life.

Many arguments,are raised by the issue of euthanasia (**B**):

B

Euthanasia – the arguments for and against

Many terminally ill patients are in great pain and/or experience a poor quality of life.

Is it right to use limited resources on expensive treatment merely to prolong the life of a dying person by a few days or weeks?

If euthanasia was openly practised, some patients would fear their doctors rather than trust them.

If someone faces life with a painful and incurable disease and wants to die, there is little difference between them taking their own life (suicide) or asking someone to help them die (euthanasia).

Some argue that pain can be controlled to tolerable levels by the use of drugs.

By making euthanasia available some people could be pressured or influenced by others.

If animals are suffering we do not hesitate to have them put down, so why not humans?

Many faith groups believe that suffering can have a positive value for the terminally ill and for the carers.

Some people who make the request are clinically depressed.

QUESTIONS

1 Look at the arguments given for and against euthanasia in figure **B**. Draw up a table with two columns – one headed 'For' and the other 'Against'. Sort out the statements under the two headings.

Despite pressure to change the present laws, active euthanasia in Britain is a crime carrying a possible prison sentence for the individual who performs it. There have, however, been several high-profile cases involving terminally ill patients requesting medical assistance in committing suicide. In the vast majority of these cases the accused individuals have been let off by the courts.

Euthanasia

Case Studies

1 A doctor treating an elderly, bed-ridden patient at home, leaves powerful sleeping tablets by the bed with strict instructions that no more than two must be taken on any account. The patient has already told the doctor that she wants to die.

2 A badly deformed baby is born and needs immediate maximum intensive care to survive. The mother also needs urgent medical care, and the doctor deliberately deals with her needs first.

3 A doctor administers a fatal dose of potassium chloride to his elderly patient. She was close to death and in great pain. After consulting her two sons, she asked her doctor to help her die painlessly which he did. The doctor noted the injection in the medical records, making no effort to conceal what he had done.

4 A brother and sister try to administer a potentially fatal overdose of a powerful pain killer after their terminally ill mother begs them to end her suffering. They immediately tell hospital staff what they have done and the mother is brought back from the brink of death only to die in terrible pain 12 days later.

QUESTIONS

1 Write down the differences between suicide, voluntary, involuntary and non-voluntary euthanasia.

2 Consider the case studies above. If you were involved in any of these cases, what questions would you be asking?

3 Was the doctor in Case study 1 right to leave the tablets, knowing how the patient felt? Is this the same as administering a normal dose of painkillers by syringe at the patient's request?

4 In Case study 2:
a Is the delay in treating the baby the same as 'causing its death'?

b Would it have been different if the mother hadn't needed such skilled medical treatment?

5 In Case study 3 the authorities accused the doctor of attempted murder. He received a suspended sentence and was allowed to continue his work. Do you agree with the verdict?

6 Do you think the medical staff in Case study 4 were correct in reversing the overdose?

The legal position

In Britain there are no laws dealing directly with euthanasia. Currently it is covered by the laws forbidding murder. The charge in test cases regarding euthanasia are often attempted murder or manslaughter. Since 1961 suicide has not been a crime in England and Wales but assisting in a suicide is still a criminal act. Two relevant sections of the Suicide Act (1961) apply to euthanasia cases (**C**):

Section 2 (1) A person who encourages, assists, or gets someone else to assist another in attempting suicide will, if convicted, face a maximum sentence of 14 years imprisonment.

Section 2 (2) If a person being tried for murder or manslaughter is proved to have encouraged, assisted, or got someone else to assist, suicide, then the jury can find them guilty of this second offence.

C The Suicide Act 1961

The position in other countries

Generally, the governments of most countries appear to avoid dealing with the issue of euthanasia. Holland became the first country to legalise euthanasia in April 2001 and many countries adopt a positive attitude to it. In Japan the courts have listed four conditions under which mercy killing is permitted:

1 The patient is suffering unbearable physical pain.
2 Death is imminent and inevitable.
3 All efforts have been made to eliminate the pain.
4 The patient wishes to have their life ended.

Under Dutch law, a patient is able to make a written request for euthanasia. This gives doctors the right to use their own discretion when patients become too physically or mentally ill to decide for themselves. The request must be made voluntarily, persistently and independently while the patient is of sound mind. The guidelines are very clear:

1 A patient must be undergoing irremediable and unbearable suffering.
2 All other medical options have been examined.
3 A second professional opinion has been sought.

The Voluntary Euthanasia Society (EXIT) set up in 1935, argues that anyone suffering from a useless and painful existence should have the right to die under their own terms. The society argues for a set of safeguards, like those used in Japan and Holland, to ensure that the procedure is not abused. Strict controls are needed to ensure that a patient is not influenced by others and that they are of 'sound mind' when they make the request. The society believes that this can be achieved if the patient has made an Advance Directive (Living Will), stating their wishes regarding health care, particularly with regards to refusal of treatment. This 'directive' might be taken into account at a future time if the patient became terminally ill and incapacitated.

Many of the arguments made against euthanasia come from religious beliefs. Almost all religions regard euthanasia as wrong, either because it is an offence against God as in the Christian, Muslim and Jewish traditions, or because it is a source of bad karma in Eastern religions such as Hinduism and Buddhism.

stop and think!

- It has been said that euthanasia is an 'open secret' in Britain. What do you think is meant by this statement, and do you agree with it?

Christianity

Many faith groups within Christian, Muslim, Jewish and other religions believe that God gives life and therefore only God should take it away. All main Christian churches strongly oppose euthanasia. In Britain the Churches united to give evidence to a House of Lords Committee on Medical Ethics and Pope John Paul II strongly condemned the practice (**D**).

Euthanasia is essentially an issue that has arisen out of the success of modern medicine in keeping death at bay. To this extent the Bible, like other sacred writings, is not directly relevant. In the New Testament, however, there are at least five different places where there is a biblical commandment, 'Thou shalt not kill'. It is upon these verses and other texts that opponents of euthanasia point to in support of their arguments. King Saul who was mortally wounded in a battle asked an Amalekite to kill him. The Amalekite later described to David how he killed Saul. David condemned his action and had him put to death. In the case of Job, he ignored his wife's advice, preferring instead to put up with his suffering. This is a key concept for many Christians – suffering enables a person to learn humility, and in so doing, they are better equipped to comfort others. Suicide and mercy killing lie in direct contradiction to biblical teaching (**E**).

 D Christian teaching

An act or omission which, of itself or by intention, causes death in order to eliminate suffering constitutes a murder gravely contrary to the dignity of the human person and to the respect due to the living God, his Creator. The error of judgement into which one can fall in good faith does not change the nature of this murderous act, which must always be forbidden and excluded.

Pope John Paul II, Catechism of the Catholic Church 1994

 E Christian teaching

Then he said to me, 'Stand over me and kill me! I am in the throes of death, but I am still alive.' So I stood over him and killed him, because I knew that after he had fallen he could not survive. And I took the crown that was on his head and the band on his arm and have brought them here to my Lord.'... David asked him, 'Why were you not afraid to lift your hand to destroy the Lord's anointed?' Then David called one of his men and said, 'Go strike him down!' So he struck him down, and he died. For David had said to him, 'Your blood be on your own head. Your own mouth testified against you when you said, 'I killed the Lord's anointed'.

2 Samuel 1:9–10, 14–16

His wife said to him, 'Are you still holding on to your integrity? Curse God and die!' He replied, 'You are talking like a foolish woman. Shall we accept good from God, and not trouble?' In all this, Job did not sin in what he said.

Job 2:9–10

Given the number of Christian denominations and their varying traditions, it is hardly surprising that not all Christians agree on ethical issues. With regard to the euthanasia issue there are a number of principles on which most denominations would agree (**F**).

Most Christian denominations do not oppose passive euthanasia. They respect the right of the individual to die with a minimum of pain. Extraordinary means to prolong life may, at times, be inappropriate. The use of painkilling drugs is clearly favoured even if they incidentally shorten life. Here the Roman Catholic doctrine of double effect can be applied – 'the distinction between that which is intended and that which is foreseen but unintended'.

 F Agreement!

- Human life is a gift from God – as such it is sacred and is his possession.
- Death is an event in eternal life, not an end in itself – whilst the physical body dies, the soul lives on.
- People should receive good terminal care – all the patient's needs, including the spiritual, should be met.

Islam

Muslim teachings about the sanctity of life influence their beliefs on euthanasia (**G**). Islamic religious law totally rejects the idea of euthanasia on the following grounds:

- Every soul is perfect even if the body is not.
- The reason for all suffering is known to Allah.
- All suffering has a purpose – Allah is not unfair.
- Allah has decided each person's life span and so the length of life is not a personal choice.
- 'Mercy killing' may not be the person's choice.
- All members of Muslim society must be honoured and cared for until the end of their life, no matter how confused or ill they may be.

It has been suggested that the problem of voluntary euthanasia is not so acute in less developed countries. The morality of keeping someone alive on a life-support machine for years rarely arises. This is because there are so few hospitals and they often lack the sophisticated medical technology to keep people alive for an indeterminate length of time.

Both the Hindu and Buddhist traditions focus on the law of karma. The quality of life in one lifetime depends on the actions of a previous life. Helping someone to die would be seen as a great sin since this is interfering with the cycle of life. This does not, however, commit Buddhism and Hinduism to the view that life must be preserved at all costs just because we have the technology to do so.

Within the Sikh, Buddhist and Hindu traditions there appears to be no consensus on the euthanasia issue. Some followers believe that in certain cases euthanasia fits comfortably with their religious teachings. In Sikhism, for example, death is not to be feared. It is not the end of life, rather it is a gateway into another life (**H**).

Some individuals point out that it is wrong to use religious arguments on the sanctity of life to decide public policy on any aspect of medical ethics. Many religious people view voluntary euthanasia as morally desirable in some cases. There are also many **secularists**, atheists, agnostics, etc. who actively disagree with the religiously based arguments put forward against what they see as a humane act of compassion.

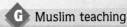 **Muslim teaching**

Nor can a soul die except by Allah's leave, the term being fixed as by writing.

Surah 3:145

The Prophet said, 'in the time before you, a man was wounded. His wounds troubled him so much that he took a knife and cut his wrist to bleed himself to death. Thereupon Allah said, "My slave hurried in the matter of his life therefore he is deprived of the Garden".'

A Hadith from the Collections of al'Bukhari

 Sikh teaching

The dawn of a new day is the herald of a sunset. Earth is not thy permanent home. Life is like a shadow on a wall. All thy friends have departed. Thou too must go.

Adi Granth 793 The Suhi of Ravidas

God sends us and we take birth. God calls us back and we die.

Adi Granth 1239

QUESTIONS

1 Choose one religion and summarise its teachings on euthanasia.

2 'We have a right to decide when to end our lives.'

Do you agree? Give reasons for your opinion, showing you have considered other points of view. How might the religion you have chosen respond to this statement?

The hospice

> Accepting death's coming is the very opposite of doing nothing.
> We have to concern ourselves with the quality of life as well as its length.
>
> *Dame Cicely Saunders*

Hospices, where pilgrims and travellers could rest and eat and where the sick were nursed, began almost 2,000 years ago. In the past shelter was often given to the poor and sick by monks in monasteries. The word 'hospice' comes from the Latin word 'hospes' meaning 'guest'.

What is a hospice?

A hospice nowadays is a place where people who have a **terminal** illness are treated until they die. The hospice movement specialises in pain control and the aim of the hospice movement is to give people suffering from terminal diseases the best possible quality of life.

A The hospice Dame Cicely Saunders established has become the model for similar centres throughout the country

Origins

In 1879 a hospital for the poor was established in Dublin by the Irish Sisters of Charity. In 1905 they set up St Joseph's Hospice in Hackney for those who were sick and could not afford to pay for care, or who were considered too disreputable for a hospital.

In 1967 Dame Cicely Saunders founded the first modern hospice, St Christopher's Hospice in Sydenham, South London. It was founded on the principle of palliative care – making suffering more bearable in the final stages of illness, researching into pain control, searching for cures for the diseases and teaching nurses and doctors how to cope with terminal disease. It was also one of the first hospitals to include the ideas of spiritual treatment as well as medical.

Cicely Saunders's work means that many of the terminally ill can die with dignity. Although she believes that medical technology can be used to promote patient well-being, she also accepts that in some situations it can have the opposite effect. She is equally clear in her opposition to killing patients (**B**).

movement

Some hospices – like St Christopher's – have a Christian foundation but are open to all. Although some of the doctors and nurses who work at the hospices may be Christian, the patients can be of any religious faith or none at all. Today there are hospices found worldwide. Many of them are run by different faith groups, but some are not faith-based. However, they all share similar values to those held by St Christophers (**C**).

B The hospice movement undermines the demand for euthanasia

It would be a grave error to perceive the Christian opposition to euthanasia as a rejection of the problems of the terminally ill. The hospice movement grew out of the concerns of Christians that people should be helped to die with dignity. It is killing, rather than caring, which denies the dignity of the dying.

Cicely Saunders

Hospices are concerned not only with the physical health of their patients but also with their quality of life. A hospice can be purpose-built, or a wing within a hospital, but it is more than just a building. Hospice care also entails specially trained nurses visiting individuals in their homes. The staff not only look after the patients, they help them cope with their dying and also help the relatives prepare for the death of their loved ones.

A hospice aims to relieve pain so that individuals can live their lives to the full. It provides an open and safe atmosphere where patients are treated with respect and allowed to express their fears and anxieties. Most importantly, a hospice is as much about living as dying – 'Hospices are places where people come to live, not to die'.

The patients

Some people need help to control the symptoms of their illness or disease. They will be given care, advice and support before returning home. Others, especially those who are living on their own, come in for a short break, to a place where all their needs are met and they have opportunities to socialise.

Whilst the hospice movement has become the expert in cancer care, they are also there for many other illnesses and diseases including, more recently, AIDS.

 C The values of St Christopher's:

To affirm life without hastening death and to regard death as a normal process.

To respect the worth and individuality of each person for whom we care.

To offer relief from pain and other distressing symptoms.

To help patients with strong and unfamiliar emotions.

To help them to rediscover meaning, purpose and value in their lives.

To offer the opportunity to reconcile and heal relationships and complete important personal tasks.

To offer a support system for family and friends during the patient's illness and in bereavement.

The hospice movement

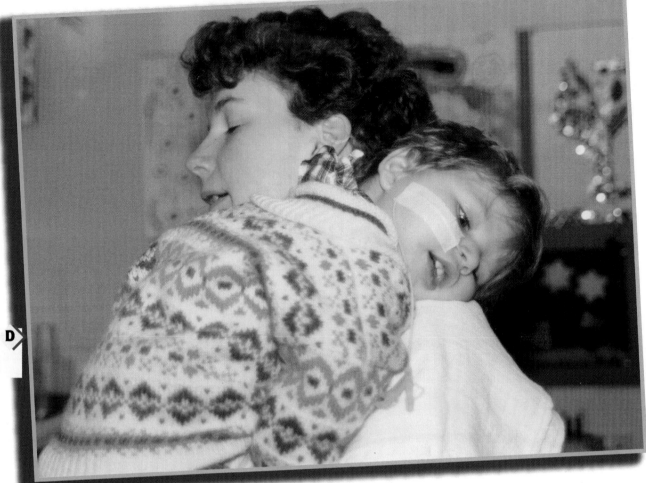

Helen House Hospice in Oxford **D**

Children are not usually cared for within the adult units. There are a few special hospices for them, such as Helen House in Oxford (**D**) and Zoe's Place baby hospice in Liverpool. Helen House was set up in Oxford by a group of nuns as the world's first hospice for children. It is especially sad to see children with terminal diseases. We expect old people to be ill, and we expect to die when we are old; but to see children dying is very distressing.

In all hospices the emphasis is on living. Some will organise candle-lit suppers or afternoon teas in the gardens. Then there are coach outings and trips to the local pub. Visitors are encouraged, and many come to teach a skill or to entertain. Friends and family can visit at almost any time of the day or night, and some visitors even bring the family pet in with them!

A central principle in the teaching of all the world faiths is caring for people, particularly those disadvantaged by age, circumstances or illness.

stop and think!

- **Why do you think people might be frightened to talk about serious illness or death?**

QUESTIONS

1 What is the main difference between a hospice and a hospital?

2 What are the main aims of a hospice?

3 Why do you think many religious people support the work of the hospice movement?

4 What sort of qualities do people need when they work in a hospice?

Sikhism

The Sikh religion believes that God cares for everyone and considers caring as part of its religious heritage (**E**). Gurdwaras (Sikh places of worship), often have medical clinics close by. Sikhs believe that the right relationship with God is based on prayer, work and charity. Service to the community (seva) entails all of these.

stop and think!

• What might further improve the way we care for people who are terminally ill?

 E Sikh teaching

There can be no worship without performing good deeds... A place in God's court can only be attained if we do service to others in this world.

Adi Granth 4, 26

Islam

In recent years some British hospices have noted an increasing number of Muslim patients. In Islamic countries, however, a terminally ill Muslim is far more likely to be cared for at home by their family rather than in a hospice. The family is central to Islam and children are taught from an early age that members of a family are there to support one another. It is a religious duty to care for parents in times of need (**F**).

Buddhism

All Buddhists recognise the virtue of goodwill (metta) which involves compassion for others and generosity especially to those in need, such as the elderly and the dying (**G**). Metta is regarded as a necessary rule of life, one which is essential to combat greed and selfishness.

 F Muslim teaching

Treat with kindness your parents and kindred, and orphans and those in need.

Surah 2:83

The Prophet said, 'He is not one of us who has no compassion for our little ones and does not honour our old ones'.

Reported by Al-Tirmidhi

 G Buddhist teaching

Let us fill our hearts with our own compassion – towards ourselves and towards all living beings. Let us pray that we ourselves cease to be the cause of suffering to each other. Let us plead with ourselves to live in a way which will not deprive other beings of air, water, food, shelter or the chance to live.

The Venerable Thich Nhat Hahn

QUESTIONS

1 Match the tops and tails of these sentences below.

Metta (the virtue of goodwill) involves	without performing good deeds
One of the Five Pillars of Islam is zakah	compassion for others and generosity to those in need
According to Sikh teaching, there can be no worship	is on living
Helen House is a hospice	which expects all Muslims to give a proportion of their savings to charity
In all hospices the emphasis	specifically for children

2 List all the things that may have made a difference to attitudes on this subject in recent times (e.g. soap operas, newspapers and television, AIDS, changing attitudes among the medical profession).

3 'In every case, care is more merciful than euthanasia.' Do you agree? Give reasons for your opinion, showing that you have considered the various different arguments put forward.

Organ transplants

- **In 1950, surgeons could not have transplanted a kidney.**

- **In 1994, an Englishman's life was saved because he had six organs transplanted into his body.**

- **At one time we would not have contemplated heart transplants because it was believed that the heart contained the soul.**

- **Today we are living with animal transplants.**

Britain

A doctor in Cambridgeshire is genetically engineering pigs in an attempt to overcome the shortage of suitable organ donors. Transplants in America in the 1980s which involved killing primates for their organs led to an outcry, so now the research has transferred to pigs. A small amount of human DNA is introduced into the pig's ovum. Two of the pig's offspring are then mated to produce pigs with organs that will be accepted by the human body. **Insulin** from pigs is already being used in the control of human **diabetes**.

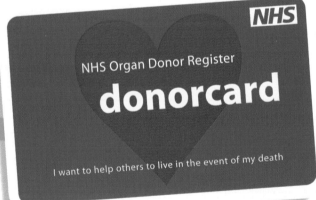

NHS Organ Donor Register

donorcard

I want to help others to live in the event of my death

 A Do you think organs should be used automatically, unless the person has specifically requested otherwise?

France

On 28 July 1991, a 19-year-old boy, Christophe, suffered a fatal accident while riding his bike. The doctors could legally have taken his organs, but consulted his parents. They agreed, but with misgivings, to his heart, liver and kidneys being used. When they saw Christophe in the mortuary, his eyes had been taken as well. His distorted face is the most vivid picture that remains in his father's mind. The publicity which followed this led to a 20 per cent drop in organ donations, and to a change in the law in 1994. Now doctors have to seek permission even if there is a relevant donor card.

India

In poorer countries like India it is legal, at present, to buy a kidney. As medical evidence shows that healthy individuals can live a normal life span with one kidney and, as the average wage is around £5 a week, the £650 paid for a single kidney means there is no shortage of donors. However, media stories about the exploitation of the poor, and concern about the moral implications have led the government to propose a change in this law. Sadly, this is likely to lead to a black market in organ sales.

The USA

In April 1995, a pharmaceutical company took organs from pigs and put them into baboons. In Cleveland, Ohio, a leading neurosurgeon has successfully transplanted a monkey's head onto the body of another monkey. Although it could see, hear and taste, it could not move because of the damage to the spinal cord. In the near future, it should be possible to repair the nervous system.

A question that frequently arises when people are faced with the decision of whether to donate their organs or those of their loved ones is: 'Will my decision be compatible with my religious beliefs?' The majority of the world faiths, in fact, have little difficulty accepting the basic philosophy of transplant surgery. In theory, a religion such as Sikhism views the human body after death as a 'shell' because the 'atman' (spirit or soul) has left it (**B**).

In practice, however, and despite recognition of the need to have a constant supply of organs for surgery, many followers are reluctant to accept the idea of donating parts of the body. Many Muslims strongly believe that their body belongs to Allah, and so they are not in the position to donate any part of it. Supporting this view, in 1983 the Muslim Religious Council rejected organ donation by its followers, but has reversed this decision since then on condition that the donor consents in writing in advance. The Muslim Law Council issued a ruling in 1995 urging all Muslims to carry donor cards, and allowing the removal of essential organs after death (**C**). The organs of Muslim donors must, however, be transplanted immediately, and not stored in organ banks.

Judaism, like many of the other religions, teaches that saving a human life must take precedence over maintaining the 'sanctity' of the human body (**D**).

B Sikh teaching

The dead may be cremated or buried, or thrown to the dogs, or cast into the waters or down an empty well. No one knows where the soul goes and disappears to.
Adi Granth 648

C Muslim teaching

We have no policy against organ and tissue donation as long as it is done with respect for the deceased and for the benefit of the recipient.
Dr Abdel Rahma Osman, Director of the Muslim Community Center in Maryland, USA

D Jewish teaching

If one is in the position to donate an organ to save another's life, it is obligatory to do so, even if the donor never knows who the beneficiary will be. The basic principle of Jewish ethics – 'the infinite worth of the human being' – also includes donation of corneas, since eyesight restoration is considered a life-saving operation.
Dr Moses Tendler, Chairman of the Bioethics Commission of the Rabbinical Council of America

stop and think!

- What are the advantages of having a donor card?

- What would be your feelings if you knew that, after your death, organs from your body would be used to save another's life or improve the quality of their life?

- How would you feel if the organs of one of your family were used?

QUESTIONS

1 Should we allow scientists complete freedom, or should there be clear internationally agreed guidelines to limit what they can do?

2 How do you feel about transplanting animal organs into human beings?

3 Will humans with animal transplants cease to be humans?

4 What will happen when we can, in theory, get a new body to replace the old worn-out one?

5 Animal rights activists say that we should not allow animal suffering caused through genetic experimentation. What do you think?

Genetic engineering

Most press reports of genetic engineering stress its incredible potential for good, mostly in terms of 'conquering' disease. The main issue is how far should the potential benefits of this new technology be weighed against the risk of unforeseeable side-effects?

When faced with difficult issues normally a religious person can draw upon the teaching of his or her faith. The problem with genetic engineering is that religious leaders, like the rest of society, can hardly keep pace with the advances that are being made let alone keep control on the progress being made. Holy books like the Bible and the Qur'an offer little guidance on issues that could never have been anticipated centuries ago.

B Frederick Sanger

Structure and organisation of DNA in the human genome. The entire DNA content of a cell nucleus is called a genome.

Billions of cells.

The nucleus of each cell contains the genetic material in chromosomes.

ATCG = bases

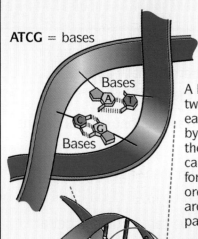

Bases

Bases

A DNA molecule consists of two long chains coiled around each other and held together by hydrogen bonds between the bases. These chemicals called bases are the 'alphabet' for the 'genetic message'. The order that the different bases are found in will determine the particular characteristic.

There are 23 pairs of matching chromosomes in each cell nucleus. 46 in total, 23 from each parent.

Each chromosome may contain up to 4000 genes. Genes determine human characteristics.

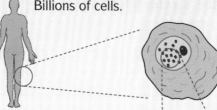

Unravelling the DNA

A gene is a segment of DNA. Each segment determines a particular characteristic, e.g. eye colour.

A The human genome

There are 40,000 – 100,000 genes in the whole cell.

In the 1950s two Cambridge scientists, James Watson and Francis Crick, unravelled the double-helix or 'spiral staircase' structure of deoxyribonucleic acid (DNA), the chemical used by animals and plants to store the information that is passed from generation to generation – the chemical blueprint of life (**A**). In 1977 Frederick Sanger (**B**) developed a technique for sequencing the genetic code of DNA.

The structure of DNA and its organisation into genes and chromosomes (**C**) has led to the current revolution in modern genetics.

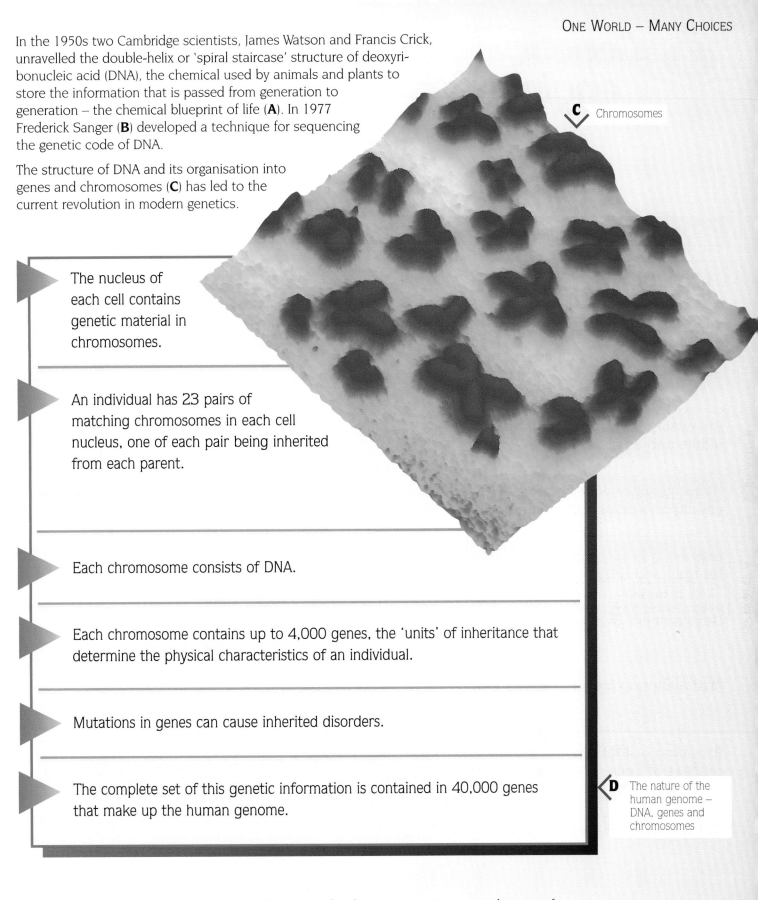

C Chromosomes

The nucleus of each cell contains genetic material in chromosomes.

An individual has 23 pairs of matching chromosomes in each cell nucleus, one of each pair being inherited from each parent.

Each chromosome consists of DNA.

Each chromosome contains up to 4,000 genes, the 'units' of inheritance that determine the physical characteristics of an individual.

Mutations in genes can cause inherited disorders.

The complete set of this genetic information is contained in 40,000 genes that make up the human genome.

D The nature of the human genome – DNA, genes and chromosomes

Every cell in an organism, whether it is a plant, animal or human, contains a complete set of genes known as the genome. The human body is made up of approximately 100 trillion cells. The genome of each human cell is made up of 23 pairs of chromosomes – 23 from each parent (**D**).

Genetic engineering

There is little doubt that medicine in the twenty first century is being revolutionised by the decoding of the human genome – the three billion letters in the human 'Book of Life'. Everyone's DNA sequence is 99.9% identical but it is the differences that become important in knowing why some people become ill, some cannot take certain drugs and some die prematurely. Knowing the full DNA sequence will enable scientists to predict disease in a person and develop tailor-made drugs.

Many scientists are excited about what they see as the numerous benefits stemming from the use of genetic engineering (**E**). They believe that the general public's concern is due to ignorance and misinformation stemming from sensational headlines in the media.

When examining genetic engineering it is helpful to divide the research being carried out into three categories, some of which are far more controversial than others (**F**):

GENETIC ENGINEERING

Treating human and animal diseases

Increasing food production from plants and animals

Reducing the need for potentially harmful chemicals such as pesticides

Improving processing techniques for food and drugs

Development in forensic science

Manufacturing fuels to replace oil

Providing insight into the growth process of cells

 E The centre of the bioethical debate. The major uses of genetic engineering.

 F Branches of genetic engineering

Somatic cell gene therapy

Somatic cells play no part in the production of sex cells so where a defective gene is repaired or replaced by a healthy gene it only effects the individual concerned. Scientists have been using this procedure since 1989 to treat genetic diseases and they are hopeful that it will be able to treat many single-gene diseases such as haemophilia, cystic fibrosis, thalassaemia and sickle cell anaemia.

Germ line gene therapy

The cells which are involved in the production of eggs or sperm are known as germ-line cells. If genetic changes are made to an individual's germ-line cells, the altered genes could be passed on to future generations.

Enhancement genetic engineering

This is where a gene is inserted in a healthy person to change physical appearance such as height, eye or hair colour. This type of genetic engineering is now technically possible for somatic cells but has not been attempted both for medical and moral reasons.

A further distinction must also be drawn in genetic engineering between therapeutic and non-therapeutic gene therapy. Therapeutic is the treatment of an inherited disease by the alteration of the genetic defect that causes it. Non-therapeutic is where normal inherited characteristics such as eye or hair colour are changed. It is not always easy to distinguish between the two – is shortness, for example, an inherited disorder or just part of normal human variation.

1 What do you understand by:

a chromosomes?

b somatic cells?

c germ cells?

d therapeutic gene therapy?

e non-therapeutic gene therapy?

f DNA?

2 Look at **E**, the major uses of genetic engineering. In your opinion, which three uses are the most beneficial and which is the least beneficial? Give reasons for your choices.

Dr Ian Wilmut led the team of scientists from the Roslin Institute which, in 1996, famously cloned **G** Dolly the sheep

In just fifty years genetics has taken us from only knowing the DNA structure to discoveries linking individual genes with specific diseases and mapping the entire human genome. The power of genetics is felt in the search for cures for potentially fatal diseases, altering the characteristics of food (see pages 144–47), understanding the inner workings of the body, improving humans and even changing the mental and physical characteristics of the unborn. We now have the potential for **gene therapy**, designer babies and cloning (**G**). No wonder the future has been described as 'a minefield and a circus of wonders!'

During the 1990s, genetic research that could not go ahead with human subjects was often carried out on animals. Animals have been created with defective human genes, such as cystic fibrosis and cancer, so medical researchers can experiment with them and gain a better understanding of the disease. Demand for human transplant organs has led to animals being genetically engineered and bred to provide suitable organs for transplant (xenotransplants). These could save many lives but there remain real dangers of disease transmission across the species.

Other less controversial areas are the experiments where there is little or no suffering to the animals and the potential human benefits are massive. **Transgenic** sheep have been genetically altered to produce human proteins in their milk. They are exactly like normal sheep except that they produce vital drugs, such as **AAT**, which is used in treating patients with emphysema, a lung disease. Goats, pigs and sheep are now seen as future 'pharm' stock.

Without doubt these discoveries generate strong feelings and arouse widespread publicity and a great deal of excitement in the media. The possibilities opened up by these scientific and medical advances raise many difficult questions. For the world religions, the field of genetics is raising many issues that must be tackled. Most religious groups are not opposed to using the skills of science to relieve suffering but problems arise when genetic research is undertaken for reasons that are not considered right and/or moral.

Many religious groups are wary of the possible misuse of such genetic experiments. In their teaching they try to get the balance right between encouraging scientific advances for the common good and voicing concerns about interfering with God's creations. Two foundation stones in all their teachings are respect for the uniqueness of human life and care for the future of the planet.

 # Genetic engineering

Islam

As far as Muslims are concerned life is a gift from Allah and only Allah can decide if and when someone is born or dies. According to the Qur'an, after the Devil tempted Adam and Eve to sin he also wanted them to change God's creation (**H**).

The consensus is that these Qur'anic verses cannot be used as a total ban on genetic engineering. If they were taken too literally many forms of **curative** surgery which involve some change in God's creation would be banned. Most Islamic scholars accept certain forms of genetic engineering (**I**).

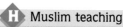 **H** Muslim teaching

It is Allah who gives you life, then gives you death.

Surah 45:26

I will mislead them, and I will create in them false desires; I will order them to slit the ears of cattle, and to deface the (fair) nature created by Allah.

Surah 4:119

 I Muslim response to genetic engineering

Applications such as the diagnosis, amelioration, cure or prevention of genetic disease are acceptable and even commendable. Gene replacement is essentially transplantation surgery albeit at the molecular level... possibilities of genetic engineering will open tremendous vistas in treatment of many illnesses and the possibilities in agriculture and animal husbandry might be the clue to solving the problem of famine...

Website – Genetic Engineering

The main concerns about this research lie in the area of the unknown future. Tampering with life forms may disturb the 'natural balance' of creation. Genetic engineering like all science, must be used responsibly. Science might think that everything is under control but this is not always the case.

Christianity

Some Christian denominations believe that genetic engineering denies the 'sanctity of human life'. The Roman Catholic position was made clear by Pope John Paul II in the encyclical 'Evangelium Vitae'. Other Christian denominations such as the Church of Scotland take a more liberal view (**J**).

 J Christian teaching

[Such research] under the pretext of scientific or medical progress, in fact reduces human life to the level of simple 'biological material' to be readily disposed of... Life itself becomes a mere 'thing', which man claims as his exclusive property, completely subject to his control and manipulation... The killing of innocent human creatures, even if carried out to help others, constitutes an absolutely unacceptable act.

Pope John Paul II – Evangelium Vitae

[We] commend the principle of production of proteins of therapeutic value in the milk of genetically modified sheep and other farm animals, but oppose, and urge Her Majesty's Government to take necessary steps to prevent, the application of animal cloning as a routine procedure in meat and milk production, as an unacceptable commodification of animals.

The General Assembly of the Church of Scotland (22 May 1997)

Judaism

There is no clear consensus in Jewish law regarding genetic engineering. The belief is that the issues that are being raised by genetic research should be discussed and debated now (**K**).

 Jewish teaching

We are standing at the edge of a new scientific era. We certainly wish to utilise the potentials of genetic engineering for the benefit of humanity... As we learn more about the nature of genetic engineering we must discuss its moral implications both with regard to animals and human beings... So we must proceed with caution. In consort with others we must set limits and provide direction.

Rabbi Walter Jacob

Genetic engineering may open a wonderful chapter in the history of healing. But without prior agreement on restraints and the strictest limitations, such mechanisation of human life may also herald irretrievable disaster... Man, as the delicately balanced fusion of body, mind and soul, can never be the mere product of laboratory conditions and scientific ingenuity.

Rabbi Immanuel Jakobovits – Genetic Screening and Gene Therapy

Like most of the other world religions, Judaism fully supports genetic research aimed at eliminating every kind of disease. Opinions are divided, however, over other uses of genetic research that can affect the whole of nature. The Rabbinical Assembly of Israel stated that just because human beings are capable of doing something does not mean they should do it. The Bible declares that man was created in the image of God but every time man tried to achieve equality with God or 'play God', it led to disaster.

The problem with genetic engineering is the scale of potential for damage. A broad spectrum of religious leaders throughout the world have serious objections to the kind of tampering with the basic patterns of life that occur in most genetic engineering research. They point out that what makes genetic engineering special is its power and very importantly, its irreversibility. Its ability to harm human, animal and plant life is much greater than other technologies and does not leave room for mistakes.

 stop and think!

- The future of genetic engineering has been described as 'a minefield and a circus of wonders!' Do you agree?

QUESTIONS

1 What are xenotransplants? Why are they so controversial?

2 What are the two 'foundation stones' found in the teachings of many religious groups concerning the possible use of genetic experiments?

3 On what grounds do some Islamic scholars accept certain forms of genetic engineering?

Hi-tech babies

There are many medical techniques for assisting conceptions, some of which continue to cause a lot of controversy.

For millions of people throughout the world, natural reproduction does not work. It is estimated that in Britain 1 in 10 couples are affected by infertility and on average around 20,000 people a year undertake fertility treatment. In recent years we have witnessed the development of medical techniques which have utterly transformed the treatment of infertility. Since the birth of Louise Brown, the first 'test-tube' baby in 1978, the development of assisted reproduction techniques have given hope to thousands of couples who were unable to have a child. Until these scientific breakthroughs were made, these couples would have either had to go through adoption procedures, or accept that they could not have children.

Today, assisted reproduction can help many childless couples and single women experience parenthood whether they are infertile, post-menopausal, lesbian or women wanting a dead partner's child. Clearly many people, including religious authorities, will argue that these techniques are unnatural and/or against the will of God. Others, however, see it as science simply giving a helping hand to a person who cannot have a baby naturally.

Assisted conception techniques

There are now thirteen ways to have a baby other than through sexual intercourse. Some of these medical techniques involve the use of genetic engineering. Many of these continue to cause a lot of controversy particularly amongst certain religious traditions.

Currently, apart from fertility drugs, the main techniques for assisting fertilisation are:

A Mrs Diane Blood with baby Liam. Her husband's name could not go on Liam's birth certificate – he was not officially recorded as the boy's father.

Test-tube babies

Officially called In Vitro Fertilisation or IVF, it was developed to enable women with blocked fallopian tubes to have children. The woman is given drugs to help her produce eggs which are collected and then fertilised by sperm under laboratory conditions. The embryo is then transferred to the uterus.

AI (artificial insemination)

Artificial insemination is a relatively simple and well-established treatment that has been in clinical use in Britain since the 1930s. Compared with other fertility treatments, it is the cheapest, involving little in the way of medical intervention and virtually no risk. Nowadays, the sperm can be tested for the AIDS virus before it is used so it can be said that sometimes artificial insemination is safer than attempts to achieve pregnancy through sexual intercourse.

There are two basic forms of artificial insemination:

AIH (artificial insemination by husband)

If a couple encounter difficulties in having a child, sperm can be taken from the husband and inserted into the wife's womb. Fertilisation then takes place naturally and the pregnancy develops normally. In 1997 Diane Blood (**A**) made history by giving birth to a child two years after the father had died. Doctors took some of her husband's sperm as he lay dying and froze it. Diane had to fight a long court battle before she was allowed to use the sperm.

AID (artificial insemination by donor)

If a woman's partner is infertile she can be fertilised by sperm taken from an anonymous donor. As British law stands at present, the identity of the donor is kept secret, and the child's birth certificate has the husband or partner's name as the father.

Gamete intra fallopian transfer (GIFT)

GIFT is a procedure in which eggs are extracted from the woman's ovary and then both eggs and sperm are injected through a catheter directly into the fallopian tube. Fertilisation may then take place normally in the body (in vivo).

Egg donation

A woman donates an egg, which is then fertilised with the semen of the husband of the woman into whose uterus the resulting embryo is transferred.

Embryo donation

Similar to egg donation except the ovum is fertilised by semen from a donor because both partners are infertile or both carry a genetic defect.

Surrogacy

The development of reproductive technologies has transformed the practice of surrogacy ('womb leasing'). In the past, this was an option for women who are able to produce eggs but unable to bear children because they have either no uterus or a condition that makes pregnancy dangerous to their health. Now there are different types of surrogacy:

- AI surrogacy where an embryo is created with the sperm of the intended father and egg of the surrogate who will carry the baby.
- IVF surrogacy where the embryo is created by the intended parents and then transferred to the surrogate.
- Donor surrogacy where the embryo is created by using either the sperm of the intended father to fertilise a donor egg or the egg of the intended mother is fertilised by donor sperm and then carried by the surrogate. In some cases neither of the intended parents are actually a biological parent.

 B Britain's first homosexual couple to father surrogate children had their twin babies baptised

Barrie Drewitt and Tony Barlow, both millionaire businessmen, have planned to fly back to the United States to add to their family next year. Mr Drewitt said, 'We have 24 embryos still on ice and we are planning to go again next year.'

The Rev Michael Blyth, defending his decision to carry out the service, said: 'The Church does not make any distinction about parents. We baptise the children of single parents and couples who are cohabiting. It is not for other people to penalise any child or shut them out'.

The couple took advantage of relaxed surrogacy laws to have the babies. The children were conceived with sperm donated by both fathers and a donated egg. The pregnancy was carried through by a Californian surrogate mother... The men, who paid £250,000 for the surrogacy had originally been turned down as suitable parents by adoption agencies in Britain.

After the ceremony Mr Barlow said, 'I am convinced it was the right thing to do. We have had a very positive response from people. And if anyone can't accept it then it's just too bad. They are in the minority.' Mr Drewitt added, 'Times change. There is no such thing as a normal family these days'.

By Thomas Harding, 'Gay couple's surrogate twins are baptised' (*The Daily Telegraph*, 15 May 2000)

Hi-tech babies

In the eyes of many religious authorities advances in medical science raise certain controversial questions. The main opposition to AI is that it is seen as a departure from the natural sexual process. AID, egg/embryo donation and surrogacy all involve a third party. If a third party is involved are these reproductive methods forms of adultery? Also questions have been raised about a number of women who have chosen these methods because they do not wish to have a relationship with a man. Numerous concerns have been expressed over surrogacy particularly when the intended parents are not the biological parents and when the surrogate is paid for her services.

QUESTIONS

1 a What is 'surrogacy'?
   b How many types of surrogacy are there? Briefly describe them.

2 Explain what might be some of the dangers and problems of particular surrogacy cases.

The Warnock Report

The Warnock Committee looked at the subject of test-tube babies, at artificial insemination, and at egg donation. It also considered freezing of test-tube embryos for future use, genetic engineering and cloning, clinical intervention in the genes and chromosomes of embryos and womb leasing. One of the most difficult issues considered was surrogacy.

The Report, published in July 1984, made several far-reaching recommendations:

● All research and treatment of infertility should be licensed by an independent body.

● No experiments should be carried out on embryos more than 14 days old and no embryo used for research should be implanted into a human womb.

● No human embryo should be implanted in the womb of another animal.

● It should be a criminal offence to set up surrogacy agencies on a commercial basis.

In recommending new legislation or regulations, the Committee sought to embody the 'minimum moral requirement' of this society.

C Some of the findings of the Warnock Report

stop and think!

● What is the difference between AIH and AID?

● Why are AIH and GIFT more acceptable to most religious authorities than other assisted reproduction techniques?

Britain and the Warnock Report

Aware of the concerns being expressed by many religious groups and other parties, in 1982 the government set up a special enquiry headed by Dame Mary Warnock to examine IVF treatments and Embryo Experimentation (**C**).

Religious viewpoints

There are several principles which are shared by most of the major religions (**D–F**).

D Buddhist teaching

Each being is related to us ourselves, just as our own parents are related to us in this life. We regard our survival as an inalienable right. As co-inhabitants of this planet, other species too have this right to survival.

The Buddhist Declaration on Nature

E Hindu teaching

I look upon all creatures equally; none are less dear to me and none more dear.

Bhagavad Gita 9:29

F Christian teaching

Right from the beginning, we are conceived and nurtured in a setting of human relatedness; if that is denied us, then a crucial aspect of personhood is denied and we are less than properly human... marriage should be understood as primarily a unique human relationship intended by God to be permanent.

Richard Jones, Groundwork of Christian Ethics, Epworth Press, 1991

 G Sikh teaching

I don't think there are any passages in the Adi Granth touching these subjects, particularly because they were not well known or an order of the day... The Sikhs these days would normally follow the general trend of society and are liberal and broadminded, excepting the very orthodox element.

Dr Chatwal, Secretary of the Sikh Cultural Society

Many people are still concerned that the teachings of the world faiths are ill prepared to deal with the breathtaking developments in medical science. Some representatives of the world religions accept the fact that their holy scriptures do not give much guidance on such matters (**G**).

Some scientists talk of a future where children could be the products of three different sets of parents: biological, **gestational** and nurturers. Religious leaders warn that if these three rroles are separated, the whole concept of parenting will be undermined (**H**).

As with other religions, Hindus would say that medical technology only fits with respect for life (Ahimsa) if the motive is totally selfless, and brings about some spiritual benefit. There are specific barriers that we cannot cross without altering the way in which we relate to others (**I**).

 H Christian teaching

There are undoubted benefits which gene therapy might bring. I do fear for the future, however, if the language of bodily human love is gradually replaced by an artificial process, if procreation becomes production, or even reproduction, and if the individual human being becomes valued as a product to be ordered rather than a gift to be received.

Cardinal Basil Hume

 I Hindu teaching

The result of a virtuous action is pure joy; actions done out of passion bring pain and suffering; ignorance arises from actions motivated by 'dark' intentions.

Bhagavad Gita 14:16

Today, scientists are pushing the technology of assisted reproduction even further. One such medical procedure is 'sex selection' giving hope to thousands of couples who are at risk of passing on serious diseases such as haemophilia (which affects only boys) to their children. Until 1990, such couples wishing to have a child were faced with a terrible dilemma of either taking the high risk of having an affected child or waiting for tests during pregnancy and then, if necessary, requesting an abortion. IVF technology means that male and female embryos can now be identified at a very early stage of development (**J**).

In the case of haemophilia, it is possible to ensure that women at risk will conceive only girls and thereby increase their chances of having healthy children. Clearly, problems can arise with this treatment if the motive for requesting it is not a medical one. For example, if a couple want to have a baby boy because they already have two daughters.

 J

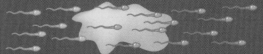

1 Sperm are covered in a DNA-staining solution. The X chromosome (in female producing sperm) contains more DNA than the Y chromosome (the male producing sperm). Therefore, the X chromosome absorbs more solution.

2 When a laser beam is shone on each sperm the stain makes it glow.

3 As the X chromosome absorbs more of the stain solution, it glows more brightly.

4 The 'brighter' sperm can be automatically separated from the 'dimmer' ones.

Hi-tech babies

3 ONE WORLD MANY CHOICES

Genetic engineering (See pages 106–111)

Research into genetic engineering is concentrating on identifying the genes that cause hereditary diseases such as **Down's Syndrome**, with the idea that these 'faulty' genes could be replaced with ones from another healthy human, or from animals.

Three areas stemming from genetic engineering and which are giving rise to many concerns are cloning, ectogenesis and the use of 'spare embryos'.

Cloning

Since the Roslin Institute in Edinburgh successfully cloned Dolly the sheep in 1996, the issue of cloning, particularly in relation to humans, has remained firmly under the media spotlight.

The genetic information about a person is carried in long, complex chains of chemicals called DNA. In theory a cell is taken from Person A, who it is hoped will be cloned, and the nucleus – including all the DNA it contains – is removed. It is then placed next to a donor egg cell that has had its nucleus removed. Gentle pulses of electricity are applied so that the egg accepts the new nucleus. If successful, the resulting embryo is implanted and develops in the uterus of a surrogate. The resulting baby would contain exactly the same DNA and be identical to Person A.

Cloning occurs naturally in the case of identical twins which share both the same genes and the same conditions in the womb. Artificial clones would not be such exact copies because some of a person's biological characteristics are not carried in their genes but are influenced by factors such as the mother's diet during pregnancy. To suggest that if we are cloned, we can live forever implies that we are no more than our DNA and we thereby deny an essential part of our humanity. We are the sum of our experiences and life histories. We are much more than our genes.

Inevitably cloning raises questions of eugenics and what makes up the 'self' and the 'soul'. At present, in Britain, the law regarding the artificial cloning of human beings was relaxed in 2001 to allow the therapeutic cloning of human embryos – producing 'spare part' tissues from cloned embryos up to 14 days old. Scientists are now able to launch research on master cells called 'stem cells' (**K**) found in human embryos which have the potential to develop into any of the body's tissue, including nerves, muscle, organs and bones. By producing a 'carbon copy' embryo of an adult patient, scientists hope to grow unlimited supplies of a variety of perfectly matched body parts from the stem cells. This could end the shortage of human organs for transplant operations and launch a new era in medicine. 'Reproductive' cloning is specifically banned but still remains a possibility in the future.

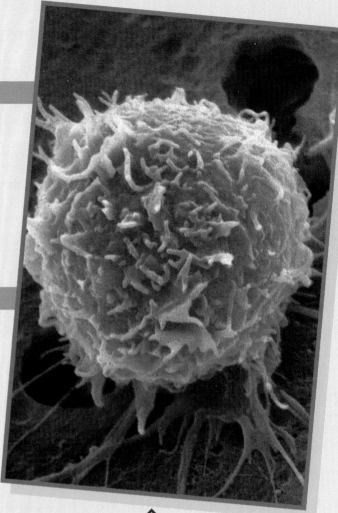

K Stem cells like these can now be taken from cloned embryos and used to treat diseases. Scientists hope, in effect, to create individualised 'body repair kits'.

stop and think!

- The various fertility methods described on pages 112–113 are considered to be perfectly acceptable by many people. What are your thoughts about them?

Ectogenesis (glass womb)

Research has produced artificial wombs capable of sustaining the life of a foetus for a few days. At the other end of the development of a child, the advances in incubator technology mean that babies born as much as three months early are now surviving.

'Spare embryos'

It must be remembered that the conception of Louise Brown came after more than 500 unsuccessful fertilisations. Even with the better assisted reproduction techniques available today, far more fertilised eggs die after unsuccessful implantation attempts than actually develop into a live-born baby. A large number of women have eggs or embryos frozen in case they are needed in future treatment. There is a legal time limit on how long these eggs and embryos can be kept. One problem is that when the time limit is reached, many women cannot be contacted to be advised that their eggs or embryos must now be used or destroyed. Some scientists also experiment on 'spare embryos' as part of their ongoing investigation in developing reproductive techniques and contraception.

Religious viewpoints

There is much agreement between the world religions with regard to developments in reproductive technology. Yet, even within the same religion there can be division.

Roman Catholics believe that an embryo's life is sacred from the moment of conception and therefore disagree with all experimentation. Along with other Christian denominations, the Church of England is more sympathetic to the views of medical bodies like the Royal Colleges and Medical Research Council that insist experimental research on 'spare' embryos provides a vital means of advancing medical knowledge.

On the subject of artificial insemination the Roman Catholic Church insists that embryos have human rights and are not to be treated as a means to an end. It describes any technique that involves a third party as 'mechanical adultery' but accepts that if the marriage act is preserved the 'various clinical techniques designed to help create new life are not to be condemned'. The Church of England views AIH and AID as acceptable practices provided that donors do not sell their sperm. It also regards IVF treatment as acceptable but like the Roman Catholic Church it is firmly set against commercial surrogacy believing that 'it violates the dignity of motherhood that a woman should be paid for bearing a child'.

QUESTIONS

BRAVE NEW BABIES

Born or made?

New agony over surrogate twins

Vatican in test-tube baby row

1 What dangers could arise if sex selection was openly available to couples?

2 'Stem cell research opens up a new medical frontier. It offers enormous potential for new treatments of chronic diseases and injuries and the relief of human suffering.'
Professor Liam Donaldson, Chief Medical Officer

'Obtaining stem cells from a human embryo is morally wrong because it involves the destruction of a human life.'
Cardinal Thomas Winning, Chairman of the Bioethics Committee of the Catholic Bishops of Great Britain and Ireland

With which statement do you feel the most sympathy? Give reasons for your answer, showing that you have considered the different points of view.

117

1 Can you think of ways that medicine has given us control over:
a birth?
b life?
c death?

2 What is meant by the 'sanctity of life'?

3 What is meant by the terms:
a birth control?
b family planning?
c contraception?

4 Do you think the Roman Catholic Church is too severe in its teachings on contraception? Give reasons for your answer.

5 How is it possible for Christians to hold such different views on birth control?

6 Should contraceptives be easily available to young people without their parents' knowledge?

7 Outline the current legal position in Britain regarding abortion.

8 Briefly explain the views on abortion held by the organisations Life and BPAS.

9 In what situations do you think a Muslim or a Hindu might consider abortion to be acceptable?

10 Try and explain, in your own words, why the Roman Catholic Church opposes abortion.

11 Apart from abortion, what other options are available to a woman who has an unwanted pregnancy?

12 'It is a woman's right to choose whether to have an abortion or not.'
a Explain how people with religious beliefs might react to the statement above.
b Do you think anyone else should be involved in the decision?

13 Why is the issue of adoption problematic for:
a Muslims?
b Hindus?

14 What is the difference between active and passive euthanasia?

15 Is there a difference between 'being alive' and 'living'? Give reasons for your answer.

16 What developments have caused the euthanasia issue to be such a problem today, compared with 20 years ago?

17 Explain the following words or terms:
a EXIT
b hospice
c living will
d PVS

18 The Sikh view is that death is only a step towards another life. Does this belief have any bearing on the issue of euthanasia? Give reasons for your answer.

19 'Why is a human being allowed to live in a state where we would have no hesitation in putting an animal to sleep?'

Should we treat humans in the same way as we treat animals?

20 'People have the right to decide for themselves whether they should live or die.'

In what ways might an individual's attitude to euthanasia be different depending on the religious faith he or she held?

21 Explain the work of a hospice. What do you think are the three most important features of hospice care?

22 Try and explain in your own words the Jewish attitude to the issue of organ transplants.

23 Muslims believe that all bodies belong to Allah and therefore individuals have no say in what happens to them after death. Do you think that this belief has any bearing on the issue of organ donation?

24 What is the difference between:

a somatic cell and germ line therapy?

b therapeutic and non-therapeutic gene therapy?

25 Explain what is meant by In Vitro Fertilisation and why it is used?

26 Why do you think the Roman Catholic Church opposes AID?

27 What is meant by surrogate motherhood, and why are some people opposed to it?

28 What were the four main findings of the Warnock Report?

29 What do scientists mean when they talk about the possibility in the future of children being the products of three different sets of parents – biological, gestational and nurturers?

30 Are there any circumstances when human embryos should be used for medical reasons?

31 'Mary had a little lamb,
    it's fleece was slightly grey.
It didn't have a father,
    just some borrowed DNA.
It sort of had a mother,
    though the ovum was on loan.
It was not so much a lambkin
    as a little lamby clone.'

What do you think are the main reasons why many religions are concerned about changing human embryos?

Introduction
One world

Unit aims

The aims of this unit are to present a range of environmental issues for you to consider and respond to. It also introduces you to some of the traditional religious beliefs relating to the care of planet earth and the advice given in teachings which are concerned about the use of the earth and its resources.

Key concepts

From space, the planet earth looks fine: white swirls of cloud moving over continents or the great oceans. Earth might look peaceful from such a distance but this is not the case. Some see the planet as something which exists purely for their convenience; others, however, care deeply about threats to the environment. The major world faiths find themselves in the difficult position of accepting that we live in a technological world but, at the same time, urging restraint and conservation.

What is this unit about?

Some religions stand accused of allowing the environment to be slowly destroyed: after all, within Christianity and Judaism there is an assumption that the human race was appointed by God to be in control of nature. Other religions, such as Buddhism, insist that instead of being superior, we should be in close harmony – part of nature.

The last twenty years have witnessed green open spaces disappearing into housing and business projects, road systems and shopping malls. Along with so called 'progress' has come the destruction of this wildlife and nature with little thought for the future. Religious leaders recognise that the earth is at risk and urge their followers to do something about it.

wonderful world?

We also contribute to polluting the atmosphere, to fouling the seas and shorelines, and to contaminating the land with poisons. Nearly all the religious teachings are quite clear on these issues: it is essential that the correct balance is achieved between progress and conservation. At the moment, the price we are paying for progress is just too high. The earth must be saved from further destruction otherwise future generations will inherit nothing.

It is ironic that we get excited about the possibility of life on other planets and yet we stand back and allow wholesale destruction of numerous species of plants and animals on this one. Some religions do not appear to take animal suffering seriously whereas others are totally committed to preserving all types of life. The conclusion must be drawn that some religious believers must share a heavy responsibility for the continuing abuse of animals in the modern world. In *Mountain Lion*, D H Lawrence wrote in 1923, 'Man! The only animal in the world to fear.'

Certain religions believe in reincarnation and most religious traditions urge followers to show kindness and compassion towards animals. Consequently vegetarianism is often regarded as the easiest way to live according to the ethical, environmental and health precepts of many world faiths.

Towards the end of the twentieth century religious leaders and teachers have had to focus their attention on the genetic modification of animals and plants. Some religions disagree totally with what is seen as 'tampering with nature' whereas others seem to have few objections. They feel that the benefits of genetic engineering, as long as it helps to preserve or improve human or animal life, should be taken into account.

Why worry?

Questions about pollution and conservation are becoming increasingly important to many people. These days, we are more aware of the consequences of our actions with regard to the health of our planet and all its living forms. People are prepared to act to ensure that the earth has a future, but even so, large numbers of once common plants, fruit and vegetables are becoming extinct every year.

Many of our environmental problems are due to greed – to people's desire to make money. If you can produce, in a laboratory, a type of apple or carrot that is ready earlier, that lasts longer and that looks nicer, this will be the one growers and supermarket chains will want to sell (**A**). Everyone will make more profit. The destruction of the hedgerows, local beauty spots, the rainforests and other huge areas of land are often largely related to man's desire to make a profit. Land is also taken to provide housing and roads connecting towns and villages.

The saying 'apple of my eye' comes from the Bible and means 'child of my eye'. It is therefore precious and a symbol of God's love for human beings.

A In the last century, we have lost over 6,000 varieties of the precious apple

B The harmful effects of acid rain

> The World's religions have done virtually nothing to help physically save the world, or to place on the central agenda of their believers the need to care for or with nature.
>
> Believing in the Environment, *Martin Palmer, from* World Goodwill Occasional Paper, *1988*

Christianity

Some people believe that the major world faiths have not done enough to prevent this wide-scale destruction (**C**).

The signs today are more optimistic. Christians, for example, accept that they have certain responsibilities towards all living things because they believe that God placed them in the position of **stewards** for his creation. It is up to the Churches, to new movements, and to leaders to take the initiative (**D**).

The problem is that many individuals believe that this stewardship allows them to exploit nature and behave irresponsibly, if they so wish.

The Catholic Agency For Overseas Development (CAFOD) and Christian Aid, recognising that the needs of people relate to a healthy local environment, have implemented tree planting schemes, and have worked to save local habitats.

Islam

Muslims believe that Allah created the world and everything in it. Human beings are the most important creation and have been given the role of 'guardians' (khalifah).

Islamic teachings make clear that Allah entrusted the planet to mankind, and it is important that Muslims play a leading part in the efforts to protect the environment. They must look after the environment and ensure that it is never spoiled (**E**).

Buddhism

A very important part of Buddhist teaching is focused on the interaction between mankind and the environment. We are part of the natural world and we should be attempting to preserve it. At the same time, Buddhists are aware of the need to live in the modern world, making use of resources of raw materials and fuel.

Buddhists believe that all individuals must actively try to protect the environment and ensure that any acts of neglect or destruction do not occur. The Buddhist view is to avoid harm to any living thing, from the largest mammal to the smallest insect (**F**).

 D Christian teaching

> Nature now belongs to us and is part of us, so that our whole life is interwoven with it... We want to be human in the world, rather than human by conquering it.
>
> Towards a Green Humanism, *Don Cupitt General Studies Review Vol. 1 No 1.*

> The Lord God took man and put him in the Garden of Eden to work it and take care of it.
>
> *Genesis 2:15*

 E Muslim teaching

> Nature and the world are a field of exploration and the object of enjoyment for the Muslim. But whether he uses them for utility or for sheer enjoyment, he must avoid waste and excess. As a responsible agent of God and a conscientious trustee, he must always be mindful of others who share the world with him and who will succeed him in the future.
>
> Islam in Focus, *by Hammudah Abdalati, 1981*

> It is Allah who has subjected the sea to you... And he had subjected to you, as from Him, all that is in the heavens and on earth.
>
> *Surah 45:12–13*

 F Buddhist teaching

> (Buddhism) attaches great importance to wildlife and the protection of the environment on which every being in the world depends for survival.
>
> *The Assisi Declaration, 29 September 1986*

> Monks and nuns may not 'destroy any plant or tree'.
>
> *Vinaya Pitaka*

Why worry?

Sae Sau, aged 48 years, works as a paid volunteer at the Reforestation Nursery run by monks. They produce seedlings and plant trees in the forest.

H

There are hundreds of organisations which encourage millions of individuals to involve themselves actively in environmental issues. The Worldwide Fund for Nature and Friends of the Earth, for example, are both important in influencing public awareness of environmental concerns throughout the world.

Every country has people who campaign about issues that affect the country they live in and issues that affect the whole world. Ajahn Pongsak, a Buddhist monk in Thailand, is trying to educate people in his country about the importance of replanting trees after more than 50 per cent of the country's forests disappeared in only 30 years.

International conferences are frequently held where environmental issues are discussed, and attempts to find solutions are made. In recent years organisations have started to join forces to tackle some of the problems that worry them most.

In the UK, another result of concerns for the local environment was the establishment of the Church and Conservation Project in 1987. Supported by the World Wildlife Fund, the Royal Agricultural Society and the Nature Conservancy Council, this project assists with the training of clergy in rural areas, and gives advice on the best ways to conserve the land holdings of the Churches. Particularly effective has been the Living Churchyard Project, which has identified burial grounds as actual and potential havens for wildlife.

stop and think!

- What kinds of problems are causing people to worry about the future of the world?

- Which environmental problems worry you most?

- Why do so many people feel so strongly about the environment that they are prepared to do more than just complain?

Whilst it is true that governments and large companies are more likely to take notice of large groups than of individuals, there are people, as we have seen, who have made a significant contribution to the environment on their own. It should also be remembered that most of the large organisations concerned with environmental issues were started by individuals prepared to act on their beliefs and ideals.

stop and think!

- We have lost 97 per cent of the varieties of vegetables that existed at the beginning of the last century. Why do you think this is?

- Why are scientists rushing to endangered rainforests to take samples of some of the rare plants that exist only in these areas?

- How does the Bible support the belief that Christians are the stewards of all living things?

- Does the future survival of human beings depend on the survival of their environment?

The United Nations (UN) 'Earth Summit' in 1992

QUESTIONS

1 Read **E**.
  a What does 'conscientious trustee' mean?
  b Why should a conscientious trustee be concerned about endangered species?

2 How practical would it be if we all tried to follow the teaching in **F**?

3 What advice do the religious teachings give us about how we should be looking after the planet earth?

4 What advantages are there for the environment if more organisations work together on one particular problem or issue?

5 What do pictures **G**, **H** and **I** tell us about the commitment some people are prepared to make because of their concerns about the environment?

6 If individuals and organisations around the world are working to save the environment, why are there still real worries about the future of this planet?

7 'What befalls the earth befalls all the sons and daughters of the earth… This we all know: All things are connected like the blood that unites us. We did not weave the web of life, we are merely a strand in it. Whatever we do to the web, we do to ourselves.' (*Brother Eagle, Sister Sky: A Message from Chief Seattle*, by Susan Jeffers, Puffin Books, 1993)

What should we be doing to ensure that we stop losing the varied life of this planet?

Poisoned planet

Pollution is not a new problem. For hundreds of years we have been aware of the devastating effects of smoke in the atmosphere. However, we seem to have ignored the lessons of history, and today, smoke is only one of the many ways in which we are poisoning the planet.

A Litter is just another way that we pollute our environment – can you think of any others?

B Christian teaching

We have no liberty to do what we like with our natural environment; it is not ours to treat as we please. 'Dominion' is not a synonym for 'domination', let alone 'destruction'.
The Rev Dr John Stott, President of Tear Fund

It is tragic that our technological mastery is greater than our wisdom about ourselves.
Pope John Paul II

We have no right to plunder, pollute, exploit, destroy, kill or in any way disrespect God's creation.
Simon Phipps, Bishop of Lincoln, November, 1986.

The air is constantly fouled by the burning of fossil fuels in homes, cars, factories and power stations. Sulphur dioxide is released into the atmosphere and then washed back down in acid rain. The amount of carbon dioxide in the earth's atmosphere has steadily risen leading to changes in the world's climates. The ozone layer, which protects us from harmful ultraviolet rays from the sun, is being eroded. This is caused by, among other things, the gases (known as CFCs) used in some aerosols, and in the exhausts of high-flying aircraft.

As well as the atmosphere, pollution also damages soil, rivers and seas. Around 70 per cent of the earth's surface is water and, in recent years, huge areas have been polluted by oil spillages, sewage and even toxic waste. When the supertanker, the *Exxon Valdez*, was involved in an accident off the Alaskan coast in 1989, over 50 million litres of oil were leaked into the sea. Beaches were covered in oil, thousands of animals died, and fishing stocks were severely affected for years.

Despite warnings from scientists that the tropical rainforests are irreplaceable and are the richest source of life on earth, they are felled at an alarming rate to provide us with fuel, timber, paper and land for farming. In addition, the mass clearing and burning of the forests contributes to air pollution and affects worldwide rainfall patterns. The land itself is threatened when it loses its tree cover. A desert may be all that remains where forests once grew.

Christianity

All the major world religions speak about the need to respect the earth and some, such as Christianity, Judaism and Islam, strongly believe that humankind has been appointed by God to be in command of nature. Since God is the creator of the world and has given human beings the responsibility for it, Christians have an extremely powerful reason to adopt a sensitive and caring policy towards nature, the environment and fellow creatures (**B**).

Hinduism

Hindus suggest that we are part of the natural world and humankind should be in harmony with it, rather than in control (**C**).

Sikhism

Sikh teachings insist that all followers should make every effort to help slow down and halt the present destructive trends in society (**D**).

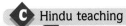

C Hindu teaching

Thou [Krishna – the Supreme Reality/Lord] art the dark blue butterfly, and the green parrot with red eyes. Thou art the thundercloud, the seasons and the oceans.
Shvetashvatara Upanishad, 4.4

The Isa Upanishad tells us that everything, from a blade of grass to the whole cosmos, is the home of God. God lives in every corner of existence. Therefore the whole creation is sacred.
Ranchor Prime, Hinduism and Ecology

D Sikh teaching

Sikhism teaches both respect and responsibility towards God's creation and the needs of future generations.
Indarjit Singh JP, Editor, Sikh Messenger

The Lord pervades all created beings; God creates all and assigns all their tasks.
Adi Granth 434

By God's will the Lord has created the creation and watches over all.
Adi Granth 1036

GREENPEACE

Greenpeace, an organisation that has actively campaigned against the poisoning of the earth, was founded in 1971 by Jim Bohlen, Paul Cote and Irving Stowe as a direct protest against the testing of H-bombs in the South Pacific. Irving Stowe introduced Bohlen to the Quakers who believe in a form of protest known as 'bearing witness'. This is a form of passive resistance that involves going to the scene of an activity you object to, and registering opposition to it simply by your presence there. Since 1971, Greenpeace volunteers have carried the symbols of ecology and peace to all corners of the earth bearing witness to the pollution and the unnecessary destruction of many forms of life.

E Greenpeace members protesting against the dumping of Shell's 'Brent Spar' oil platform in the North Sea

stop and think!

- In what ways has Greenpeace continued to 'bear witness'?

- Might a person's religious beliefs prevent involvement with an organisation like Greenpeace?

- What do you feel strongly enough about to want to 'bear witness'?

QUESTIONS

1 In what ways are we poisoning the planet?

2 Was Pope John Paul II right when he said that we do not have the wisdom to match our technological abilities?

3 'One of the UK's largest and longest-running schemes for monitoring the effects of acid rain may be discontinued following a threat by the Department of Environment to remove funding... The news comes as more evidence of the **detrimental** effects of acid rain on wildlife is surfacing.' *BBC Wildlife Magazine, Vol 14. No. 4.* What is your immediate reaction to this extract?

Conservation

The Beauty of the World: Antarctica – even in the driest, highest, coldest and windiest continent the wonders of nature can be clearly seen

A

Scientists tell us that life first appeared on earth about 3,000 million years ago. Since then it has evolved into literally millions of different forms. All these species live in a natural balance with one another but one species threatens to unsettle this balance… Humans.

Many people today believe that the planet earth is becoming less pleasant to live on. By covering more and more of the planet with our cities, farms and waste we have damaged and reduced the natural resources that took millions of years to develop. We have failed to use them effectively and, ultimately, the earth simply will not be able to support life.

Post-quake landscape. This earthquake in Taiwan registered 7.6 on the Richter scale.

B

The climatic changes which were recorded throughout the second half of the twentieth century are clear evidence of man's stupidity. In the last half of the twentieth century the planet has been hit by over 250 great natural disasters, killing at least 1.5 million people. The late 1980s and 1990s had four times as many natural catastrophes than in the 1950s. Experts believe that as the world's population continues to grow and increasing numbers of people pack into large and vulnerable coastal towns and cities, the number of disasters will climb still higher.

A rise of half a metre in sea levels over 100 years may not sound very much, but when a country's land is less than 2 metres above sea level, it matters a great deal. Hundreds of populated atoll islands are threatened each year. In 1950, only one city, New York, had more than 10 million inhabitants. By 2000 there were 20, of which 16 were in the developing world (**C**). The problems associated with living in these 'mega-cities' are enormous. Places like Tokyo, Bombay and Dhaka cannot cope with millions of tons of household refuse. Breathing the air in New Delhi is equal to smoking 10–20 cigarettes a day! All kinds of waste including human sewage, toxic chemicals and nuclear waste contaminate our land, rivers and seas.

Throughout the 1990s and the start of the twenty first century, religious leaders have expressed their concerns and repeatedly warned of the dangers of abusing the gifts of nature. They point to the threats posed by man-made climate change and the senseless exploitation of the earth's resources. In all religions there is the feeling that human beings are just part of the natural world and they should not force change upon it. The major world religions believe that all humans are stewards, responsible for looking after the planet.

C The growth of large cities

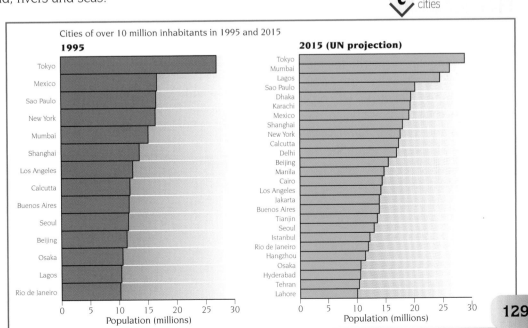

Cities of over 10 million inhabitants in 1995 and 2015

1995

Tokyo
Mexico
Sao Paulo
New York
Mumbai
Shanghai
Los Angeles
Calcutta
Buenos Aires
Seoul
Beijing
Osaka
Lagos
Rio de Janeiro

Population (millions)

2015 (UN projection)

Tokyo
Mumbai
Lagos
Sao Paulo
Dhaka
Karachi
Mexico
Shanghai
New York
Calcutta
Delhi
Beijing
Manila
Cairo
Los Angeles
Jakarta
Buenos Aires
Tianjin
Seoul
Istanbul
Rio de Janeiro
Hangzhou
Osaka
Hyderabad
Tehran
Lahore

Population (millions)

Conservation

In 1992 leaders from 178 nations met in Rio de Janeiro for the Earth Summit, in an effort to make agreements that would help protect and preserve the global environment. Unfortunately, on many of the critical issues, words failed to be backed up by action. Five years later leading environmental experts, scientists and politicians gathered for a 10 day summit in the Japanese city of Kyoto. At the top of their agenda was a campaign of action to prevent what they saw as the main threats to the world environment: global warming, ozone depletion, deforestation and desertification. All four threats are interconnected and must be addressed if further damage to our environment was to be avoided. In 2000, however, when officials from 160 countries met in The Hague, Holland, they failed to reach agreement and talks about greenhouse gas emission collapsed mainly because the USA refused to take the necessary action to meet the target set in Kyoto.

Six years before the Rio conference, representatives of all the main world religions met in Assisi on 29 September 1986. The event marked the 25th anniversary of the World Wide Fund for Nature. The conference took place in Assisi, Italy, a place chosen in recognition of the work of St Francis of Assisi. For centuries, his teachings on conservation have been widely admired, and in Christian circles he is acknowledged as the 'patron saint of ecology' (**D**). In response to the environmental dangers facing the world, the religious leaders who took part in this event produced a programme of education, action and reflection – the Network on Conservation and Religion. The success of Assisi was followed by further conferences: in 1995 at Ohito in Japan, for example, and at Windsor Castle, where the Summit on Religions and Conservation adopted the Ohito Declaration.

D

We, members of major world religions and traditions, and men and women of good will, are gathered here, in this marvellous Church of St Francis, to awaken all people to their historical responsibility for the welfare of Planet Earth, our Sister and Mother, who in her generous sovereignty feeds us and all her creatures.

Father Lanfranco Serrini – The Assisi Declarations

stop and think!

- In what ways can we contribute to conservation?

Islam

From their reading of the Qur'an, Muslims accept that responsible stewardship is essential and that they all must play a leading part in protecting the environment. Allah has created the planet and humans have the responsibility of looking after all of the other creations on the planet (**E**). Life on earth is established with natural balance and Allah has made things in nature available for the use of man. For example, the healthy effects of salt water and fresh air are well known and yet, man seems to continue destroying them.

E Muslim teaching

For the Muslim, mankind's role on earth is that of a 'khalifa', vice-regent or trustee of God. We are God's stewards and agents on earth. We are not masters of this earth; it does not belong to us to do what we wish. It belongs to God and He has entrusted us with its safekeeping... His trustees are responsible for maintaining the unity of His creation, the integrity of the earth, its flora and fauna, its wildlife and natural environment.

The Muslim Declaration on Nature

It is He who sends down rain from the sky. From it you drink, and out of it (grows) the vegetation on which you feed your cattle. With it He produces for you corn, olives, date palms, grapes and every kind of fruit... He has made subject to you the Night and the Day; the Sun and the Moon; and the Stars are in subjection by His command... If you count up the favours of Allah, never would you be able to number them.

Surah 16:10, 12 and 18

QUESTIONS

1 What do you understand by the following words/terms:
  a environment?
  b mega-city?
  c deforestation?
  d ozone depletion?
  e global warming?
  f desertification?

2 Some conservationists believe that it is a race against time to save the planet earth from destruction. Outline three serious problems that suggest this may be so.

3 Looking at the photographs on pages 126–129, explain the religious reasons why people should be concerned about the dangers to the environment shown.

4 What meeting took place on 29 September 1986? What was significant about the choice of venue for this meeting?

5 What is meant by a 'khalifa'? Write down what Islam teaches about the correct treatment of the environment.

In November 1991 a meeting on environmental protection took place in Ohito, Japan. The conference was organised by the Christian Orthodox Church but eight representatives of other world religions also took part. The Ohito Declaration on Religions, Land and Conservation published guidelines for future action caring for the planet earth (**F**):

 **F** Recommended courses of action

1 We call upon religious leaders to emphasise environmental issues within religious teaching: faith should be taught and practised as if nature mattered.

2 We call upon religious communities to commit themselves to sustainable practices and encourage community use of their land.

3 We call upon religious leaders to recognise the need for ongoing environmental education and training for themselves and all those engaged in religious instruction.

4 We call upon people of faith to promote environmental education within their community especially among their youth and children.

5 We call upon people of faith to implement individual, community and institutional action plans at local, national, and global levels that flow from their spiritual practices and where possible to work with other faith communities.

6 We call upon religious leaders and faith communities to pursue peacemaking as an essential component of conservation action.

7 We call upon religious leaders and communities to be actively involved in caring for the environment to sponsor sustainable food production and consumption.

8 We call upon people of faith to take up the challenge of instituting fair trading practices devoid of financial, economic and political exploitation.

9 We call upon the world's religious leaders and world institutions to establish and maintain a networking system that will encourage sustainable agriculture and environmental life systems.

10 We call upon faith communities to act immediately, to check and review these policies on conservation issues on a regular basis.

More recently the World Bank has recognised the important role that the world religions can play. A meeting of religious leaders from nine world faiths took place in February 1998 at Lambeth Palace. It was jointly chaired by the Archbishop of Canterbury and the President of the World Bank, to discuss, amongst other things, responsibility for the environment.

The Christian Church makes clear in its teachings that care for planet earth is crucial if the human race is going to survive. Working in some of the poorest countries in the world, Christian aid agencies such as Tear Fund, CAFOD and Christian Aid draw attention to the misery caused by the unjust way that the earth's resources are distributed.

From the two meetings held in Assisi and Ohito it has become clear that although many different beliefs exist about the environment, religious groups express concern and agreement over four areas (**H**):

G Christian teaching

Praised be my Lord God for all his creatures, especially for our brother the sun who brings us the day and who brings us the light... praised be my Lord for our sister the moon, and for the stars, which he has set clear and lovely in heaven. Praised be my Lord for our brother the wind, and for the air and clouds, calms and all weather by which you uphold life in all creatures...
The Canticle of the Sun – St Francis of Assisi

When I consider your heavens, the work of your fingers, the moon and the stars, which you have set in place, what is man that you are mindful of him, the son of man that you care for him?
Psalm 8:3–4

 Religious agreement!

Planet earth is sacred.

Nature should not be exploited.

Humans must look after the planet.

Humans should work alongside nature and not against it.

It is now essential to involve religious followers at large in the discussion and implementation of these four principles. Since the meetings at Assisi and Ohito, clear guidelines have been given on conservation. In the past the world faiths have done little about the situation preferring to leave it to international agencies and governments. Today, many faith communities are setting up projects that help preserve the natural resources of planet earth, taking positive action to protect and conserve nature. They realise that it is essential that everyone responds to these concerns.

 World religious leaders gathered together in Assisi

stop and think!

- **How can we help to preserve the planet's resources?**

QUESTIONS

1 Look through the list of guidelines produced in the Ohito Declaration on Religions, Land and Conservation. In your opinion which three are the most important recommendations? Give reasons for your choices.

2 Describe and explain how Christian teaching might affect attitudes to the environment.

3 Explain why so many religions feel that humans have been given responsibility for the earth.

4 Take any one religion and describe some of the positive steps it is taking towards safeguarding the environment.

5 'The Lord God took the man and put him in the Garden of Eden to work in it and take care of it.' (Genesis 2:15)

   Explain what most Christians believe is the purpose of humans in the world. State one way this teaching might affect the way believers treat the resources of the natural world.

Animal rights

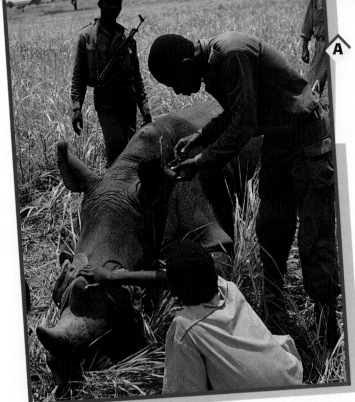

A Helped to survive! An endangered White Rhino is radio-tagged to protect it from poachers

Certain species of animals are near extinction because of hunting, urbanisation and agriculture. Huge numbers of wildlife are threatened because their natural habitats are being damaged as roads, houses and industrial sites are built. As fields are ploughed, levelled, fertilised and re-seeded many animals and plants are destroyed.

Over the last two centuries thousands of species of animals have become extinct and, even today, hundreds of animals are on the endangered list. Under pressure from environmental groups such as Greenpeace, Friends of the Earth, WWF and RSPCB, some nations are now beginning to act to ensure the survival of endangered species (**A**).

There appear to be seven main areas of concern regarding the poor treatment that animals face at the hands of humans (**B**):

B The seven main areas of concern

Work

Fur

Hunting

Food

Medical experimentation

Cosmetic experimentation

Entertainment

Some of these areas appear to be more controversial than others. In recent years killing animals for fur, cosmetic experimentation and hunting are largely frowned upon. Using animals for food, work, or medical experimentation however, seems more acceptable. Most people believe that animals should be protected and not harmed unnecessarily but clearly animals are still being mistreated, exploited and killed for what many regard as immoral reasons.

Even today, despite widespread education and media attention, many animals such as the chiru, a rare Tibetan antelope, face extinction. The wool of the chiru is used to make shahtooshes, a kind of scarf or shawl (**C**). The shahtoosh is very fine and incredibly light because the chiru's hair is seven times thinner than human hair. During the 1980s shahtooshes became a must-have for wealthy women and a few men who were happy to pay £650 for a scarf and from £2,000 to £10,000 for a shawl. Despite being protected by a United Nations ruling there are now only 75,000 chiru left in the world when just 100 years ago there was well over one million!

Animals are often treated as little more than 'machines' on factory farms. Every year millions of animals are crammed together in tiny spaces. In factory farms chickens have their beaks cut off, cattle are often dehorned and castrated and many animals are branded and their tails are cut off without the use of anaesthetics. Dairy cows are kept constantly pregnant through artificial insemination so they keep producing milk. Due to the overcrowded conditions on factory farms diseases quickly spread and so farmers routinely feed or inject the animals with antibiotics. They are often sprayed with pesticides and to fatten them up quickly they are fed growth hormones. Despite widespread protests, wild animals like mink are still kept in captivity for their fur and other animals are bred to be used in experiments or exported abroad in appalling conditions (**D** and **E**).

Followers of all the world faiths are clearly expected to show respect for all parts of creation and there are clear guidelines laid down about the treatment of animals. Generally these can be summed up as follows:

- Animals should be treated well and properly looked after.
- If an animal is to be killed it should be done humanely.
- Animals must only be used for food or other beneficial purposes.
- Animal breeding or experimentation for luxury goods is forbidden.

C Animal cruelty. Chiru hair used for scarves and shawls.

D Up until 2001, farms in England slaughtered over 100,000 mink for fur

E Ban live exports!

135

Animal rights

Buddhism

One world religion is consistent in its views on animal rights. As far as Buddhists are concerned, killing an animal for any purpose is wrong. Buddhists try to practise five basic guidelines known as the Five Precepts. The First Precept of Buddhism is 'Do not kill, but rather preserve and cherish all life'. The Buddhist teachings, set out by the Zen Buddhist monk and peace activist Thich Nhat Hanh, make clear that all life is sacred and must be cared for (**F**).

 F Buddhist teaching

Aware of the suffering caused by the destruction of life, I undertake to cultivate compassion and learn ways to protect the lives of people, animals, plants and minerals.

Thich Nhat Hanh – The First Precept: Reverence for Life

Protecting human life is not possible without protecting the lives of animals, plants and minerals... While practising the protection of humans, animals, plants and minerals, we know that we are protecting ourselves. We feel in permanent and loving touch with all species on Earth... The practice of the First Precept is a celebration of reverence for life. When we appreciate and honour the beauty of life, we will do everything in our power to protect all life.

The First Precept: Reverence for Life

QUESTIONS

1 State two things humans have or do that make them different from animals?

2 Look at the seven main areas of concern regarding the treatment of animals (**B**) and answer the following questions.

   a In your opinion, which area of concern is the most controversial?

   b Do you agree with using animals for experiments? Give reasons for your answer.

   c Write an article on the following statement: 'In view of the fact that so many species of wildlife are threatened zoos are a good thing.' Remember you do not have to agree with the statement but you must support your comments.

3 What are the Five Precepts and why does the First Precept have a direct link to animal rights issues?

G Do humans need animals more than animals need humans?

Apart from Buddhism most religions have been criticised for not being sympathetic to animal protection concerns. Many religious traditions for example accept that scientific experiments on laboratory animals that might find cures for human illnesses should be allowed. Likewise the use of animals for work, as pets and for producing food raise few objections as long as the animals are not subjected to pain or discomfort because this would break the religious laws forbidding cruelty to animals. Almost without exception, religious traditions object to animals being killed or experimented upon for reasons that are not considered right and/or moral such as hunting or cosmetic research.

Islam

Muslim teachings regarding the welfare of animals is set out in the Qur'an. All of the Qur'an's 114 chapters except one begin with the phrase 'Allah is merciful and compassionate'. The prophet Muhammad forbade cruelty to animals (**H**). He condemned the branding, beating or imprisonment of animals as well as hunting them for sport and forbade the setting up of animals to fight each other. The teachings of the Qur'an make it quite clear that animals should not be treated as mere resources for humans. Practices on factory farms, for example, contradict the Prophet's teachings to cause no pain to an animal before it is killed.

The Qur'an does permit meat-eating but many Muslims have concluded that animal products should not be consumed. Given these traditions, many Shi'ite Muslims and the Islamic mystics such as the Sufis, choose vegetarianism as the proper diet. The majority of Muslims however eat halal meat, that is meat prepared according to specific dietary laws. According to Muslim law, animals must be killed according to the halal method where the jugular vein is cut with a sharp knife, allowing the maximum drainage of blood. When the animal is being killed the name of Allah is invoked in a prayer (Tasmiyyah) to show that the animal's life is being taken solemnly, with the permission of God and the act must be done out of sight of any other animals that are going to be killed.

H Muslim teaching

[The Prophet] said, 'One who kills even a sparrow or anything smaller without a justifiable reason will be answerable to Allah'. When asked what would be a justifiable reason he replied, 'To slaughter it for food – not to kill and discard it'.
Reported by Ahmad and Al-Nassa'i (The Muslim Educational Trust)

There is not an animal (that lives) on the earth, nor a being that flies on its wings, but (forms part of) communities like you.
Surah 6:38

Christianity

Animal rights is an issue on which Christian traditions vary. Many devout Christians such as St Francis of Assisi and Dr Albert Schweitzer have encouraged respect and reverence for all life. The description of Jesus as the 'Good Shepherd' reinforces to Christian followers the need for a caring attitude towards animals. All Christians would agree that cruelty to animals goes against the will of God. Opinions, however, remain divided over certain issues. Whereas some Christians support the use of animals for food or scientific experiments, others, such as the Quakers, actively campaign to stop such things as experimentation, blood sports and the live transportation of animals.

Recognising that animals are an important part of God's creation, some Christian churches now set aside time in the religious calendar for 'pet or animal services'. People, especially children, are encouraged to bring their animals to church to receive God's blessing. Ely Cathedral, for example, has an annual pet service for the Wood Green Animal Shelter.

In the past, many world faiths have been accused by animal rights supporters of ignoring the cruelty and poor treatment that many animals face at the hands of humans. Despite these criticisms all the world faiths show great concern for animal welfare and the responsibility that humans have to look after them. As far as supporters of 'animal rights' are concerned, however, many religions such as Christianity, Judaism and Islam are guilty of saying one thing and doing another.

QUESTIONS

1 Explain how religious followers might do more for animal welfare in order to fulfil their responsibilities as 'stewards' or 'custodians' of the earth.

2 Why would you expect a Buddhist to be actively involved in saving endangered animals?

3 'Everyone, whether they are religious or not, should be actively involved in the animal rights issue.' Do you agree? Give reasons or evidence for your answer showing that you have thought about more than one point of view.

Vegetarianism

Today many religious followers believe that eating meat conflicts with their teachings of kindness and compassion to animals.

A Ganesha, Nandi and Hanuman

Hinduism

Hinduism bases its teachings on the oldest and most sacred writings – the Vedas. Vedic texts repeatedly urge Hindus to act non-violently towards humans and animals. Animals figure very prominently in the Hindu religion. Many of the Hindu gods take the form of animals (**A**).

A Ganesha, Nandi and Hanuman

Nandi, the sacred bull

The elephant-headed god, Ganesha

Hanuman, the monkey-god

B A traditional image of Indian cattle

To be a Hindu, only two things are required; that a person looks for the truth and practises ahimsa, which means avoiding harm to other living things. Consequently, most Hindus are vegetarians because causing the death of anything that breathes is contrary to ahimsa. As far as Hindus are concerned God is present in all things and there is no clear difference between humans and animals. They believe that like humans, animals have feelings and souls that are reincarnated into different life forms over time. Certain Hindu gods such as Hanuman (the monkey-god) and Ganesha (the elephant-headed god) play major parts in some Hindu stories. Other animals such as the eagle, swan, bull, mouse, peacock, elephant, and tiger are regarded as sacred. The last three animals are some of the most protected animals in India.

In the Hindu religion there is a strong link between humans and animals. Various groups of Hindus have their own sacred animals but the most sacred of all the animals is the cow. In India, it is quite commonplace to see cows wandering through the streets of most Indian towns and cities, mingling with the traffic and nosing through the rubbish skips in the markets (**B**). The cow symbolises the special care that exists between all humans and animals. Even those Hindus who are not **vegetarian** do not usually eat beef.

One branch of Hindu religious life is Jainism, which can still be found today in parts of northwest India. Its followers, take five vows, the first of which is to avoid harming any living being. The importance they attach to this vow sets them apart from other religious groups and even, strict vegetarians. All of India's seven million Jains are vegetarian and they go to extreme measures to make sure they do not harm or injure any creature. A Jain will wear a scarf or mask over their face to ensure not only that they do not accidentally swallow an insect but also to avoid disturbing any insects with their breath. They will gently sweep the ground in front of them as they walk in case they tread on an ant or any other insect in their path (**C**). Jains are forbidden even to eat vegetables that grow underground such as carrots and onions. This is because pulling them up will cause harm to the soil and numerous very small creatures.

C Two Jains taking care not to injure anything as they walk

Vegetarianism

Buddhism

The First Precept of Buddhism states the need to protect animals and to avoid killing them. One of the sacred writings, the Diamond Sutra teaches that it is impossible to distinguish even between **sentient** and **non-sentient** beings. In other words, even if we take pride in being a vegetarian, we must accept that the water in which we boil our vegetables contains many tiny micro-organisms.

It is clear that vegetarianism is seen by Buddhists as a step in the right direction. By adopting this practice, we appreciate the beauty of life and do everything in our power to protect life (**D**).

 D Buddhist teaching

We cannot be completely non-violent, but by being vegetarian, we are going in the direction of non-violence. If we want to head north, we can use the North Star to guide us, but it is impossible to arrive at the North Star. Our effort is only to proceed in that direction.

Thich Nhat Hanh The First Precept: Reverence for Life

The simple underlying reason why beings other than humans need to be taken into account is that, like human beings, they too are sensitive to happiness and suffering; they too, just like the human species, primarily seek happiness and shun suffering.

Venerable Lungrig Namgyal Rinpoche – The Buddhist Declaration on Nature

QUESTIONS

1 Give an account of the practices of cow-protection and vegetarianism amongst Hindus.

2 Explain how the teachings and practices of the Jains could influence people's attitudes to animals today.

3 What difficulties are there in following Buddhist and Jain principles in the world today? Discuss this in pairs or small groups and write down some ideas.

 stop and think!

- **What do you think of the measures that Jains go to in order to avoid harming or injuring any creatures?**

Clearly, not all religious people go to these extremes. In some religions such as Christianity, Judaism, and Islam vegetarianism is an individual choice rather than a religious duty. Increasing numbers of religious followers now believe that eating meat, dairy products and eggs, conflicts with religious teachings about kindness to animals. In addition, many reports suggest that the animal industries contribute to large scale environmental pollution, destruction and, more recently, have introduced many potentially fatal human diseases associated with food poisoning (**E**).

E-COLI OUTBREAK

Listeria

E Watch what you eat!

CJD/BSE

Salmonella

Islam

Muslims are increasingly concerned that factory-produced meat may not be halal (lawful or permissible). We now know that cattle, sheep, chickens and pigs are routinely fed the ground-up bodies of other animals as well as other waste products. This would immediately make most meat haram (forbidden) to Muslims for two reasons:

1 The animals may have eaten pork.

2 Animals that are fed the bodies of other animals could be described as carnivorous and carnivorous animals are generally forbidden food for Muslims.

The guidance found in the Qur'an says only that permitted meats may be eaten if a Muslim wishes to. Nowhere in Islam are Muslims encouraged or recommended to eat meat (**F**).

F Muslim teaching

Say: I find not in the Message received by me by inspiration any (meat) forbidden to be eaten by one who wishes to eat it, unless it is dead meat, or blood poured forth, or the flesh of swine.

Surah 6:145

O you who believe! Eat of the good things that We have provided for you and be grateful to Allah if it is Him you worship. Indeed, what He has forbidden to you is the flesh of dead animals and blood and the flesh of swine, and that which has been sacrificed to anyone other than Allah. But if one is compelled by necessity, neither craving [it] nor transgressing, there is no sin on him: indeed, Allah is forgiving, Merciful.

Surah 2:173

Some Muslims believe that the modern methods of raising animals for food contradict the teachings of the Prophet Muhammad about kindness to animals. All vegetables are halal and therefore vegetarian food is acceptable to Muslims as long as it does not contain alcohol and is not cooked in the same oil used for haram items such as pork sausages. Adopting a **vegan** diet (free from meats, dairy products and eggs) is seen by many Muslims, as the easiest way to live according to the ethical, environmental and health precepts of Islam.

141

Christian and Jewish teaching

Although Jews and Christians may be vegetarians if they choose, both the religions' sacred writings allow followers to eat meat if they wish. Quakers, for example, were among the first to commit themselves to vegetarianism in the nineteenth century. Unlike the majority of Christians, Jews have very specific food laws. In Judaism food which is allowed is called kosher. Food that they cannot eat is called terefah (forbidden). All plants are kosher but certain animals are not. Restrictions about certain animals are clearly outlined in the Torah. These banned animals are set out in Chapter 11 of the Book of Leviticus (**G**).

 Jewish teaching

These are the regulations concerning animals, birds, every living thing that moves in the water and every creature that moves about on the ground. You must distinguish between the unclean and the clean, between the living creatures that may be eaten and those that may not be eaten.

Leviticus 11:46–47

If meat is to be eaten, the animal must be killed using the least painful method available. This is called shechitah, cutting the animal's throat with a razor sharp knife. According to Jewish authorities, if shechitah is performed properly the animal's carotoid arteries are severed and the animal immediately loses consciousness before it is able to feel any pain. This method of killing is similar to that used by Muslims producing halal meat. In fact, if no halal meat is available, kosher meat is acceptable to Muslims.

In order to remove the blood from the meat before it is cooked it is soaked in cold water and sprinkled with salt. Just like the Islamic teachings, the animals must never feel physical pain or even fear. Clearly many modern farming methods and slaughterhouse conditions are a violation of Jewish moral principles. Similarly, many Christians who choose to be vegetarians do so in the belief that methods used in meat production are cruel and inhumane.

stop and think!

- In what ways are the Jewish dietary laws similar to those of Islam?

stop and think!

- Do you think that special rules about what people can or cannot eat are an advantage or a disadvantage for religious followers today?

QUESTIONS

1 What is meant by the following words:
 a ahimsa?
 b halal?
 c vegan?
 d kosher?
 e terefah?
 f schechitah?
 g haram?

2 Why would Muslims object to animals being fed waste products and the ground-up bodies of other animals?

3 What must Muslims do to ensure that all vegetarian food is halal?

4 Referring to at least two religions, look at the attitudes that religious followers adopt to eating meat.

5 'Then God said, "I give you every seed bearing plant on the face of the whole earth and every tree that has fruit with seed in. They will be yours for food".' (Genesis 1:29)

Explain how some people might see this as a strong case for being a vegetarian. What is your opinion? Give reasons for your answer showing that you have considered different points of view.

Genetic modification

In the early 1990s the use of genetic engineering in humans created much controversy but in the last few years attention is also turning to the genetic modification of animals and plants. Scientists are now able to alter the genetic make-up of some of the foods we eat.

It is argued that these genetically engineered plants and animals can provide the world with increasing amounts of much needed food and medicines. By using genetic engineering, plants can be developed that grow faster, produce bigger fruit, survive harsher weather and even resist disease. To avoid dependency on oil-based plastics, some scientists have even genetically engineered plants that produce plastic within their stems! The same techniques can also increase animal breeding programmes. Animals have been engineered to produce more milk, meat, wool or eggs and some have already been redesigned (transgenic) to secrete useful drugs into their milk and blood.

A The double-muscled 'Belgium Blue' cattle can scarcely walk and its calves are so big they have to be delivered by caesarean

B These lambs produce valuable AAT in their milk which can be used to help emphysema sufferers

Genetically modified (GM) crops

Some experimental breeding policies have proved disasterous, others beneficial! (A and B)

In 1995, scientists discovered how to 'switch off' the gene that makes tomatoes go soft and squishy. The Calgene's Flavr Savr tomato, was sold widely in grocery outlets in the United States with the claim that it had a better flavour and a longer shelf life. Genetic engineering can develop new plant varieties with built in defences against pests and diseases. Whole crops of potatoes can be wiped out because of potato blight so scientists developed a potato that 'committed suicide' the moment it was infected! Scorpion poison genes have been added to cabbages to kill caterpillars. Scientists now talk about producing a banana that when eaten vaccinates against hepatitis B, and tomatoes that contain a cholesterol-lowering protein.

At the same time, however, warnings are made about so called 'Frankenstein foods' (**C**). Many people believe there is a need for caution because genetic engineering is not a precise science and mistakes will be made which could lead to unexpected, and possibly dangerous, side-effects (**D**).

Many religious leaders are worried that we are experimenting with nature and they question the benefits of genetic engineering in the plant and animal world. Many Buddhists, for example, believe that the genetic modification of food is not supported by the teachings of Buddhism. Genetic engineering of food is regarded as potentially dangerous and unnecessary tampering with the natural patterns of the world. They point out that already, there are 'super pests' emerging that can resist the genetically engineered, pest-resistant crops. The genes that give GM crops resistance to disease, insects and herbicides could cross-pollinate and produce 'super weeds.' New plant viruses, not anticipated by scientists, could wipe out whole crops with terrible consequences for those whose lives depend on the harvests.

D GM crops have become a focus for protesters who want more research on safety

E Genetically modified poplar seedlings designed for resistance to insects and rot

C

FRANKENSTEIN'S VEGETABLES

Yesterday's science fiction is today's reality

What are you eating?

GM CROPS DESTROYED BY PROTESTORS

Without doubt these discoveries have raised strong feelings and have been given widespread publicity. Generally the major religions are not opposed to genetic research aimed at relieving suffering. The search for cures for illnesses and diseases is encouraged but concerns are expressed with what is regarded as the possible misuse of genetic experiments.

In 1993 these worries led to the British Government setting up a Committee headed by Reverend Dr John Polkinghorne. The Report on the Ethics of Genetic Modification and Food Use reflected the views of representatives from the world faiths. The Committee found that:

> Most Christian and Jewish groups find genetic modification acceptable in principle; Muslims, Sikhs and Hindus have objections to consuming organisms containing copies of genes from animals that are subject to religious dietary restrictions. Some vegetarians would object to consuming plants into which copy genes of animal origins had been added.

stop and think!

- What is the general attitude adopted by various religious groups to genetic modification?

One criticism levelled at scientists is that they are 'playing God' and 'tampering with nature'. Muslims draw on the Qur'anic teachings which state that the created world should not be interfered with (**F**). They believe that all 'life forms' have been created by God in the 'best design', and should never be changed by humans except to correct 'deviations' back to their original form. A distinction is drawn between 'natural' cross breeding and genetic modification which might unbalance a species. Together with the Buddhist and Hindu communities, Muslims see evolution and selective breeding as controlled and gradual unlike the instant changes brought about by genetic modification which may go out of control and be irreversible.

Many, but not all Christians and Jews approve of genetic modification as long as it helps to preserve or improve human or animal life. Nature can be used for our benefit as long as we also nurture and protect it and safeguards are in place to ensure safety and animal welfare.

F   Muslim teaching

> So set thy face steadily and truly to the Faith: (Establish) Allah's handiwork according to the pattern on which He has made mankind: No change (let there be) in the work (wrought) by Allah.
> *Surah 30:30*

> Say: 'Of your "partners", can any originate creation and repeat it?' Say: 'It is Allah who originates Creation and repeats it: Then how are you deluded away (from the truth)?'
> *Surah 10:34*

QUESTIONS

1 Make a list of the advantages and disadvantages of genetic engineering in the animal and plant world. What is your view on the subject? Do you think the advantages outweigh the disadvantages or vice versa? Give reasons for your answer.

2 What particular concerns would Muslims raise about scientists 'playing God'?

3 What is the main difference between Muslim, Hindu and Buddhist views about genetic modification and those of Christianity and Judaism?

As was highlighted in the Polkinghorne report, most religious groups are concerned with three issues (**G**):

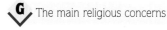

G The main religious concerns

A the transfer of human copy genes to animals

B the transfer of genes from animals forbidden by dietary laws

C the introduction of animal genes into food crops

The various religious traditions have different views regarding concerns **A** and **B**. All the world faiths oppose cannibalism. In the eyes of some people, eating an animal that has had human genes transferred into it would be the same as cannibalism. Some religious groups, including Hindus, Sikhs and especially the Muslim community would refuse to eat any GM food involving the transfer (transgene) of either human copy genes or genes from forbidden animals. Generally Jews and Christians have fewer concerns. The reason for these varied positions is that, for a Muslim, the transgene keeps its human nature. Jews, on the other hand, believe that the host organism rather than the donor remains the dominant species.

The dietary laws of some religious communities are also important. Sikhs and Hindus who are not vegetarian refuse to eat beef or any food where a gene transfer from cattle has been involved. Although the eating of pork is forbidden for Muslims and Jews they adopt different positions regarding the transfer of genes from forbidden animals. Muslims would refuse to eat any animal which had a pig gene transferred into it. Jews, on the other hand, do not believe that an introduced gene from a pig into a host animal turns that animal into some kind of pig.

The positions taken by the various religious groups regarding the transfer of animal genes to plants are the same and, in addition, there is the issue for vegetarians and vegans to avoid the eating of all animal products. Vegetarians who refuse to eat meat because of concerns for animal welfare are not so decisive when faced with GM plants containing animal copy genes. Some, like many religious believers, will find the transfer of copy genes unacceptable in any circumstance.

Clearer labelling on foods was recommended by the Polkinghorne Committee. This allows the various religious groups to make informed choices. There is however no requirement to label medicines containing GM ingredients or animal products. Despite the specific dietary laws of certain religious groups their position in relation to medicines or transplants of animal organs is less rigid. Virtually all faiths take the view that saving life is the first priority. Generally, a Jew will accept an organ transplant even from a pig if it saves a life. Muslims take a stricter view and would regard any product from a pig as unacceptable but there are exceptions. For example, if a Muslim doctor agrees that the product is essential to sustain life.

All these difficulties reveal that there are no universally agreed conclusions across the religious groups. Some see genetic modification as unacceptable and others seem to have few objections. Many religious communities cannot offer clear views because, like the Law, they are often struggling to keep up with the flood of medical advances.

QUESTIONS

1 What were the three main religious concerns highlighted in the Polkinghorne report?

2 Explain why certain religious traditions have different views regarding these three concerns.

3 Describe the different positions adopted by Jews and Muslims regarding the transfer of genes from animals forbidden by dietary laws.

4 Why do the world faiths have so much difficulty in offering definitive views about genetic modification?

5 'Developments in science, medicine and technology should be closely monitored.' Do you agree with this statement? Give reasons for your answer, showing that you have considered other points of view.

147

Question bank

1 Briefly describe what the following words/terms mean:

    a extinct   **d** pollution

    b CAFOD   **e** CFCs

    c conservation

2 In connection with environmental issues, explain what being a good steward is.

3 On what biblical teachings is stewardship based?

4 Make a list of things people are doing to reduce the problem of pollution.

5 Describe the work of an organisation committed to environmental issues.

6 Describe the Christian teachings and the teachings of one other religion on stewardship and creation. Discuss whether you think this is a good way to think about our responsibilities.

7 Describe and explain how the Jewish teaching opposite might affect our attitudes in caring for the environment.

> Our ancestor Abraham inherited his passion for nature from Adam. The later rabbis never forgot it. Some twenty centuries ago they told the story of two men who were out on the water in a rowboat. Suddenly, one of them started to saw under his feet. He maintained that it was his right to do whatever he wished with the place which belonged to him. The other answered him that they were in the rowboat together; the hole that he was making would sink both of them.
>
> *From The Jewish Declaration of Nature made at the Assisi Conference by Rabbi Arthur Hertzberg*

8 In which four areas do religious groups express concern and agreement with regard to responsibility for the environment?

9 'It's worth putting up with a few environmental problems if people can be given jobs and earn a salary.' How do you think religious people might respond to this comment? In your answer, try and look at different points of view.

10 'God made the Earth so he should look after it.'

Do you agree? Give reasons to support your answer and show that you have considered different points of view.

11 Read this extract from a Greenpeace publication.

> Think of the planet earth as a 46-year-old.
> The earth is thought to be around 4,600 million years old, an almost inconceivable timespan. For the moment, think of it as someone in middle age, 46 years old.
> This person is a late developer. Nothing at all is known about their first seven years and only sketchy information exists about the next 35 years. It is only at the age of 42 that the earth began to flower. Dinosaurs and the great reptiles did not appear until a year ago, when this planet reached 45.
> Mammals arrived only eight months ago. In the middle of last week, human-like apes evolved into ape-like humans, and at the weekend the last ice age enveloped the earth.
> Modern humans have been around for four hours. During the last hour we discovered agriculture. The industrial revolution began just a minute ago. During those sixty seconds of biological time, humans have made a rubbish tip of Paradise.
> We have caused the extinction of many hundreds of species of animals, many of which have been here longer than us, and ransacked the planet for fuel. Now we stand like brutish infants, gloating over this meteoric rise to ascendancy, poised on the brink of the final mass extinction and of effectively destroying this oasis of life in the solar system.

What is your reaction to this article?

12 'There is enough in the world for everyone's need, but not enough for everyone's greed.' Frank Buchman

'The earth has skin and that skin has diseases; and one of its diseases is called man.' Friedrich Nietzsche

Describe in your own words the messages of these two statements.

13 'Animals can be exploited.'

   a Describe seven different examples of this.

   b Are any of these acceptable? Give reasons for your answers.

   c Explain the attitudes towards animals of any one religion you have studied.

14 Explain religious attitudes concerning the acceptability of eating meat and using products tested on animals. Refer to at least two different religions.

15 Describe the example of the Prophet Muhammad concerning responsibility to animals.

16 Why do many religious followers adopt vegetarian diets?

17 Why would some modern methods of raising animals for food go against Jewish/Muslim moral principles and dietary codes?

18 On what grounds do some religious traditions approve of genetic modification? Do you agree? Give reasons to support your answer.

Introduction
One world

Unit aims

There are two main aims of this unit: to consider how religion is portrayed in the media and the arts, and how it contributes to these; also to consider how the world's religions affect the community at local and worldwide levels, with special attention given to their role in caring for the disadvantaged.

Key concepts

The major world religions have made enormous contributions to the areas of art, literature and music. Almost all western art and sculpture until the Middle Ages had religion as its subject, and many of the greatest musical works ever written were religious in inspiration. Islam has given us the most beautiful **calligraphy** and design, and religious architecture is some of the most impressive in the world.

The modern-day media in all of their many forms have had an impact on the modernisation of many religious ideas and, in turn, have been influenced by the different faiths. Religions are less suspicious of the media nowadays and, similarly the media are learning to take more care instead of making sweeping generalisations. A healthy respect between the religious and the **secular** is now beginning to exist.

Poverty remains a global issue and religious people realise that whatever happens in one part of the world will affect another part. All the world religions work towards helping the needy and appreciate that only a commitment to share the world's resources more equally will overcome the global issue of poverty. Religious people are urged to think about their lifestyles and examine their attitudes towards others. It can be difficult for people to live up to the expectations that are set by particular religious traditions. Clearly, some material possessions are necessary but wealth should be more fairly distributed and help should be offered to the less fortunate. Where the State cannot help, religious groups and charities do their best to care for people in need. Followers of all the world religions are expected to respond with compassion to the problems of poverty and work to relieve the suffering of millions.

many religions

What is this unit about?

In this unit, you will find images of religion portrayed in a variety of media such as television, newspapers, film and the internet, and you will see how religious ideas have permeated nearly every part of our lives. You will see, too, how society is gradually becoming more tolerant of 'foreign' ideas and attitudes.

This unit also shows the work of charitable religious groups such as Muslim Aid, CAFOD and Tzedek which have responded to global poverty by providing relief to the needy regardless of race and religion.

Religion in

Baroness Margaret Thatcher (Prime Minister of the UK 1979–90) was reported to have once said that people were only individuals, and not part of a bigger group (**A**). Yet, much earlier, the poet, John Donne, pointed out that no one can be completely alone (**B**).

A

> There is no such thing as a community, only a group of individuals.
> *Margaret Thatcher*

B

> No man is an island, entire of itself. Every man is a piece of the Continent, a part of the main.
> *John Donne, 1573–1631,*
> *Devotions XVII*

stop and think!
- What do you think about Baroness Thatcher's statement? How do you think her statement would be viewed by: a politician? a minister of the church? a housewife? an elderly person? a shopkeeper?
- What do you think John Donne meant by 'entire of itself?'

stop and think!
- Which 'communities' do you belong to?
- Do some of your answers surprise you?

People belong to many different types of groupings or 'communities', some more formalised than others. For example, people can belong to the community of the school, or the work place, the community of the local area in which they live, or the 'faith' community.

Communities vary considerably depending on what draws them together. You can choose to belong to a particular group, but there is less choice about who becomes your neighbour.

Some communities are linked to others that share the same faith or ideals as themselves. However, it is important to note that there can be different opinions and ideas even within the same community. Much will depend on what people consider to be the 'authority' behind their beliefs and attitudes.

Areas which can cause problems in the workplace, in schools and in the wider community, are the observance of religious holy days and festivals, specific laws and practices. Fortunately, in our communities we now accept the need to recognise such events, and there is evidence of far greater tolerance on all sides. Religions, too, have adapted as far as they can, emphasising that they must respect and keep the laws of the country in which they are living.

Islam

The vast majority of Muslims are actively involved in their community. However, living in a country where most of the population do not share the same religious beliefs can be a challenge. It is not always easy to keep the beliefs, values and traditions of your religion if they bring you into conflict with the wider community (**C**).

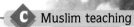

C Muslim teaching

Employers should show sensitivity towards their employees and ensure that they are able to take leave on these days, as they form an integral part of their religious practices.

The Muslim Educational Trust

Buddhism

Many religious leaders have pointed out that it is not easy to have a firm religious conviction and yet to be tolerant of those whose views are different from one's own. Buddhists have achieved this kind of tolerance to a large exent, although many do not find it easy to live within a society whose aims are particularly **materialistic** (**D**).

D Buddhist teaching

The Western way of life and Buddhism I don't think mix terribly well together. We are far too materialistic – I am far too materialistic. I spend all my time at work, wondering how to get more money, and that does worry me, because I don't think you can live properly in the West and be a good Buddhist.

Worlds of Faith,
by John Bowker, Ariel Books, 1983

Christianity

In Britain, every village, town and city skyline appears to be dominated by church spires or towers. Although attendance in churches appears very low, there is little doubt that the Christian influence runs through every community. Most Christians believe it is their duty to be involved in their local communities, for example, organising charitable relief. They hope, as would any member of a religious tradition, that they offer a visible model of the way people can live in the community in more loving and just ways (**E**).

E Christian teaching

Let no debt remain outstanding, except the continuing debt to love one another, for he who loves his fellow man has fulfilled the law… Let us behave decently…

Romans 13:8,13

ONE WORLD
5
MANY RELIGIONS

Religion in the community

stop and think!

To understand any place of worship, you need to watch what goes on and ask certain questions about what you see.

- Is there a notice-board outside?

- Do you notice that different ages or different genders attend at particular times?

- Do all those who attend dress similarly?

- Can you hear anything?

- Is the inside of the building always arranged in the same way?

- Are there particular rooms set aside for particular activities?

The public face of the community

People know who lives in your house because they see who goes in and out regularly. They may even know something about your circumstances by what you wear, for example, a school uniform or police uniform, or by the times you leave home and return, for example, as a shift worker. This is also true at a place of worship, which will be the centre or 'home' of a particular faith community.

QUESTIONS

1 Think about the places of worship in your community. What makes you aware of them?

2 What might give you clues about the regular activities that happen there?

F A gurdwara, a place of worship for the Sikh community

What information can you find from this notice-board about the services that occur within this church?

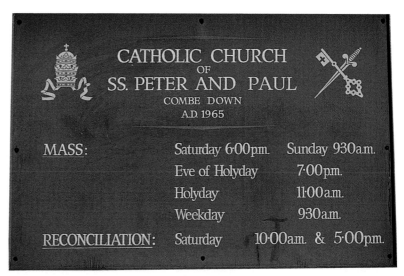

A visit to a place of worship will answer a lot of these questions, but it needs to be well organised. It is important to think about:

- exactly what you want to know
- the questions you will ask to get this information
- the best person to show you round
- how you will record the information

There will be times when a place of worship becomes a hive of activity. Usually, there will be only one main act of worship in a week, but there will also be weddings, funerals and christenings. In fact, some people only attend a place of worship for an important family event like this. These events tend to be more noticeable in the local community.

Festivals are also times when celebrations spill out into the local community or draw people in who might not usually attend.

QUESTIONS

1 Choose a local area you know and draw a sketch map of it, like the one here. Mark on it:
   a any well-known local landmarks
   b any local amenities e.g. library
   c any places of worship

2 What good things can you conclude about the neighbourhood you have considered?

3 What do you think might be missing from the community? How could you make any improvements?

4 Which festivals are celebrated in the community? How are they celebrated?

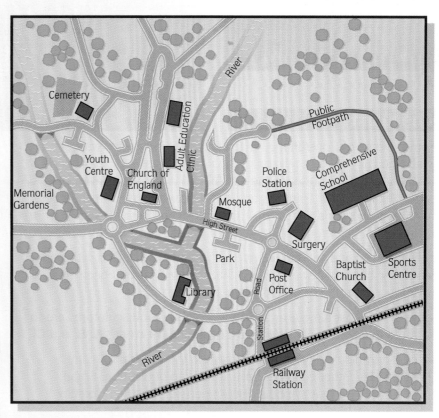

Art and music

Throughout the history of humankind, art has been used to express beliefs, to worship, to teach and to inspire.

A A stained-glass window

B The ceiling of the chapel in Wurzburg, Germany

C An icon of Jesus and the Virgin Mary

Christianity

From the time of Constantine the Great, when Christianity was established as the state religion of the Roman Empire, art has been used to glorify God, to teach the faithful and to help to convert others to the Christian faith. Paintings and statues can be found in churches throughout the world. In Christian Orthodox churches icons are used to help worship. These are holy pictures of Christ, Mary and the saints.

Early churches and cathedrals were built as a house of God with perfect **geometry,** because it was believed that the universe had been created by God according to certain mathematical rules.

Some of the most famous architecture, paintings and sculptures are to be found in places of Christian worship around the world (**A**, **B** and **C**).

Banners may also play an important part in the worship of many Christians (**D**). Other churches have little of no decoration. Some Christians believe that symbols distract people from their worship.

D A Christian banner

stop and think!

- Why was it so important in the early history of the Christian Church for art to be used to tell people about the life and teachings of Jesus?

- Which of the pictures best expresses Christian beliefs, in your opinion?

Islam

Islamic art is very different from Christian, partly because it is forbidden to draw, paint or sculpt the human figure. This prohibition is because Muslims believe that any danger of **idolatry** should be avoided. Drawings or statues could easily become objects of worship. Instead, Muslims make use of geometric shapes and create elaborate patterns (**E**). Muslims believe that art glorifies Allah, celebrates creation and that artists should work through prayer.

One of the art forms that has always been important in Islamic countries is calligraphy. Muslims believe that 'calligraphy is the geometry of the spirit'. They also believe that writing any part of the Qur'an should be considered a religious experience.

E The most beautiful geometric art is often found in a mosque

Buddhism

In Buddhism, art plays an important part in expressing beliefs. This can be seen through the main forms of the Buddha, mandalas, and the Zen gardens (**F**). Meditation is also an important part of Buddhism. In a zen garden, the fine gravel is raked to form patterns around larger stones. Sitting quietly and looking at a garden like this might help a person to meditate – to feel calm and peaceful.

F Zen garden

QUESTIONS

1 Why does Islamic law forbid any image of the human figure?

2 'Art and religion are means to similar states of mind.' (Clive Bell, English art critic)

   a What do you think Clive Bell means?

   b In what ways do you agree or disagree with him?

G A Gospel choir – one of the many forms of Christian music

With some exceptions, religious, or sacred, music is vocal music, but there is considerable variety within each of the main religious traditions.

Christianity

In the Christian tradition, the earliest vocal music is the hymn. In the fifth century, 'hymn' was defined as a religious composition sung by a stationary chorus.

To begin with, the **Psalms** formed the basis for all hymns, and the early church decided that only hymns using the words of the scriptures were to be used during services.

As the Roman Catholic Church and the Church of England did not encourage the use of hymns, it was not until the eighteenth century that hymns became an important part of Christian worship. Isaac Watts and the Wesley brothers were responsible for writing some of the most powerful songs still used in Christian services.

There are approximately 950,000 Christian hymns in existence, although only a small number of these are in use today.

Gospel music as we know it had its roots in the American Negro spirituals. The 'Golden Age' of Gospel started in the 1920s and 1930s when Thomas Dorsey began composing songs based on familiar spirituals and hymns, mixed with blues and jazz rhythms. These brought a much needed message of hope to the churches during the depression in the USA.

One of the best known religious texts set to music is that of the *Passion*. This enacts the Passion of Jesus Christ during Holy Week. It is based on the old miracle and Passion plays which were semi-dramatic presentations of New Testament stories. J.S. Bach's The St Matthew Passion is a fine example of this type of composition. One of the most famous Passion plays is performed every ten years at Oberammergau in Bavaria, Southern Germany.

Christian music today combines the traditional influence of the scriptures with every imaginable form of music (**G**).

Islam

Islam has extremes of belief in the importance, or otherwise, of music in religion.

The **Orthodox** tradition within Islam states that 'Islam has no music'. Yazid III, a noted Umayyad Caliph, warned, in 740 BCE, 'Beware of singing for it will steal your modesty, fill you with lust and ruin your virtue.'

Whilst the call to prayer is based on the Arabic scales used for all Arab music, it is not considered music. A court case in Cairo in 1977 decreed that the reciting of the Qur'an was an act of worship, and did not involve innovation. It follows therefore, to actually deliver the Qur'an through music is considered a sin.

However, as with all the main world religions, there is considerable variations of belief within Islam. **Sufism** is a mystical movement which moved away from the more traditional Muslim faith, and within this sub-sect, music plays an important part in worship. Religious poetry set to music, called **qawwali**, is used to arouse mystical love, central to the experience of Sufism.

Nowadays, Muslim youth around the world also sings to express its beliefs, as do all young people (**H**).

Judaism

The dispersion of the Jews has meant that very little traditional music has survived. It is believed that the **Yemenite** Jewish music is the nearest to the original ancient **Hebrew**. This ancient Jewish community is believed to date back to 585 BCE. Vocal music such as the *Lamentations of Jeremiah* is believed to be closest to that belonging to the earliest Jews (**I**).

*As progress marches on
People get so busy
That they forget their duty
To pray to God five times a day
They are so drunk with progress
They think the computer is God (you're kidding!)
When they talk about the world
They're wonderfully clever
But talk to them about religion
And suddenly they're allergic.*

Rhoma Irama, 'Qur'an dan Koran' from 'Indonesian Popular Music 2', Smithsonian Folkways

H The lyrics of a popular Indonesian song

stop and think!

'Music recognises no religious differences – indeed it is something of a religion in its own right.' From *World Music: The Rough Guide*, Penguin, 1994

- **What role do you think music plays in religion?**

I Traditional Jewish musicians

QUESTIONS

1 'Music has always had its critics: just think about rock, heavy metal, punk, grunge and rap music.' Why is music regarded by some people as dangerous?

2 Why do you think the Orthodox tradition within Islam is unhappy with any involvement in musical activities?

159

Religion in

A Some forms of the media

The word 'media' is a term used to describe different forms of communication. There are many ways to communicate within society – through newspapers and magazines, books, television, radio and the internet.

The media are part of our everyday lives, and as such, are all around us, and taken for granted. Quite often, we do not realise how much we are influenced by them, how powerful they are, and what effects they have on our lives. We need only look at how the media were manipulated and used to create hatred towards Jewish people in the 1930s and 1940s to realise how powerful they can be.

stop and think!

- How many types of 'media' can you see around you at the moment?

- Which form of media do you think is the most important? Why? Remember to consider which media forms are most easily available to people.

It is clear that the media exert enormous influence on us and are often criticised for various reasons. Major criticisms are that the media focus on negative aspects of life, that they are biased, and that they create and use stereotypes. No matter how hard the media try to show a true picture of society, they can never succeed.

Religion, in particular, appears to be a difficult area to cover and, all too often, while covering religious aspects of life, the media confirm prejudices by putting forward powerful images. Newspapers and television focus on 'sensational' stories such as religious hatreds, cults and scandals (**B**). These sell far more papers, than, for example, profiles of the work of Christian Aid or Muslim Aid.

the media

stop and think!

- What 'images' do these headlines give their readers?
- Is it fair to say that many of these headlines are more about politics than religion?

Having acknowledged the negative aspects of the media, it is also important to recognise that they play a very important role in religious life. Documentaries on individuals such as Mother Teresa and Bhagat Puran Singh often promote interest, concern and most importantly, greater tolerance.

Even where the issues are controversial, many will argue that it is a good thing for religions to be examined and to have a much higher profile. In recent years this has been seen in the area of sport. The spectacular refusal of the athlete Eric Liddell (featured in the film *Chariots of Fire*) to race on a Sunday was not an isolated event. Until 1960, Rule 25 of the Football Association stated that 'matches shall not be played on Sundays… A player shall not be compelled to play on Sundays… on Good Friday or Christmas Day.'

In the 1990s, a large number of sports personalities have been profiled in the media for their religious beliefs. For example, Mike Tyson, an ex-World Heavyweight Boxing champion who converted to Islam; and Michael Jones, one of the best All Black rugby players in New Zealand who refused to participate in sport on Sundays. Such individuals are often seen as 'role models' and their influence, particularly among young people, cannot be underestimated. By seizing on certain examples, the media highlight the difficulties faced by a believer trying to reconcile traditional items of belief with modern day standards.

For the Algerian, Hassiba Boulmerka, a World Champion and Olympic 1500 metres gold medallist, home became a no-go area. Her Muslim beliefs and values clashed with her commitment to sport. In an interview she stated: 'You cannot wear the **hijab** in the stadium, just as you cannot wear shorts in the mosques. Each has its rules… I have studied the Qur'an. I have evaluated my life through its teachings. I am committed to it, and happy to be so.'

Her views led to confrontation with a number of Islamic religious leaders. From their point of view, she was guilty of insulting conduct because she was ignoring the strict law of the Qur'an that women should keep their bodies covered by the **chador**. For this reason, several Muslim nations do not enter women's teams at international competitions. Episodes like this, eagerly reported in the media, can, in fact, be educational. Many people now better understand some of the problems of having a religious faith. Although media coverage is often biased, nowadays there is a greater effort towards balance and towards an understanding of the clash between religious tradition and modern lifestyles.

THIS POTENT MIXTURE OF GUNS AND GOD

Rabbi calls for suicide bombings

Satellite TV station devoted to religion

BURNINGS, BEATINGS, TORTURE…
ANOTHER WEEKEND IN SIERRA LEONE

Church failing to attract young as congregations fall by 500,000 in decade

Muslims demand equality in law

B A typical selection of newspaper headlines covering 'religious' issues

Religion in the media

In the past and, to some extent, even today, the media have tended to present **fundamentalist** Islamic views as the 'norm'.

One example of this kind of 'misrepresentation' occurred in the case of Salman Rushdie's book, *The Satanic Verses*. This was described by many Muslims as blasphemous, as an attack on their faith. Fundamentalist Muslims insisted that the author should die, whereas other Muslims have urged followers not to resort to violence. As newspapers at the time pointed out, it is important to remember that, in an Islamic State, Islam *is* the State, and not just the state religion. Rushdie's work was seen by many as an act of treason, punishable by death (**C**).

Public awareness is becoming greater as people become better educated, and it now seems far more acceptable to acknowledge that there are divisions within the same religious traditions, or that certain terrorist groups use religion as an 'excuse' to carry out their activities, or that the media very often focus on negative aspects of a situation in order to boost circulation or to attract audiences.

Two films that have highlighted religious standpoints **D**

C A balanced report?

A MILLION-DOLLAR bounty was placed on the head of author Salman Rushdie last night as the furore over his novel *The Satanic Verses* echoed around the world.

The chilling offer was made by one of the Ayatollah Khomeini's aides on Iranian TV, hours after a screaming crowd of 2,000 had stoned the British Embassy in Tehran.

Senior Muslim churchman Hassan Sanei said his June Fifth charity foundation would pay the money – £570,000 – to any foreigner killing the Indian-born writer who lives in Islington, north London.

An Iranian assassin would stand to collect triple bounty – three million dollars – for what Sanei termed 'this holy crusade'.

Rusdie, 41, who was born in Bombay and educated at Cambridge, has reaped the whirlwind since the publication by Viking of *The Satanic Verses*, which Muslims say is blasphemous and which has already led to riots in which six people died in India and Pakistan.

(Only a few weeks ago the author, bearded and sardonic, posed for a photographer from the American Elle magazine to publicise a US tour.

Last night he was clean-shaven,

frightened and under armed police guard at a secret hideout. Detectives say he must be protected around the clock for the foreseeable future as Muslim fanatics seek chances to carry out the Ayatollah's execution decree. There are even suggestions that the author may have plastic surgery and emigrate to avoid the Iranian death squads.)

Muslim religious leaders in Britain were yesterday urging their 1.4 million followers not to resort to violence and to observe the law.

But experts believed at least one Iranian hit team may already be on Rushdie's trail. (A sleeper unit of fanatics has probably been activated, according to Ian Geldard, a reseacher at the Institute for the Study of Terrorism.)

He estimated that there were up to 1,000 radical Khomeini supporters in Britain, mainly students or people on short visas. (The main centres were London, Bradford, Leeds and Manchester, particularly among Iranian university students.) 'This is a very serious threat indeed,' added Mr Geldard. 'Khomeini has issued a command – not a suggestion or a hint. A fanatic would obey it to the letter.'

By Anthony Doran, (Daily Mail, *16 February 1989*)

In literature today, thousands of titles could be cited to prove that religions play a significant role in the poetry, fiction and drama of even the most non-religious of societies. Many films could also be cited to exemplify the same point. But the world of cinema no longer only produces films based on biblical themes restricted to Christian or Judaic history, as it used to. Nowadays, films tend to examine the world faiths in a more realistic and sympathetic way (**D**).

World religions now make far greater use of the media, instead of the media making use of them. It is not uncommon for religious leaders to be invited to give interviews to the press and television and to be encouraged to speak out about the problems in society. In the United States, religious groups have actually bought television channels, and now broadcast their own programmes to high audience figures.

Finally, we now find God on the internet. Religions are being drawn into making use of the World Wide Web, where ideas of faith, religion and spirituality can be freely examined and discussed. Not everyone approves of this, but there is no doubt that it is important.

On the Web, all the world faiths, as well as tiny religious sects, now have a 'home page'.

Clearly, computer telecommunications are now seen as opportunities to spread religious beliefs and religions are now using a variety of media in a positive way. Some even hope that this global network may bring people together in a way that other forms of the media have failed to do. Television, for example, has tended to take people away from their communities and has encouraged a passive, receptive audience. The internet, it is argued, is creating spiritual communities on a world-wide basis, and placing religious faith firmly in people's lives.

E Religion and the media through the ages

QUESTIONS

1 Read through **C** again, then answer the following questions:

a What do the words 'bounty' and 'furore' mean? (Paragraph 1)

b What does the term 'reap the whirlwind' mean?

c Do you think that the article gives a well-balanced account of Muslim attitudes? Give examples from the text in your answer.

2 Select one of the films in **D** and find out what it was about. Comment, in particular, about the theme of the film and the religious concepts and beliefs central to the plot.

3 Either

a Compare two different newspapers of the same date. Look through them carefully to find any reference to religions or religious topics. For each newspaper, copy and complete a table like the one below to show your findings.

	1	2
Name of newspaper		
Number of religious topics		
Which religion(s)?		
Title of article(s)		
How much detail is given?		
Is the article(s) positive, negative or balanced?		

or **b** Look at a weekly television or radio magazine. Carefully look through it to find any reference to religions or religious topics. Copy and complete a table like the one below to show your findings.

	Television	Radio
Number of programmes about religions or religious topics		
Which religion(s)?		
Names of religious service programmes		
Names of religious documentary programmes		
Names of religious comedy programmes		

4 'Television always presents religious people as out of touch with the modern world.' Do you agree with this statement? Give reasons for your answer.

Poverty in the developing world

Lupang Pangako (Philippines) – A home on a rubbish dump. Over 5,000 tonnes of rubbish is dumped here every day. The people who live here have to put up with the sickening smell of rotting rubbish as well as facing the obvious health dangers.

A

It is a depressing fact that 1.2 billion people are living on less than one dollar a day and poverty sends over 11 million children to their deaths every year. It is not easy to grasp what statistics like these mean in real terms. Poverty has always existed but in the twenty first century communication through the mass media means that we are much more aware of it – no longer can we say, 'out of sight, out of mind'.

The faces of absolute poverty

B▷ Hong Sorcerers (China) – Here over 40 'cage people' live in 50 square metres of space. Their 2 by 2 metre cubbyholes are divided by plywood partitions. There is no ventilation, barely any light and they become unbearably hot in the summer.

Poverty is struggling for the basic necessities of life. Although the idea of poverty seems fairly straightforward, arguments about poverty can easily become bogged down in 'word games', and contact is lost with the very real issues of hardship facing millions of people today.

In any discussion of poverty it is essential to make a clear distinction between the two terms: 'relative' and 'absolute'. In Britain and the developed world there are families who can be described as living in relative poverty. Being poor in this context is seen as having a standard of living below the normal acceptable level in any given society. When examining the issue of relative poverty it is important to remember that what were regarded as luxuries in one era, for example a fridge or central heating, can easily be seen as essentials of the next era.

When compared, however, with the poorest in the developing and less developed countries, people living in relative poverty are regarded as quite well off. For the inhabitants of many countries throughout the world every day is a struggle to survive, scraping a living from land that is totally inadequate. Millions of people in the less developed world live in absolute poverty (**A** and **B**). This means that they do not have sufficient money or food to supply their everyday basic needs. For example, they lack sufficient food to avoid starvation, adequate shelter to avoid freezing, or basic medicine to avoid preventable illness and disease.

stop and think!

- Should it matter to us in Britain that people endure lives of great poverty in other parts of the world?

Wealth is not evenly distributed in the world and many countries are extremely poor. There are many reasons for this poverty (**C**).

C Absolute poverty

Unable to trade

Natural disasters

Politically unstable

Absolute poverty

Debt repayment

Increasing populations

Involvement in wars

Everybody has heard comments like 'the trouble with these countries is overpopulation' or 'they should spend less money on weapons and more on food'. The importance of population and military spending should not be underestimated but it is clearly misleading to view these two factors as the main causes of poverty. Family planning programmes are making an impact and population experts believe that if this can be sustained it should be possible to stabilise the world's population at around 8 billion in 2050. Previous estimates set the figure at around 12 or 13 billion.

What is undoubtedly true is that millions of people find themselves facing massive food shortages and are at the mercy of a combination of factors such as war, natural disasters and economic collapse often caused by the massive debts owed to the greedy rich nations.

In 1980 an influential report named the 'North-South: A Programme for Survival' (the Brandt Report) was produced which examined the enormous problems of world poverty and put forward suggestions to resolve the issue. The North or 'developed' world refers to rich countries with a high standard of living (North America, Western Europe, Japan, Australia and New Zealand). The South or developing world are the poorer countries with a lower standard of living (most of Africa, Asia and South America). Whereas the North has a quarter of the world's population and four fifths of its income, the South has three quarters of the world's population and just one fifth of its income.

The Brandt Report made ten main suggestions:

▶ An end must be found to mass hunger and malnutrition. Money must be found to develop agriculture, irrigation, crop storage, fertilisers and other aids.

▶ Ensure that money goes into direct help rather than weapon production.

▶ Increase overseas aid.

▶ Developing countries should increase their earnings by having more say in the processing, marketing and distribution of their exported goods.

▶ More attention should be paid to educating the public about the need for international co-operation.

▶ An emergency programme is essential to help the world's poorest nations particularly in the poverty belts of Asia and Africa.

▶ Greater international support for family planning programmes.

▶ An international 'income tax' to spread wealth more evenly.

▶ The international monetary system must be changed to give the developing countries a greater advantage.

▶ A World Development Fund could be developed to distribute the resources raised on a universal and automatic basis.

The world religions realise that for millions of adults and children, hunger, suffering and hardship is a reality of life and that the need for charity remains greater than ever before. Religious believers all over the world see it as their duty to give to those in need.

QUESTIONS

1 Explain what is meant by the following terms:
   a absolute poverty.
   b relative poverty.

2 Name three developed countries and three developing ones.

3 Many people in this country would consider themselves poor if they did not have certain items such as a fridge, video, TV, hi-fi, computer, mobile phone, car, etc. Yet 50 years ago most people lived perfectly contented lives without them.
   a Describe which of the above items you could not live without and explain the reasons for your choice.
   b If you could only have two items which would you choose? Which one could you do without the most?

Poverty in the developing world

Christianity

Christian teaching clearly sets out the need to help the poor (**E**). There are numerous examples of responses both on an individual basis and through groups such as Christian Aid, CAFOD and Tear Fund. Many denominations support the work of Christian Aid which was originally founded to help refugees after the horrors of the Second World War. Gradually the organisation's help grew throughout the world and it now works in over seventy countries. Fundraising activities help to raise essential money which is used for disaster relief, education and, most importantly, development work.

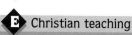

E Christian teaching

For I was hungry and you gave me something to eat, I was thirsty and you gave me something to drink, I was a stranger and you invited me in, I needed clothes and you clothed me, I was sick and you looked after me, I was in prison and you came to visit me.

Matthew 25:35–36

True happiness is not found in riches or well-being, in human fame or power, or in any human achievement... God blesses those who come to the aid of the poor and rebukes those who turn away from them... Rich nations have a grave moral responsibility towards those which are unable to ensure the means of their development by themselves.

The Catechism of the Catholic Church

Islam

Islam teaches that all charitable acts should be done through love rather than duty. Charity is an important part of Muslim life and because of their beliefs Muslims often take an active part in raising money. Red Crescent, Islamic Relief and Muslim Aid are three charities that uphold the Islamic principles of helping others in need, working discretely, not embarrassing those who receive help (**F**). These organisations help to bring humanitarian relief to over 150 countries throughout the world.

Red Crescent is the Islamic section of the Red Cross international relief agency. Islamic Relief, founded in 1984, is an independent charity working to bring help particularly to those areas devastated by natural and man-made disasters. Muslim Aid was set up in 1985 and supports projects in over 40 of the poorest countries in the world. Like many other charities, people are helped regardless of race, colour or religion and great emphasis is placed on long-term development work so that the needy are able to help themselves.

F Muslim teaching

O you who believe! Cancel not your charity by reminders of your generosity or by injury – like those who spend their substance to be seen of men, but believe neither in Allah nor in the Last Day. They are in parable like a hard barren rock, on which is a little soil; on it falls heavy rain, which leaves it (just) a bare stone.

Surah 2:264

And whatever you spend in charity or devotion, be sure Allah knows it all. But the wrongdoers have no helpers. If you disclose (acts of) charity, even so it is well, but if you conceal them, and make them reach those (really) in need, that is best for you: It will remove from you some of your (stains of) evil. And Allah is well acquainted with what you do.

Surah 2:270–271

D A young boy in Bosnia receives some bread distributed by Islamic Relief

Christian and Muslim Aid Agencies in Seville, Spain

Judaism

In 1990 a group of young Jews formed Tzedek, a charity based on the important Jewish principles of justice, compassion, respect and partnership (**H**). Its aim is to respond to global poverty by providing relief to the needy regardless of race and religion. Like many other charities it raises funds in order to support development programmes overseas, particularly in Africa and the Indian subcontinent.

H Jewish teaching

One man gives freely, yet gains even more; another withholds unduly, but comes to poverty. A generous man will prosper; he who refreshes others will himself be refreshed.

Proverbs 11:24–25

Speak up for those who cannot speak for themselves, for the rights of all who are destitute. Speak up and judge fairly; defend the rights of the poor and needy.

Proverbs 31:8–9

QUESTIONS

1 What was the 'Brandt Report'?

2 Evaluate different responses, at least one of which should be religious, to the problems of less developed countries.

3 **a** Name two Muslim charities that work to bring relief to Less Developed Countries.

   b Give two reasons why they do this work.

4 Describe how Tzedek works to relieve poverty in the world, showing how it bases its actions on Jewish teachings.

Poverty remains a global issue and religious people realise that whatever happens in one part of the world will affect another part. Millions of people in the developing world are starving, disease-ridden and living in absolute poverty. It is easy to blame this situation on population growth and general lack of development. This view is too simplistic. It is hypocritical to talk about over-population in the developing countries, while ignoring over consumption in the developed countries. All the world religions work towards helping the needy and appreciate that only a commitment to share the world's resources more equally will overcome the global issue of poverty.

The Gorbals area of Glasgow became infamous in the 1930s for tenement slums such as these

Poverty in the developed world

'**Homeless, Hungry, Help Me' cards everywhere. But that doesn't hide the pain, the suffering, the awfulness of sleeping on the streets. The dreadful feeling of not being as good as the people walking by. The terrifying fear of another, yet another night hiding in a corner hoping you won't be noticed, hoping you don't matter but praying you do.**

(Anonymous poet in Crisis News)

During the Great Depression of the 1930s many people were unemployed, living on the bread line and facing great difficulties. Most managed to survive on charity handouts and the support of relatives and friends. Then and now – poverty, conflict and hardship continue to bring hardship to children and adults alike. Today there is a general recognition that wealthy countries like the United States and Britain should be able to look after its poorest members. Yet, there are still millions living in poverty in these countries.

Just after the Second World War, amid mounting concern about poverty, the Welfare State was created. A report in the early 1950s suggested that poverty had come close to disappearing in Britain because of the emerging Welfare State. The majority of people in the country survive comfortably although admittedly some are much better off than others. Yet, there are individuals and families today living in relative poverty. For these people, not having a job or being poorly paid means they have great difficulty in changing their situation.

Nowadays government officials prefer to use the term 'below average income' rather than 'poverty'. Definitions of relative poverty focus on income levels said to be 'poor' in relation to the average or normal standards of living regarded by the majority as acceptable. Whatever one calls it, there are families who feel the serious effects of hardship and poverty and are in need of welfare benefits. Yet despite these state benefits, food handouts and begging are still in evidence in most major cities throughout Britain. The effects of being relatively poor will vary for particular individuals but are likely to include some of the side-effects set out below:

- Living in a home that is cold or damp or not suitable for your needs.
- Not eating a healthy diet.
- Going hungry so your children do not.
- Suffering from poor health related to your living conditions and diet.
- Feelings of being alone and nobody caring.
- Living in run down areas with poor facilities.
- Feeling of being on the 'outside' of society and being helpless to do anything about it.
- Not bothering to vote because you believe nothing will change.
- Wearing clothes which are unsuitable or do not fit.
- Having no faith in the 'system'.
- Anger, frustration and desperation.

One definition of poverty describes a set of five minimum standards linked to a lack of adequate income which are seen as basic requirements of 'citizenship'. If a person is deprived of any of these requirements they are described as 'poor by exclusion' (**C**).

B A homeless man and his dog in central London

Poverty by exclusion

Lack of an adequate diet

Lack of good health

Lack of access to transport

Lack of participation in community life

Lack of opportunities to socialise

 Poverty by exclusion

171

Poverty in the developed world

We have to remember that the everyday needs in a wealthy developed country are not the same as those in a poor country. The word 'poverty' does not have the same meaning in different parts of the world. It is easy to point the finger of blame but in a developed country like Britain poverty is inexcusable. Most individuals and successive governments claim to be committed to getting rid of poverty but only actions will demonstrate this and ensure a future where all people can enjoy life, free from poverty.

Many religious organisations are devoted to the relief of the poor and the **destitute** in their own countries as well as sending overseas aid and relief. They help to keep the problems firmly in the public's view. Within religious communities in Britain there is a tradition of looking after not only close family and friends but also caring for all people in need. One of the fundamental principles that guide all the major religious traditions is sharing with others. Followers are encouraged to set an example, raising money for charity and finding time to help the poor and sick.

stop and think!
- **What do you think is meant by the term 'poverty trap'?**

QUESTIONS

1 Describe some of the side-effects of being relatively poor in Britain.

2 What are the five minimum standards which are regarded as basic requirements of 'citizenship'? Which, in your view, is the most important? Give reasons for your choice.

 D Muslim teaching

If the debtor is in a difficulty, grant him time till it is easy for him to repay. But if you remit it by way of charity, that is best for you if you only knew.

Surah 2:280

'Sadaqah is the responsibility of every Muslim.'
His companions said, 'O Prophet of Allah. What about a person who has nothing to give?'
He said, 'He should work, earn and give in charity'.
They said, 'If he has nothing in spite of this?'
'He should help a distressed person, one who is in need.'
They said, 'If he is unable to do this?'
He said, 'He should do good deeds and not do bad things, this is charity on his part'.

Bukhari Hadith 24:31

Islam

Central to Islamic law, Muslims who have a certain amount of income and savings are required to give money to the poor (normally 2.5%). The giving of Zakah is not an act of charity, it is an obligation, an act of worship and is one of the five pillars of Islam. The income raised by Zakah can only be spent on certain things like providing food, housing, clothing, medicine and education for the poor, the elderly, the disabled and the sick. Wealth must always be put to good use. Showing off or extravagance are not Islamic qualities. Generosity and extra charitable donations called Sadaqah are encouraged and reinforced by religious teachings (**D**).

During the month of Ramadan Muslims are required to fast. This serves as a reminder of the needs of the poor throughout the world and helps to promote understanding and sympathy.

Judaism

Similar to the Islamic commitment to Zakah, all Jews are required to give one tenth of their earnings to charity. Even poor people are expected to contribute something. Jewish teachings make clear that everyone has a responsibility to help the poor (**E**). In Britain there are several Jewish care agencies, some of which were founded over 300 years ago. They are funded mainly through voluntary contributions. Jews are urged to support not only specific Jewish organisations such as Jewish Care and Chai-Lifeline, but also any deserving cause.

In Judaism a distinction is made between two types of charity: Tzedaka ('righteousness') and Gemilut hasadim. The former involves giving financial support to the poor. Many Jewish homes have collecting boxes (pushkes) in which money is put for charities. From an early age children are taught to think about others, less fortunate than themselves.

Gemilut hasadim refers to acts of kindness, showing compassion towards those in need of help, and echoing the words of Moses Maimonides: 'The best way of giving is to help a person help themselves so that they may become self-supporting'. Emphasis is always placed on long term aid that promotes self-help. All these acts of charity must be done anonymously so those who receive the money are not embarrassed and can keep their self-esteem.

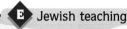 **Jewish teaching**

Is it not to share your food with the hungry and to provide the poor wanderer with shelter – when you see the naked, to clothe him, and not to turn away from your own flesh and blood?

Isaiah 58:7

If there is a poor man among your brothers in any of the towns of the land that the Lord your God is giving you, do not be hardhearted or tightfisted toward your poor brother... there will always be poor people in the land. Therefore I command you to be openhanded toward your brothers and toward the poor and needy in your land.

Deuteronomy 15:7 and 11

QUESTIONS

1 What is Zakah?

2 Describe Muslim teachings on wealth and poverty, charitable giving and charity.

3 Name any Jewish organisation that helps the needy.

4 Why does Ramadan remind Muslims of the needs of the poor?

5 In Judaism, what is the difference between Tzedaka and Gemilut hasadim?

Every religion has its own distinctive set of beliefs but there are important concerns that all the world religions share and one of the main ones is to encourage believers to help and show compassion to the poor. All the religious sacred writings and teachings are quite clear – looking after the disadvantaged is everyone's problem and priority must be given to ensuring that people are given every opportunity to escape the 'poverty trap'.

stop and think!

• 'To claim to be religious without helping those around you who are in need is useless.'

How far do you agree? Give your views about this statement, showing that you have considered other points of view.

Wealth

Without doubt, we all need money to survive. In many countries throughout the world the obvious signs of success are bound to the material benefits that you have (**A**).

Countries in the developed world often stand accused of being materialistic, valuing possessions and money far above things of much greater significance such as justice and kindness. In some countries, however, the desire for possessions and wealth are not so evident or as important because people are just intent on surviving. For millions of people life can be very miserable.

 Contrasting Fortunes! Two families outside their homes, surrounded by all their possessions. The Natomo Family, Kouakourou, Mali (left) and the Ukita Family, Tokyo, Japan (above).

Although their practices may be very different, the main world religions all believe that wealth encourages greed and selfishness. Central to all their teachings is the belief that actions, rather than possessions or money, determine the true value of a person. Consequently, wealth should be more equally distributed and helping those who are less fortunate should be encouraged.

Wealth

Christianity

All Christian traditions agree that it is a religious duty to help the needy. Much of Jesus' teachings encouraged his followers to give up material possessions and to share their wealth with the poor (**B**). During his lifetime, society did not accept Jesus' views easily. Wealth and good health were regarded as blessings from God, whereas poverty and ill health were clear signs of God's disapproval.

B Christian teaching

When Jesus heard this, he said to him, 'You still lack one thing. Sell everything you have and give to the poor, and you will have treasure in heaven. Then come, follow me… How hard it is for the rich to enter the Kingdom of God! Indeed it is easier for a camel to go through the eye of a needle than for a rich man to enter the Kingdom of God!'

Luke 18:22, 24–25

For we brought nothing into the world, and we can take nothing out of it. But if we have food and clothing, we will be content with that. People who want to get rich fall into temptation and a trap and into many foolish and harmful desires that plunge men into ruin and destruction. For the love of money is a root of all kinds of evil. Some people, eager for money, have wandered from the faith and pierced themselves with many griefs.

1 Timothy 6:7–10

The example and teachings of Christian leaders such as Martin Luther King, Dom Helder Camera and Mother Teresa have inspired Christians throughout the world to try to help the poor and the oppressed (**C**).

Mother Teresa founded the Sisters of Mercy – a Roman Catholic order of nuns who work to help the poor in India and other parts of the world

Islam

In Islamic teaching, the important thing is not whether people are rich or poor, it is what they do in the situation they find themselves in. On Judgement Day a Muslim is answerable on two matters concerning wealth: how it was earned and how it was spent.

All Muslims are encouraged to earn a livelihood to support themselves rather than rely on others (**D**). The Prophet Muhammad once said to one of his companions: 'To leave your children well off is better than leaving them poor which makes them ask other people for charity'. This hadith (tradition) sums up the Islamic attitude to wealth. The Prophet praised money that comes from a good source to a good person and encouraged people to be responsible with their wealth. If you earn your money in a lawful way, and use it for lawful (halal) purposes such as providing for your family and being mindful of the need of others, then wealth is likely to increase your reward from God. People must not, however, earn their money by doing anything forbidden (haram) such as cheating, gambling, theft or exploiting others. A Muslim's income cannot include earning interest (Riba) on money.

stop and think!

- In light of the religious viewpoints you have studied, what responsibilities do the wealthy have towards the poor?

D Muslim teaching

It is better that a person should take a rope and bring a bundle of wood on his back to sell so that Allah may preserve his honour, than he should beg from people (regardless of) whether they give to him or refuse him.

The Prophet Muhammad reported in Sahih Al-Bukhari

That which you lay out for increase through the property of (other) people, will have no increase with Allah: But that which you lay out for charity, seeking the countenance of Allah, (will increase): it is these who will get a recompense multiplied.

Surah 30:39

QUESTIONS

1 Look at the two photos in **A**. What are the most obvious differences that you can see? Are there any items, owned by the Ukita family, that could be useful to the Natomo family?

2 What do Christians believe is the right attitude to wealth?

3 Describe and explain how Christian teachings on wealth and poverty could help relieve the problems of world development.

4 Describe the work of a religious individual or organisation which helps the poor and needy.

5 'The love of money is a source of all kinds of evil.'

Give your views about this statement, showing that you have considered other points of view.

Wealth

Buddhism

According to Buddhist scriptures too many people search for happiness by acquiring wealth and material possessions. This pursuit of material wealth brings about a lot of unhappiness. The Buddha taught that everything is dependent on other things. Just like Hindus and Sikhs, Buddhists believe in the law of karma – that what a person does effects their own life as well as the lives of others. Buddhists believe that our present wealth is determined by our actions in the past. The way we use our wealth will affect our circumstances in the future. Those people who are rich and refuse to share their money will eventually be poor (**E**).

Being wealthy does not guarantee happiness but on the other hand living in poverty means barely surviving. Buddhism aims at achieving a balance between wanting more and not having enough. The Buddha urged his followers to have few possessions and follow a life where greed and jealousy are minimised. In his teachings he encouraged generosity and a life of moderation. His 'middle way' between the two extremes is the example for all Buddhists to follow (**F**).

E Giving alms to a Buddhist monk

Buddhist teaching

And which are the six ways for dissipating [wasting] wealth? Drink; being in the streets late; fairs; gambling; being with bad friends and idleness... there are six ways of idleness: A man says, it is too cold, and does no work; he says it is too hot, and does no work; he says it is too early... too late and does no work. He says, I am too hungry and does no work... too full and does no work. And while all that he should do remains undone he makes no money and such wealth as he has dwindles away.

Sigalavada Sutta

Better it were to swallow a ball of iron, red hot and flaming, than to lead a wicked and unrestrained life eating the food of the people.

The Dhammapada

stop and think!

- 'In a world where many people are starving, religious people cannot be true to their faith and stay rich.' Give your views about this statement, showing that you have considered other points of view.

Like many other religious traditions, Buddhism teaches the importance of avoiding harm to others and not earning a living through the suffering of others. Consequently certain types of work should be avoided. For example, manufacturing weapons, cruelty to animals, producing harmful drugs and poisons and slavery are all contrary to the Buddhist guidelines set out in the Eightfold Path of right livelihood.

Religious people are urged to think about their lifestyles and examine their attitudes towards others. It can be difficult for people to live up to the expectations that are set by particular religious traditions. Clearly, some material possessions are necessary but wealth should be more fairly distributed and help should be offered to the less fortunate. Followers of all the world religions are expected to respond with compassion to the problems of poverty and to use their personal wealths to relieve suffering.

QUESTIONS

1 Briefly outline the Buddhist attitude to wealth and poverty.

2 How does the law of karma relate to this attitude?

3 What was the 'middle way' taught by the Buddha?

1 In Romans 13:13 it states 'Let us behave decently'. What do you think the writer means by 'behaving decently'?

2 Give three reasons why a place of worship is regarded as the centre of a faith community.

3 What are the three main reasons given for the use of artwork in the Christian tradition?

4 Why are there no pictures, statues or photographs of human beings in a mosque?

5 Why is calligraphy such an important feature of Islamic faith?

6 Explain what is meant by meditation.

7 Briefly describe what is meant by:
a hymns
b gospel music
c qawwali

8 'The media normally portrays religions in a negative way.' Do you agree or disagree with this statement? Give examples to support your viewpoint.

9 Explain why religious parents might control the television viewing of their children.

10 What particular problems does a female athlete face if she comes from a Muslim background?

11 One headline (page 161) states that the Church is failing to attract young people. Do you think this is true? Give reasons to explain your answer.

12 Why do you think fundamentalist views are so often portrayed in the media?

13 Why do you think the internet is being increasingly used by religious groups?

14 Give your own response to 'You don't need to go to a church to be a good Christian'. Give reasons for your answer.

15 What are the six main reasons that are given to 'explain' absolute poverty?

16 Describe and explain how Christian and Muslim teachings could help to relieve the problem of homelessness.

17 Why have groups such as Muslim Aid or Christian Aid been reluctant to give just money to help the poor in the developing world?

18 The following things are sometimes described as signs of poverty in Britain. Select four of these and explain how they can affect the quality of a person's life.

- relying on social security
- poor health
- living in a high crime-rate area
- unemployment
- not having a car
- poor housing
- little educational success
- domestic problems

19 Describe the work of one agency working for the poor.

20 Explain why the main world religions all believe that wealth should be more equally distributed and the less fortunate should be helped.

21 Briefly outline the Muslim attitude to how money should be earned.

22 'In a world where many people are starving and homeless, religious people cannot be true to their faith and remain rich.'

Do you agree with this statement? Give your views showing that you have considered different points of view.

Introduction One world

Unit aims

The aims of this unit are to introduce you to some of the greatest problems facing the human race today. As the range of religious viewpoints is closely examined, you will find that even within the same religious tradition there is close agreement on some issues, but that in other areas, there are important differences.

Key concepts

All the major religions have similar views on the relationship between good and evil and the way in which God thinks people should behave. Yet, within any one particular religious faith there has never been a unanimous agreement about the use of violence. Most religions condemn those who use violence, but with some notable exceptions, it is generally accepted that when there is a war members of the armed forces may kill. Despite numerous statements to the contrary, many of the world religions stand accused of promoting religious intolerance and racism. On the subject of crime and punishment, we have to accept that although certain religions may appear to have harsh penalties for certain crimes, each of them urges people to show forgiveness and soften the penalties. As we explore these various issues, we shall see how different religious teachings relate to them.

What is this unit about?

We can see from history that some of the most fanatical wars have been brought about by religion. This unit examines the attitudes to war that we find in the teachings and writings of the world religions. All of them recognise their responsibility for promoting peace, for reconciliation and forgiveness. And yet, in practice, it is clear that religious people remain as divided as everyone else about war.

many problems

In today's world, there are clear indications that millions of people are deprived of the human rights and fair treatment that most of us tend to take for granted. Religious leaders are increasingly concerned with injustice, prejudice, discrimination and the pursuit of human rights. All the religions agree that the rules of justice have to be applied in the same way to all similar cases.

Every religion provides guidelines as to how people should behave. Many of these rules are demanding and not easy to follow. Every society has based its 'laws' on such guidelines but inevitably there will be 'law breakers' and we need to be protected from such individuals. The question which often arises is how to enforce the set laws and deal with people who break them. All the teachings are agreed that no one should be above the law or beneath the protection of the law.

The ultimate punishment is clearly the death penalty and, within this unit, arguments 'for' and 'against' are clearly set out. Although the vast majority of religious faiths firmly oppose the taking of life, certain religions permit the use of execution. To understand this apparent contradiction we have to examine their teachings very closely and bear in mind that, in certain countries, the religion *is* the state, not the state religion. In other words, state and religion are tied together and if execution is the policy held by the government of a country then the religious leaders are not in a position to oppose it.

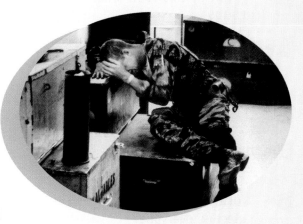

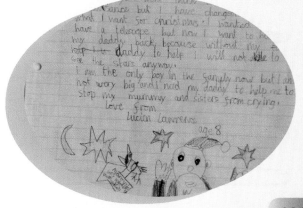

War and

A The different levels of conflict

▶ **Personal**

▶ **Two people**

▶ **Within or between small groups**

▶ **Within or between large groups, or small groups against large groups**

▶ **National** (within one state)

▶ **International** (involving two or more states)

▶ **Worldwide/global** (affecting everyone)

B Christian teaching

A time to kill and a time to heal, a time to tear down and a time to build... a time to love and a time to hate, a time for war and a time for peace.

Ecclesiastes 3:3, 8

... Nation will not take to the sword against nation, nor will they train for war any more.

Micah 4:3

C Muslim teaching

To those against whom war is made, permission is given (to fight), because they are wronged.

Surah 22:39

Central to the teachings of all the world religions is the concept of peace, and yet throughout history, religious people have been divided over whether it is right to use violence or be involved in war or armed conflict.

Every day, newspaper headlines and television heat up this debate with reports of conflicts, and gruesome or sensational events. This makes for large audience figures and increases the circulation figures, so editors find themselves pressurised into continuing to satisfy this morbid fascination.

The word 'conflict' is often used to denote violent physical acts, but it also can be used in many situations, such as disputes, competition and conflict of interests. Wars occur when the level of conflict reaches a national, international or global sphere (**A**).

Put simply, there are three possible views of war that a religion might adopt:

- The pacifist view: all killing and violence are wrong.

- Belief in a 'Just War': some wars are right because they are in the interests of justice – and should therefore be fought according to just rules.

- Belief in a 'Holy War': religious followers are asked or commanded by their leaders to defend their religion against those who do not believe in that religion and pose a threat to them.

Christianity

Initially, Christians were pacifists, opposing any form of resistance – to the extent of not even defending themselves when they were being persecuted and facing death in the Roman arenas. Yet, after the conversion of the Emperor Constantine to Christianity, it became acceptable for Christians to be in the army, and, some time later, all serving soldiers were expected to be Christians! Today, there is still much debate over the issue of war, and opinions remain divided even among followers of the same religion (**B**).

Islam

A misleading image of Muslims engaged in conflict is frequently promoted in the western media. To assume that the Muslim religion is typified by the activities of extreme fundamentalist groups would be as unfair as stating that the IRA represents the Catholic Church. All Muslims believe that it is their duty to defend themselves against any threat to Islam.

The word jihad, so frequently associated with war, is misapplied and misused in the West. Contrary to popular belief, it does not mean 'holy war'. It means 'to strive or struggle in the name of Allah'. In the warfare sense, jihad is permitted in self defence, to protect an individual's life, family and home, and also to fight oppression (**C**).

peace

Buddhism

A Buddhist must have compassion for any living creature, even to the extent of not killing an insect! It is clear, therefore that any aspect of war is unacceptable (**D**).

> All (wars) stem from our lack of human understanding, of mutual trust, and of mutual respect, based on kindness and love for all beings.
>
> *The Dalai Lama*

D Buddhist teaching

What is the enduring meaning of Buddhism? Basically, I think, it is compassion, not limited to human kind, but extended to all the living creatures. I think that is the essence, the compassion. Without that, I think there is nothing else.

Worlds of Faith, by John Bowker, Ariel Books, 1983

stop and think!

- How do the Buddhist teachings support Christian beliefs in pacifism?

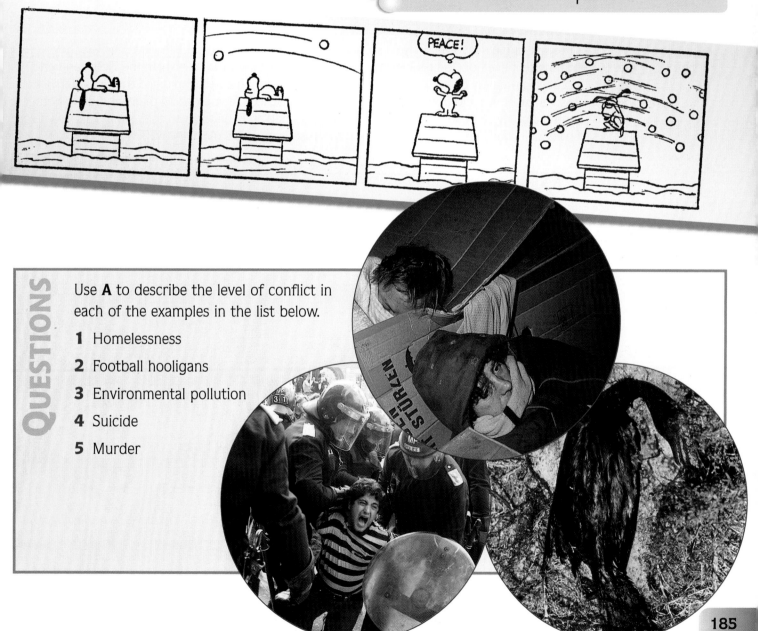

QUESTIONS

Use **A** to describe the level of conflict in each of the examples in the list below.

1 Homelessness
2 Football hooligans
3 Environmental pollution
4 Suicide
5 Murder

185

6 Religions and

It is rare when there is a single, clear cause for the outbreak of war. Wars have been fought out of fear, protest against injustice, and because of the actions of evil individuals or corrupt governments.

Many wars have been fought with religion as their stated cause, and with peace as their hoped-for end. Some of the most fanatical struggles have been inspired and legitimised by religion. The results in each case are the same: loss of life, destruction, mental and physical suffering, enormous debts and a huge refugee problem. Of course, religious beliefs are often complicated. Individuals and groups within each religion often have different views.

The Crusades

Christian soldiers involved in the Crusade campaigns in the 11th to 13th centuries felt they were fighting on behalf of God against the **infidels** or **pagans** who were living in the Holy Land and occupying the holy city of Jerusalem. It was Pope Urban II himself who urged the Crusaders to 'rescue the Holy Land from that dreadful race'. He added: 'All men going there who die, whether on the journey or while fighting the pagans will immediately be forgiven their sins.' This was a very powerful incentive for some men to join the crusading armies (**A**).

Emperor Frederick II of Germany leads the Sixth Crusade into Jerusalem in 1229 **A**

stop and think!

- What do C and D tell us about the Muslim and Sikh views of war and peace?

teachings on war

Christianity

It has been argued by certain Christian denominations, such as the Society of Friends (Quakers) and the Anabaptists, that the only true position a Christian can adopt is one of absolute pacifism. Teachings such as **B** reinforce their views. Most Christians believe that war should be avoided but accept that there are times when going to war is a necessary evil.

Islam

Islam is a religion of peace and war is seen only as a last resort. The Qur'anic teachings allow for the establishment of justice, self-defence and the protection of one's family.

The concept of 'holy war' (Harb al-Muqadis) allows Muslims to fight but they are forbidden from starting the conflict. They must also look to end the war as quickly as possible. As soon as peace is offered the fighting must stop (**C**).

Sikhism

The first Sikh community founded by Guru Nanak followed a simple disciplined way of life, committed to strict pacifism. As Sikh fortunes fluctuated, later Gurus taught their followers that they should be prepared to defend themselves. The 'Kirpan', originally a sword used by Sikhs to defend themselves, has become a symbol of dignity and self-respect, and a reminder of the need to protect the individual's religious freedom. The tenth and last Guru, Guru Gobind Singh was a general as well as a Guru. In order to strengthen the military discipline of the Sikhs at a time of great persecution, he organised the khalsa – the Sikh brotherhood.

B Christian teaching

You have heard that it was said, 'Eye for eye and tooth for tooth'. But I tell you, Do not resist an evil person. If someone strikes you on the right cheek, turn to him the other also.

Matthew 5:38–39

'Put your sword back in its place,' Jesus said to him, 'for all who draw the sword will die by the sword.'

Matthew 26:52

C Muslim teaching

But if the enemy incline towards peace, do you (also) incline towards peace, and trust in Allah: for He is the One that hears and knows (all things).

Surah 8:61

If you overpower your enemy, treat your forgiveness of him as an expression of gratitude for defeating him.

Ali ibn Abi Taleb (Cousin and son-in-law of Prophet Muhammad)

D Sikh teaching

The Khalsa – pure ones – shall rule, no hostile powers shall exist... Those who enter the Khalsa for shelter will be protected. Without power, justice does not flourish, without justice everything is crushed and ruined.

Dasam Granth

When all efforts to restore peace prove useless and no words avail, lawful is the flash of steel, it is right to draw the sword.

Guru Gobind Singh

QUESTIONS

'Positive and effective non-violence is the alternative we offer to warfare.' (Quaker Peace Testimony For Today)

1 What price are we prepared to pay for peace?

2 Are there any circumstances when it is morally right for Christians to take part in a war?

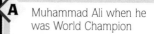

A Muhammad Ali when he was World Champion

Opinions on war and peace

From the outside, it often appears that followers of Christianity or Islam do not hold a consistent or coherent attitude when considering the topic of war. Every individual is unique and similarly, each person's responses to a particular situation will vary.

Teachings in these two religions are consistent but can be interpreted in differing ways. Some choose to adopt the stance of individuals such as Dr Martin Luther King, the black Civil Rights leader in the USA (1929–68), and 'Mahatma' Gandhi, the Indian leader (1869–1948). Others clearly believe that war can be justified in self defence to fight oppression, or to put right injustice.

We clearly see the different viewpoints when we examine the stand taken by two individuals: Muhammad Ali (**A**) and Leonard Cheshire (**D**).

Muhammad Ali

Muhammad Ali (formerly known as Cassius Clay) became the World Heavyweight Boxing Champion in 1964. He converted from Christianity to Islam, and was totally opposed to the fighting going on between the USA and North Vietnam. He soon found himself at the heart of a nation in upheaval, and became a spokesperson against the politics of war, religion and race that were tearing America apart in the 1960s.

One act of defiance was to cost Ali his Heavyweight Crown and three and a half of his best years banned from the ring. In 1966, as the US Army's need for manpower grew, Ali was called up in the draft of young men aged 18 to 24 years. He refused, and by doing so, gave up everything he had won and earned – his boxing titles, his career and his fortune. He had been one of America's favourite heroes, but now he became one of the most hated.

On 28 April 1967, he turned down his final chance, stating at a press conference: 'No. I will not go 10,000 miles from here to help murder and kill another poor people simply to continue the domination of white slave masters over the darker people of the earth.'

The US Court had no sympathy for his religious scruples and he received a maximum ten thousand dollar fine and five years imprisonment (later suspended on appeal). Ali's response was typically defiant: 'Clean up my cell and take me to jail!'

Overnight, he became a civil rights **martyr**. Reactions to him were mixed. According to some, Ali had 'given up being a man' when he did not support the war effort. Others felt that he had every right to be a **conscientious objector**. Muhammad Ali lived for fame but threw it all away when it was against his religious principles. His courage in the boxing ring was never questioned, but like so many other conscientious objectors, he was regarded by some as cowardly and unpatriotic.

Leonard Cheshire

Leonard Cheshire was Britain's official observer when the second atomic bomb was dropped on Nagasaki, in Japan. Cheshire was one of the RAF's youngest and most decorated Group Captains, and had established himself as one of the greatest bomber pilots of the Second World War. He was awarded the Victoria Cross for four years of 'sustained heroism', flying over 100 bombing missions, which inevitably caused deaths.

Yet the same man, years later, was described in a newspaper article as 'closer to sainthood than any other person in Britain this century'. So, how did this change come about?

What he witnessed on the 9 August 1945 shocked him. Over Nagasaki, he saw a huge ball of fire rushing upwards, leaving behind it a mushroom-shaped cloud. This is how he described the event:

'There was this really awesome sight… you could not think of the city, you could think of nothing. Your eyes were riveted by this fireball rocketing upwards. The fire died out and became a kind of yellow sulphurous cloud and it was suspended on a column and my impression was that the column was symmetrical not jagged like high explosive. It was almost finely sculptured and it was rising at an enormous speed but effortlessly and there was something all the more frightening in it because it was so effortless… bubbling like a cauldron… suddenly your thoughts would stop and cut and you would think about the people underneath.'

After the Second World War, Cheshire became a Roman Catholic, and dedicated his life to helping disabled people, setting up Cheshire Homes throughout the world. With very little money, he set out to find support for his idea of nursing homes for disabled people. He discovered a new role for himself, and in so doing, brought new life to many who would otherwise have suffered in their final years.

D Leonard Cheshire

Unlike Muhammad Ali, Cheshire had made a large contribution to the war effort, and he was able to reconcile this with his religious beliefs. Ali, on the other hand, intent on hurting his opponent and knocking him out in a boxing ring, was sure that fighting in a war was against his religious beliefs.

It is easy to feel confused by quotes from various religious scriptures that are sometimes misused to justify or denounce war. It often appears that followers of the world religions do not have a consistent or coherent attitude when considering war. This is clearly seen in **E** below.

stop and think!

- Looking at E, can you explain why there is no clear agreed view of 'just war' among religious people?

E

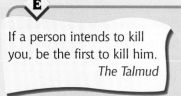

If a person intends to kill you, be the first to kill him.
The Talmud

Turn from evil and do good; seek peace and pursue it.
Psalm 34:14

Teachings can always be interpreted in different ways. Some individuals known as conscientious objectors cross all the religious barriers in their opposition to wars, holding a view similar to that held by Buddhists.

In the past, people who refused to fight in a war because of their principles often faced criticism and abuse. Some individuals during the First World War were imprisoned, and many received a white feather which represented cowardice. In the United States, the people who protested against the Vietnam War and refused to fight are still regarded with suspicion today. Young men who ignored the draft, like Muhammad Ali, were described as unpatriotic, and some were severely punished for their beliefs.

F Would you be willing to go to prison for your beliefs?

THIS IS JOE... HE'S A CONSCIENTIOUS OBJECTOR

HE DOESN'T WANT TO SHOOT.. HE DOESN'T WANT TO KILL..

HE DOESN'T WANT TO DROP BOMBS..

SO WE PUT HIM IN JAIL

WHY?

HE'S A THREAT TO SOCIETY.

QUESTIONS

1 Nuclear bombs and other weapons which maim and kill indiscriminately oppose the concepts of all world religions because it is inevitable that innocent people will suffer. Non-combatants must be spared and the environment must be protected. Does the threat of nuclear war make any difference when assessing the conditions set out for a just war? (See pages 192–3)

2 It has been argued that the atomic bombs brought the Second World War to a quick end thereby avoiding further bloodshed. In view of this, do you think the bombings of Hiroshima and Nagasaki were morally justified? Give your reasons.

3 Many Christians fought in the Second World War against Nazi Germany. On what grounds might they argue that their actions were morally justifiable?

4 How would you feel if you were called up to fight in a war?

5 Do you think conscientious objectors could be described as cowards?

6 In what circumstances, if any, would you be prepared to die for your beliefs?

A just war?

Throughout history, millions of lives have been affected by warfare. Some people, as we have seen, do not believe that it is right to fight under any circumstances. Others are content to judge the 'morality' of each war by a set of rules – the conditions of war.

Conditions for a just war

The two original conditions for a just war (**B**) were set out by St Augustine and a third condition (**D**) was added by St Thomas Aquinas. A fourth condition was added in the 16th century by Francisco de Vittoria. For several centuries these conditions seemed satisfactory, but by the 19th century, three additional conditions were needed (**E**). It is important to remember that in the modern world, nations possess weapons capable of total devastation, weaponry which was not foreseen by St Augustine and St Aquinas.

A

St Augustine (354 to 430 CE) was a writer of great importance. His ideas shaped the development of Christianity and his thought dominated the Middle Ages.

B The two original conditions for a just war

1 There is a just cause. In practice, this can only happen when a country is attacked and has to defend itself. Armed conflict is only justified if an aggressor refuses to restore what has been seized.

2 The war can only be declared and controlled by the ruler or governing body of the country concerned [i.e. it cannot be waged by private citizens].

St Augustine

C

St Thomas Aquinas (c.1225 to 1274 CE) became the official theologian of the Roman Catholic Church. He is credited with interpreting St Augustine's original thinking, formulating the Just War criteria.

D A further condition for a just war

3 The war has a clear and just aim and all fighting must stop once that aim has been achieved. It also means that the ultimate goal must be to restore good relations with the enemy, not to humiliate him.

St Thomas Aquinas

stop and think!
- Do you think that the conditions set out by St Augustine and St Aquinas would be helpful to nations today faced with the possibility of war?

E Four further conditions for a just war

4 It is waged in a just way. In other words, limits must be put in place: first by restricting the amount of force to the maximum needed for the objectives to be achieved: second, by ensuring the safety of all non-combatants and all those not directly involved in the war effort.

Francisco de Vittoria

5 There is a reasonable chance of success. Obviously it would be wrong to lose thousands of lives, knowing that there was no chance of winning.

6 Every other possibility of solving the conflict has been tried before the war is declared – this must include detailed and wide-ranging negotiations at every stage. War can only be declared as a last resort.

7 The good achieved as a result of the war must outweigh the evil which led to the war. Even suffering on a mass scale might be a lesser evil than allowing an aggressor to continue a murderous regime.

 F Hindu teaching

If you do not fight in this just war, you will neglect your duty, harm your reputation and commit the sin of omission. Having regard to your duty, you should not hesitate, because for a warrior there is nothing greater than a just war.

Bhagavad Gita 2:31,33

 G Muslim teaching

Fight in the cause of Allah those who fight you, but do not transgress limits... if they cease, let there be no hostility except to those who practise oppression.

Surah 2:190, 193

Broadly speaking, the three major religions that have their roots in India (Hinduism, Buddhism and Sikhism) share the idea of non-violence – ahimsa. The three world religions with their roots in the Middle East (Judaism, Christianity and Islam) adopted at some stages of their history, the ideas of 'Holy War' as well as that of 'Just War'.

Despite the commitment of Hinduism and Sikhism to ahimsa, not all Hindus and Sikhs share the same views. Buddhism has perhaps the best record of all religions for non-violence. However, Buddhists in Sri Lanka have been criticised for oppressing the Tamil minority there because the majority of Tamils are Hindu.

Similar themes of the just war can be seen in the teaching of world religions as diverse as Hinduism (**F**) and Islam (**G**).

The Gulf War

War in the Arabian Gulf prompted a debate within the Christian Church about whether it was a 'just' conflict. The Pope condemned the 'terrible logic of war' and declared the Gulf War unjust. Other Church leaders disagreed, believing that the war was justified because a people had to be liberated. In the Arab world, thoughts were divided and Muslims were set against Muslims.

Distinguishing between political, economic and religious ideas is not easy, and it would be fair to say that very few wars, from the Crusades to modern-day conflicts, could honestly be described as 'Holy Wars' or 'Just Wars'.

QUESTIONS

1 Look through the statements below and decide which ones are part of the Just War theory.

a There must be a reasonable chance of success.

b The war must be fought to protect religion.

c The war must not be fought against poor countries.

d Only sufficient force must be used and civilians must not be targeted.

e The war must be fought with the intention to establish good or stop evil.

2 Research any war. Using the seven conditions in **B**, **D** and **E**, decide whether or not this war can be described as 'just'. For each condition, explain how it was or was not satisfied.

3

I want to know who the men in the shadows are
I want to hear somebody ask them why
They can be counted on to tell us who our enemies are
But they're never the ones to fight or to die.
From the song *Lives In the Balance* by Jackson Browne

What do you think Jackson Browne is saying in his song above?

Letters from

A

This country is so beautiful when the sun's shining on the mountains. The farmers in their paddy fields with their water buffalo and palm trees, monkeys, birds and even the strange insects... For a fleeting moment I am not in a war zone at all, just on vacation but still missing you and the family.

A soldier fighting in Vietnam

These extracts are from letters sent home by young soldiers fighting in Vietnam.

D A Marine weeps at the end of a mission in which four of 17 helicopters were shot down

B

He called me, and I went to his side and began treating his wounds. As I applied bandages to his wounds, he looked up at me and said, 'Doc, I'm a mess'. He then said: 'Oh God, I don't want to die. Mother, I don't want to die. Oh God, don't let me die'. We called a helicopter to take him and the rest of the wounded to the hospital. Richard died before the ship arrived.

I did everything in my power to save Richard. Every skill known to me was applied. I often wonder if what we're fighting for is worth a human life!

C A Vietnamese mother and children swimming to safety

E

Dear Mum
The days are fairly peaceful but the nights are pure hell. I look up at the stars. It's so hard to believe the same stars shine over you in such a different world.
All my love
Al

F

Dear Mum
Anyone over here who walks more than fifty feet through elephant grass should automatically get a Purple Heart [highest bravery award]. Try to imagine grass possessing razor sharp edges, 8 to 15 feet high, so thick as to cut visibility to one yard. Then try to imagine walking through it while all around you are men possessing the latest automatic weapons who desperately want to kill you. You would be amazed how much a man can age in one patrol.

Vietnam

G With all the death and destruction I've seen in the past week, I've aged greatly. I feel like an old man now. I've seen enough of war and its destruction. I'm scared by it but not scared enough to quit... Please pray for us all here at Khe Sanh.
Your son, Kevin

H We are all scared. One can easily see this emotion in the eyes of each individual. One might hide it with his mouth, while another might hide it with his actions but there is no way around it – we are all scared. They say when fear is in a man, he is prepared for anything. When fear possesses the man, he is prepared for nothing.
As of now, fear is in me. I hope I can keep it from possessing me.

J Well, you learn everyday the mistakes you are making but the biggest one is to get too attached to any one person. Not over here at least! Things happen so quickly and one minute he's fine, the next he's not. But old Don is pretty lucky – knock on wood! Home I'll come I'm sure.
Love Don
(Days later, 2nd Lt Donald Jacques, along with 22 of his men, was killed in an ambush just outside Khe Sanh.)

I US soldiers brutally torturing a Vietcong prisioner

stop and think!
• How do all the accounts in these letters contrast with the images of war seen in films?

QUESTIONS

1 What do you think is the main difference between **A** and **F**?

2 In **B**, **F**, **G**, **H** and **J** what images of war are the writers portraying?

3 The following is an extract from *The Tarnished Shield* by George Walton (Dodd, 1973). This is a true account of the My Lai massacre by American troops led by Lt William Calley:

'Within My Lai Four, the killings had become more sadistic. Several old men were stabbed with bayonets and one was thrown down a well to be followed by a hand grenade. Some women and children praying outside... were killed by shooting them in the back of the head with rifles. Occasionally a soldier would drag a girl, often a mere child to a ditch where he would rape her... the young were slaughtered with the same impartiality as the old.'

'In war, anything goes.' Do you think it is possible to win a war in a humane and honourable way? Give reasons for your opinion, showing you have considered another point of view.

6 Religious tolerance

A Prejudice and discrimination takes many forms

- Ability or disabilities
- Colour
- Differing lifestyles
- Race
- Gender
- Age
- Social Class
- Wealth
- Political views
- Religious views

PREJUDICE AND DISCRIMINATION

Our everyday lives are affected by prejudice and discrimination. Prejudice is an attitude, prejudging someone or something. It means having an opinion not based on fact. Discrimination is an action. It is best described as treating someone unfairly – prejudice in action. This unfair treatment can take a variety of forms (**A**).

Some forms of persecution and oppression that existed in the past have to a certain extent been eliminated from our society but others remain. In today's world, there are clear indications that millions of people are deprived of the fair treatment that most of us take for granted.

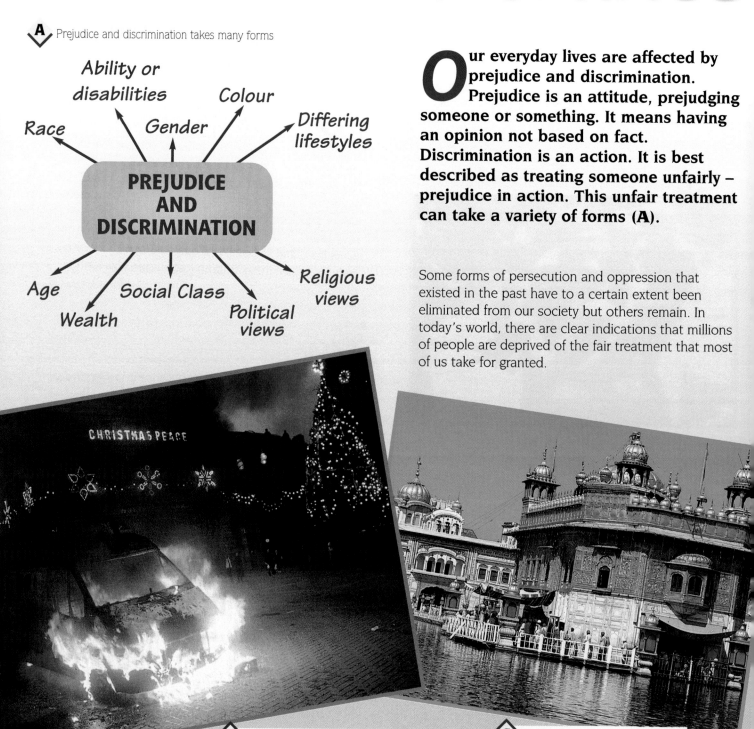

B Tension in Northern Ireland

CHRISTMAS PEACE

C The Golden Temple in Amritsar

World religions attract followers from many different countries and races. Christianity and Judaism teaches that human beings are made in the image of God and that all people are equal. All the world faiths teach that although human beings may appear different, they should be treated with equal consideration and respect. Unfortunately, theory is not always turned into practice. Despite teachings to the contrary, the world faiths have been seen at times to encourage religious intolerance which has often led to prejudice and discrimination. Rather than breaking down barriers religions often stand accused of creating divisions.

In Northern Ireland, for example, differing Roman Catholic and Protestant beliefs have been regarded as the underlying cause of tension which has led so often in the past to bombing campaigns, violent protests and sectarian murders (**B**). For many years, in India there have been clashes between Hindus, Muslims and Sikhs. In 1984 the Indian prime minister, Indira Gandhi was assassinated by members of the Sikh religion. This act was in retaliation for an attack she ordered on the most sacred Sikh shrine – the Golden Temple in Amritsar (**C**). Many Sikhs were killed by Hindus seeking revenge for the death of their leader.

In the Middle East, since its creation in 1948, Israel has been involved in many conflicts with several of its Arab neighbours.

Just a glance at the history books will show that belonging to a religious faith often means having to face prejudice and discrimination. Certain religious groups have been hated so much that attempts have been made to exterminate them. Tibet, for example, is a Buddhist country but for years it has been threatened by its Chinese neighbours. The Dalai Lama who is the leader-in-exile has urged his followers never to resort to violence and racism because this would destroy the Buddhist values that the Tibetans are trying so hard to defend. With the rise of Christianity, the Jews and Muslims were often targeted and discriminated against (**D–F**). The treatment of the Jews is known as anti-Semitism and reached a terrible climax in the last century when the Nazi Party, led by Adolf Hitler, singled out the Jews and murdered over six million of them (**D**).

D Jewish survivors of Auschwitz

E The Crusaders massacred the Muslim, Jewish and even Christian populations of Jerusalem after capturing it in 1099 CE

F The Inquisition – thousands of Jews and Muslims were tortured and executed in the name of Christianity

197

Religious tolerance

In March 2000 Pope John Paul II apologised for 2,000 years of violence, persecution and mistakes. He asked forgiveness for sins committed against Jews, heretics, women, gypsies and native peoples (**G**).

The early Christians were also victims of persecution from both the Romans and the Jews. A reading of the New Testament soon reveals that attitudes towards others were a problem for the early Church. In the Gospels we can read accounts of people who refused to mix with non-Jews (gentiles). Many other prejudices can also be seen against Samaritans, tax collectors and sick people. Jesus, himself, was a victim of discrimination but through his teachings and actions his message was very clear – 'love your neighbour as yourself' (**H**). St Paul was a tireless worker for the Christian cause but before his conversion, he ruthlessly persecuted the Christians. In the case of St Paul, the persecutor became the persecuted!

 G

'We are asking pardon for the divisions among Christians, for the use of violence that some have committed in the service of truth, and for the attitudes of mistrust and hostility assumed towards followers of other religions.'

Pope John Paul II

 H Christian teaching

And he sent messengers on ahead, who went into a Samaritan village to get things ready for him, but the people there did not welcome him, because he was heading for Jerusalem. When the disciples, James and John saw this, they asked, 'Lord do you want us to call fire down from heaven to destroy them?' But Jesus turned and rebuked them, and they went to another village.

Luke 9:52–56

'But I tell you who hear me: Love your enemies, do good to those who hate you, bless those who curse you, pray for those who mistreat you. If someone strikes you on one cheek, turn to him the other also. If someone takes your cloak, do not stop him from taking your tunic. Give to everyone who asks you, and if anyone takes what belongs to you, do not demand it back. Do to others as you would have them do to you.'

Luke 6:27–31

 stop and think!

- What problems does living in a multi-faith society cause for religious believers?

QUESTIONS

1 What do you understand by:
   a prejudice?
   b discrimination?

2 Explain the different types of prejudice which exist and the reasons for them.

3 State three things which may cause people to be treated differently or unfairly.

4 Show how the example of Jesus might help Christians facing persecution today.

stop and think!

- How far do you think followers of different religions should try to overcome their differences and work together for the good of everyone? Is this a realistic aim?

For Muslims, the teachings of the Qur'an make clear that all people are of equal worth in the sight of Allah. Protection of the rights of non-Muslims to worship is an important part of Islamic law (**I**).

I Muslim teaching

Allah forbids you not, with regard to those who fight you not for (your) faith nor drive you out of your homes, from dealing kindly and justly with them: for Allah loves those who are just.

Surah 60:8

Let not some men among you laugh at others: It may be that the (latter) are better than the (former): Nor let some women laugh at others: It may be that the (latter) are better than the (former): Nor defame nor be sarcastic to each other, nor call each other by (offensive) nicknames.

Surah 49:11

These teachings help to explain why non-Muslim societies and religious places of worship have flourished all over the Islamic world. History provides many examples of Muslims' tolerance towards other faiths. For example, for centuries before the Spanish Inquisition, Christians and Jews lived and prospered in Andalus (Spain) under Muslim rule. As Sayyeda Fatima al-Yashrutiyya stated: 'The different religions are like a tree. There is one root and many branches. On each branch there is a light, and the lights are of differing colours. But they all draw their light from one root. We all need to keep our own light bright.'

Followers of Islam are drawn from many nations and all races and have settled in different countries throughout the world. Almost inevitably however, in countries where they are in the minority, Muslims have encountered discrimination both on national and local levels because of their different religious beliefs and customs. In Britain, for example, Muslims as well as Jews and Sikhs had, until fairly recently, been refused permission to set up voluntary-aided schools, even though there were many Roman Catholic and Church of England schools. In Britain, since May 1997, maintained minority faith schools have been given government approval (**J**).

J Pupils at Guru Nanak school which, on 30 November 1999, became the first state Sikh school in Europe. Boys wear the traditional turban and girls the long-flowing falwar kameez, with a blazer.

Religious tolerance

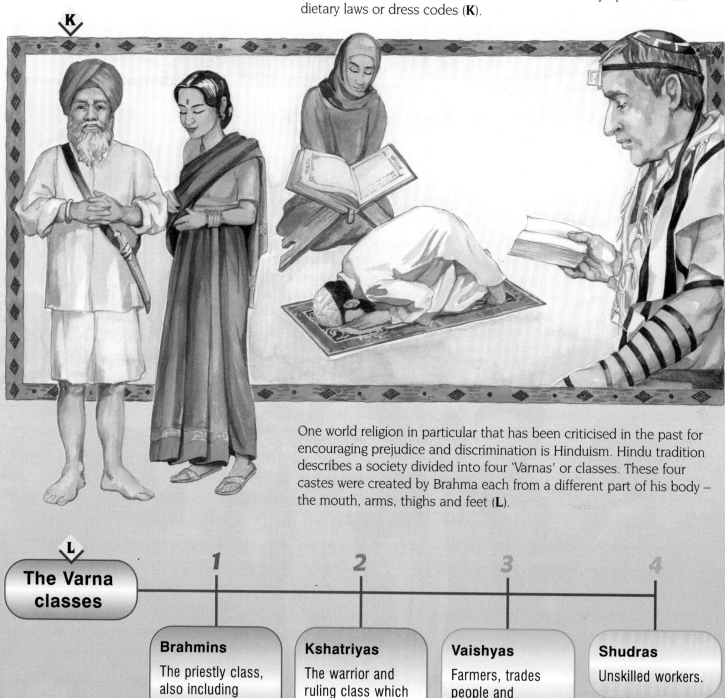

Employers are not always sympathetic to employees from different religious faiths taking time off for observance of religious festivals and little effort has been made to understand or even sympathise with dietary laws or dress codes (**K**).

One world religion in particular that has been criticised in the past for encouraging prejudice and discrimination is Hinduism. Hindu tradition describes a society divided into four 'Varnas' or classes. These four castes were created by Brahma each from a different part of his body – the mouth, arms, thighs and feet (**L**).

The Varna classes

1

Brahmins

The priestly class, also including teachers, scientists, doctors, etc.

2

Kshatriyas

The warrior and ruling class which includes civil servants and local authority workers.

3

Vaishyas

Farmers, trades people and craftsmen.

4

Shudras

Unskilled workers.

Below these four groups are the pariahs or chandela, the 'outcasts' or 'untouchables' who do the menial jobs.

Religious support for the varna system can be found in the Bhagavad Gita and in the Rig Veda and yet, there are many writings and stories in the Hindu scriptures which emphasise the equality of individuals (**M**). The great Indian leader and peace campaigner, Mohandas Gandhi, spoke out for the 'untouchables' in Indian society, those people regarded as the lowest of the castes. Largely thanks to his efforts, the Indian government passed a law in 1948 to give equal rights to all members of society and gradually barriers have been broken down and people are more free to mix socially. Admittedly, in practice, this is not always the case and struggles still continue to establish the rights of the 'untouchables'.

Like the other religions, Hinduism teaches that prejudice and discrimination are always unjust and therefore should not be tolerated by followers.

Religious laws do not allow for any form of prejudice and discrimination, yet, as we have seen the world religions often stand accused of those very things. The teachings are clear enough but it would be fair to say that, unfortunately, the interpretation and application do not always match up.

 Conflicting Hindu teachings?

I look upon all creatures equally; none are less dear to me and none more dear...
Those who come to me for refuge, no matter if there birth is low, women, workers and servants, along the highest way shall go. I am the same to every being none is disliked or dear to me, they are in me and I in them who worship me and lovingly.

Bhagavad Gita 9:29, 32

When the Primal Man was divided the Brahmin [priest] arose from his mouth, the Kshatriya [soldier] from his arms, the Vaishya [merchant] from his thighs and the Shudra [unskilled worker] from his feet.

Rig Veda, Purusha Hymn

QUESTIONS

1 State two reasons Muslims give for believing all human beings are equal.

2 Give an account of the traditional Hindu view of society as divided into four castes (varna).

3 Explain why Mohandas Gandhi regarded untouchability as a 'blot on Hinduism'.

4 State the teaching from one religious tradition about a person's duty to other fellow human beings.

5 Some people have said that they do not understand why schools teach about religions. How does the information in this unit help us to see why learning about others is so important?

6 'Religion has caused as much prejudice as it has solved.' How far do you agree with this statement? Give reasons to support your answer showing that you have considered other points of view.

6

Racism

A The slave trade and mass murder

Racism is the belief in the superiority of one race above all others. Most people would like to pride themselves on being tolerant and open minded but unfortunately racism still exists today and is the root cause of tremendous suffering for millions of people who are discriminated against because of their race or colour.

Until fairly recently in the earth's history the different races were kept apart by geographical barriers such as the oceans, mountains and deserts. This isolation enabled different groups of people to develop different national and racial characteristics such as physique, colour, language, etc. As people began to travel more widely continents were opened up for discovery. From the sixteenth century onwards the conquests of Africa, the Americas and Asia led to the destruction of cultures and civilisations. Racism was used to justify the slave trade that led to the forced removal of millions of people from Africa as well as the exploitation of their lands (**A**).

One of the main problems in examining the issue of racism is that different people use different words when talking about the same things and sometimes the same words are used but mean different things. Racism is brought about by prejudice, discrimination, and stereotyping. These three terms are central but not unique to the racism debate. All can be applied to aspects such as sex, social class, age, etc.

stop and think!

• What is your own view of racism and the way people treat each other?

B The racism route

Prejudice

This is an attitude of mind where someone prejudges others from a different racial group. It is a way of thinking about other groups of people which will not change even in the light of new experience.

Discrimination

This is basically prejudice in action. Discrimination occurs when a person is unfairly treated because of the colour of their skin.

Sterotyping

This involves creating a fixed image (stereotype) in three different stages:

a take some easily identified features that a group supposedly has.
b make these features the dominant characteristics of the group.
c suggest that all members of the group possess these features.

These 'stereotypes' are then used as a basis for racial abuse and help reinforce particular prejudices.

Like most animals, humans feel safest when they are surrounded by their 'own kind'. The problem of racism lies in attitude, in the fear and ignorance people have of others who do not look the same as they do. It is important to remember that racism is not limited to prejudice and discrimination against black or coloured people. The Holocaust, when over six million Jews were murdered, represents one of the most barbaric examples of racism ever seen.

In the past, in Britain, the Law Courts have been accused of not taking vicious and dangerous racial abuse seriously enough. The 1976 Race Relations Act strengthened the two previous laws of 1965 and 1968 so that every person is legally protected against racial discrimination in employment, housing, education and the provision of goods and services. The Act also outlawed any threatening or abusive words in public that could stir up racial hatred and made it illegal to publish anything likely to cause racial hatred. Prosecutions, however, are still relatively rare and despite the efforts of many organisations and the authorities, racism is still apparent in Britain today (**C**).

Racism appears to be universally condemned in all the major world religions. Nearly all of them, however, have been accused in the past of encouraging or ignoring racism. If a person belongs to the Christian faith it means they are committed to the belief that all people, regardless of colour or race, are equal. The teachings are quite clear on this issue (**D**) and yet many Christian missionaries in the eighteenth and nineteenth centuries turned a blind eye to slavery. The **apartheid** system in South Africa which was finally dismantled in 1994 was actively supported by the Dutch Reformed Church. Even today, 'white power' groups such as the Ku Klux Klan and the Aryan Brotherhood in the USA incite racial hatred and yet describe themselves as 'true Christians!'

C Racism – It couldn't happen here! Look closely, and the signs are there.

D Christian teaching

From one man he made every nation of men, that they should inhabit the whole earth; and he determined the times set for them and the exact places where they should live.

Acts 17:26

There is neither Jew nor Greek, slave nor free, male nor female, for you are all one in Christ Jesus.

Galatians 3:28

Racism

Both the Christian and Jewish faiths talk about the equality of human beings and the fact that we are all God's creatures (**E**). Judaism teaches that all humans can be traced back to Adam and Eve. One Biblical passage in the Book of Genesis (Chapter 10) describes all the known peoples of the world forming one huge family, descended from the three sons of Noah. There are many teachings in the Tenakh about God's care for the oppressed and the need to oppose any form of prejudice or discrimination based on race, poverty or social class.

The Nazis' attempt to destroy the Jewish race in the Holocaust makes it impossible for Jews to see racism as anything other than evil. The Jews regard themselves as God's chosen people but this does not mean that they look down on other races or treat them differently.

> Adam named his wife Eve, because she would become the mother of all the living.
>
> *Genesis 3:20*

> When an alien lives with you in your land, do not mistreat him. The alien living with you must be treated as one of your native-born. Love him as yourself, for you were aliens in Egypt. I am the Lord your God.
>
> *Leviticus 19:33–34*

QUESTIONS

1 What do you understand by:
   a racism?
   b racial discrimination?
   c stereotyping?

2 Using examples, explain the difference between prejudice and discrimination.

3 Outline the main parts of the 1976 Race Relations Act. Why do you think prosecutions against people who break this law are so rare?

4 What teaching is given about prejudice and discrimination in the sacred texts of Christianity?

F Passing out from officer training at Sandhurst

Racism is still very much alive throughout the world today but there are many examples of committed religious people campaigning against racial discrimination. One of the most famous individuals who campaigned against racism in his country was the Christian Baptist minister Martin Luther King. Throughout the 1950s and 1960s Dr King led the civil rights movement in the United States (**G**). Using the example set by the great pacifist Indian Hindu leader, Mohandas Gandhi, King used non-violent protest and peaceful boycotts as a way of achieving his aims. He closely followed the Christian teachings about non-retaliation and love: 'Love your enemies, do good to those who hate you, bless those who curse you, pray for those who mistreat you. If anyone strikes you on one cheek, turn to him the other also... Give to everyone who asks you, and if anyone takes what belongs to you, do not demand it back. (*Luke* 6:27–28, 31)

In Britain the Church of England's Race and Community Relations Committee and CARJ (The Catholic Association for Racial Justice) actively campaign against racism and examine issues such as immigration laws and unemployment levels in ethnic minority groups. In recent years they have drawn attention to the fact that very few blacks and Asians have been promoted to the highest levels of Britain's political, economic and social life. For example, at the beginning of the twenty first century all 96 high court judges and all 194 Chief Police Officers were white, under 1% of officers in the regular forces came from ethnic minority groups and there were only two black or Asian people in the top four grades of the Civil Service (**F**).

G A man committed to pacifism – Martin Luther King

Islam

Equality is a key principle running through Islam beginning with the account of the creation of humankind. Under no circumstances can an individual be badly treated simply because he or she comes from a different race. A sign of the power of Allah is the fact that people vary in colour and speak different languages. It is clear from some of the sayings of the Prophet Muhammad and verses in the Qur'an that racism, whether open or hidden, is regarded as an evil aspect of life. Differences in colour, race or traditions cannot be used as excuses for unfair treatment (**H**).

The multiracial aspect of Islam is best seen in the Hajj – the annual pilgrimage to Makkah. Here Muslims of all races gather together with one purpose in mind – to worship Allah. Muslims from all races belong to the 'family of Islam'.

It seems that all the major world religions believe that we should take action to make sure that everyone is treated fairly. This is not always an easy goal to achieve but most religious followers realise that racial prejudice and discrimination is both unjust and unworthy of the beliefs and values to which they subscribe.

H Muslim teaching

And among His signs is the creation of the heavens and the earth, and the variations in your languages and your colours; verily in that are signs for those who know.

Surah 30:22

O mankind! We created you from a single (pair) of a male and female, and made you into nations and tribes, that you may know each other (not that you may despise each other). Verily the most honoured of you in the sight of Allah is (he who is) the most righteous of you.

Surah 49:13

QUESTIONS

1 Describe Christian views on racism and write about the life and work of someone who fought against it.

2 What is the key principle running through Islam?

3 Why is the Hajj a good example of the multiracial aspect of Islam?

4 'All religious people should fight against racism.' Do you agree? Give reasons for your answer, showing that you have considered other points of view.

Crime and punishment

An individual can break a moral law by lying. Misusing God's name would be breaking a religious law – a sin. Neither constitute a crime unless the state has made a law which forbids such actions. According to the Oxford Dictionary a crime is 'an offence punishable by law'. In order to ensure the smooth running of a society, there has to be some kind of legal system based on laws, law enforcers and punishment. This sounds straight-forward enough, but not everyone agrees with the ways in which crime is interpreted and recorded. More importantly, there is a great deal of controversy concerning the punishments handed out to offenders.

A A letter from Lucien Lawrence, Philip Lawrence's son, highlights the pain and grief caused to a victim's family

> Dear Father christmas,
> I hope you are well and not to cold. I hope you wont think that I am being a nuisance but I have changed my mind what I want for christmas. I wanted to have a telescope but now I want to have my daddy back because without my daddy to help I will not able to see the stars anyway.
> I am the only boy in the family now but I am not wery big and I need my daddy to help me to stop my mummy and sisters from crying.
> love from
> Lucien Lawrence
> age 8

The death of Philip Lawrence, a headmaster murdered just outside his school in 1996 trying to stop one of his students from being attacked, provoked a public outcry concerning what is perceived as the 'state of youth today'.

All the world religions agree that an offender must not be allowed to get away with a crime, but all too often they disagree over the aims of punishment.

The teachings of some religions imply that the punishment should match the crime as closely as possible. Both Muslim and Jewish teachings seem to suggest that revenge is an important aim of punishment, but this can be misleading. The Muslim teaching in **B** emphasises the need for forgiveness and the often quoted Jewish teaching in **C** was designed as a restraint from excessive revenge and punishment.

B Muslim teaching

The recompense [reward] for an injury is an injury equal thereto (in degree); but if a person forgives and makes reconciliation, his reward is due from Allah.

Surah 42:40

C Jewish teaching

If anyone takes the life of a human being, he must be put to death... If anyone injures his neighbor, whatever he has done must be done to him: fracture for fracture, eye for eye, tooth for tooth. As he has injured the other, so he is injured.

Leviticus 24:17, 19–20

D Inmates from Strangeways prison riot because of the poor conditions in prison and alleged brutal treatment

It is important not to misinterpret such sayings. It would be wrong to imply that Islamic or Jewish laws on crime and punishment are unduly harsh. In these societies, these laws are to ensure that not only is justice done, but also that it is seen to be done.

While accepting that any crime which **destabilises** society is viewed seriously, most of the world religions appear to question whether it is ever right to hurt others, no matter what they have done. Buddhists, in particular, try to steer a path between punishment and forgiveness (**E**).

E Buddhist teaching

(Punishment) – the methods used only create more problems, more suffering, more distrust, more resentment, more division. The result is not good for anyone.

The Dalai Lama, Voices of Survival

stop and think!

• Is the Buddhist viewpoint realistic in this day and age?

QUESTIONS

1 What do such headlines tell us about the way in which the media reports crimes?

LIFE FOR THE 'VULTURES' WHO MURDERED

TOWN OF TERROR

2 When passing sentence on an offender, should the court take into account any of the following:

a previous record?
b state of health?
c home background?

d age and gender?
e psychiatric report?

Society faces a problem with some of its members who do not want to adhere to the rules. The aims of punishment are to find a way to deal with criminals and at the same time, protect society and the individual.

Studies suggest that harsh punishments do not always get the best results. Offenders build up resentment towards the 'system', and, when released, try to seek revenge on society. This situation can easily spiral to become a vicious circle (**B**).

Traditionally, punishment has six purposes, and most sentences handed out to offenders are a mixture of several of these.

The aims of

Punishment

1 Deterrence
It is hoped that the punishment will discourage the person from repeating the crime. It is also hoped that the fear of a punishment will stop other individuals from committing crimes.

4 Reform
Punishment should not only stop people from continuing to commit crimes, but should help them to become responsible members of society.

2 Protection
Punishment by locking someone up is a way of protecting society from the anti-social behaviour of some people. Some types of punishment also attempt to protect the offender as well as society.

5 Reparation
If someone breaks the law, they must be prepared to make amends, in other words, pay back something to the victim or to society.

3 Retribution
Based on the idea of an eye for an eye. If someone has done something wrong they should be given a punishment that fits the crime.

6 Vindication
For people to live together the law must be respected and be seen to be just.

A The scales of justice: are they always fair?

It is possible to find elements of these six aims of punishments in most religious teachings. The emphasis is nearly always on protection and reforming the criminal but in western society the remaining aims are often regarded as equally, if not more, important.

stop and think!

- Look at the religious teachings in C and then try to match them up to the six aims of punishment set out on the opposite page.

B Harsh punishment can lead to a vicious circle

1 minor offence

2 harsh punishment

4 major offence

3 revenge

punishment

C Christian and Jewish teachings

Rescue me, O Lord, from evil men; protect me from men of violence. Keep me, O Lord, from the hands of the wicked; protect me from men of violence who plan to trip my feet.

Psalm 140:1, 4

If a man steals an ox or a sheep and slaughters it or sells it, he must pay back five head of cattle for the ox and four sheep for the sheep.

Exodus 22:1

But if there is serious injury, you are to take life for life, eye for eye, tooth for tooth, hand for hand, foot for foot, burn for burn, wound for wound, bruise for bruise.

Exodus 21:23–5

Do not withhold discipline from a child; if you punish him with the rod, he will not die. Punish him with the rod and save his soul from death.

Proverbs 23:13–14

Then all the men of his town shall stone him to death. You must purge the evil from among you. All Israel will hear of it and be afraid.

Deuteronomy 21:21

Appoint judges and officials... and they shall judge the people fairly. Do not pervert justice or show partiality. Do not accept a bribe, for a bribe blinds the eyes of the wise and twists the words of the righteous. Follow justice and justice alone.

Deuteronomy 16:18–20

stop and think!

- What is meant by the term 'vicious circle'?
- When punishing offenders how can we try to minimise their resentment?

Religions and teachings on punishment

All the world religions accept the need to protect individuals from criminals, and urge their followers to lead law-abiding lives. References can be found in many of the religious teachings which emphasise the need to treat people in a humane manner even if they have committed crimes.

All religions accept that, on occasions punishment may have to be given to those who refuse to abide by society's rules. The aims of revenge and retaliation have little place in their teachings. The key aims must centre on reform and protection, and the punishment must distinguish between the demands of justice and the need for forgiveness and mercy (**A**).

Justice is about sorting the innocent from the guilty. If you do not have a fair trial you have what is really just a punishment system. If innocent people are in danger of punishment, or if the punishments are too severe and do not 'fit the crime' there is no real justice (**B**).

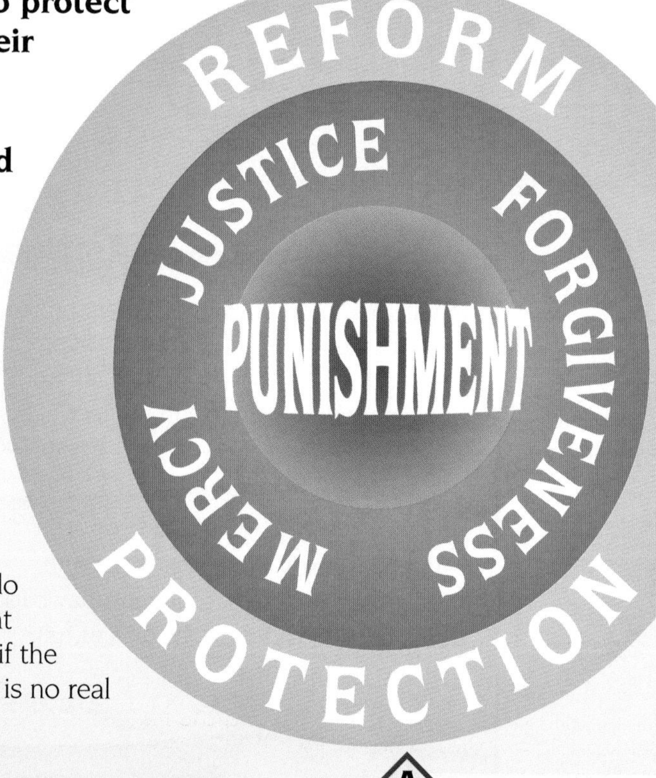

REFORM
JUSTICE
FORGIVENESS
PUNISHMENT
MERCY
PROTECTION

A The aims of punishment

Buddhism

According to the Buddhist view, in order to make a society secure and safe, everyone should have respect for the rights of others to live happily and possess property. Buddhism's approach to crime and punishment is based on the premise that 'prevention is better than cure'. According to Buddhism an individual has to take the responsibility for their own actions. A criminal is a fool (bala) while a law abiding person is wise (pandita). Buddhist teaching is clear about what will happen to those who break the law (**C**).

 B The punishment fits the crime!

 C Buddhist teaching

Here he suffers. Hereafter he suffers. In both states the evildoer (the criminal) suffers. Furthermore he suffers having gone to a woeful state... Therefore should a person commit an evil he should not commit it again and again. He should not find pleasure therein. Painful is the accumulation of evil.

Dhammapada 117

Like most religions, the Buddhist aims of punishment centre on reforming and rehabilitating the criminal to be a good citizen. There should never be any motive of retaliation or revenge.

Islam

The Islamic approach to punishing criminals is not always understood by the western press which often labels it 'barbaric'. There is no separation of religion and state. Islamic law is known as Shari'ah law and is based on teaching in the Qur'an and the Hadith. It controls, rules and regulates all public and private behaviour.

The first and most important element of **Shari'ah** Law is the Qur'an. A second element is known as the Sunnah, the 'way of life' and teachings of the Prophet Muhammad not recorded in the Qur'an. The Sunnah is based upon the sayings of Muhammad which are called Hadith. The Hadiths provide advice on how Muslims should put into practice the teachings set out in the Qur'an. The third element is the Ijma. Religious scholars (Ulamas) can be consulted on an issue and if they reach an agreement it is interpreted as an Ijma. The Qiyas are a fourth element of Shari'ah Law. These are new case laws decided by a judge. For example, a computer crime is not found in the Qur'an or Sunnah so the judge may create a new ruling.

D Muslim teaching

As to the thief, male or female, cut off his or her hands: a punishment by way of example, from Allah, for their crime... But if the thief repents after his crime, and amends his conduct, Allah turns to him in forgiveness.

Surah 5:38–39

The recompense for an injury is an injury equal thereto (in degree): but if a person forgives and makes reconciliation, his reward is due from Allah... indeed if any show patience and forgive, that would truly be an exercise of courageous will and resolution in the conduct of affairs.

Surah 42:40, 43

Religions and teachings on punishment

Under Islamic law all crimes can be broken down into four categories:

Hadud crimes

There are seven crimes (adultery, false accusation, theft, drinking alcohol, rebellion against the state, apostasy and highway robbery) that are regarded as the most serious and have fixed punishments found in the Qur'an. No judge can change or reduce the punishment for these crimes.

Al-Jynayaat crimes (Qisas)

If a person commits a Qisas crime, the victim has a right to ask for revenge. The exact punishment for each Qisas crime is set out in the Qur'an. Punishment can come in many forms and may also include 'Diya' (blood money) paid to the victim or in the case of death, to the victim's family.

Al-Ta'azir crimes

These are less serious crimes which are not part of the Hadud or Qisas but affect the right of the community such as shouting in the street or cheating people. A judge is free to decide on the punishment for the offence.

Al-Mukhalafat

This covers the rights of the State such as breaking the speed limit or parking rules. Again the judge will decide the punishment.

Although Islam may have harsh penalties for certain crimes it teaches that it is always considered better to be charitable and forgive (**D**).

Christianity

Christian views on crime and punishment are greatly influenced by Jesus' teaching on forgiveness and non-violence. He taught that keeping the law was important but what also mattered was what people were like inside. Criminal thoughts were as wrong as the acts themselves. He was critical of people who were quick to judge other people's crimes while ignoring their own (**E**).

In his teachings Jesus set out an ideal. Clearly in today's society, where so many innocent people are harmed by criminal acts, some religious teachings are considered unrealistic, however, many Christians do try to uphold these ideals. For example, after his daughter was killed by an IRA bomb at a Remembrance Day parade in Enniskillen, Northern Ireland, Gordon Wilson appeared on national news to publicly forgive her killers.

Broadly speaking, all the world religions try to balance punishment and forgiveness. The majority would argue that society ideally should reform criminals rather than just punish them.

E Christian teaching

You have heard that it was said, 'Eye for eye, and tooth for tooth.' But I tell you, Do not resist an evil person. If someone strikes you on the right cheek, turn to him the other also.

Matthew 5:38–39

Do not judge, or you too will be judged. For in the same way you judge others, you will be judged, and with the measure you use, it will be measured to you.

Matthew 7:1–2

QUESTIONS

1 What do you understand by:
   a Bala and pandita?
   b Sunnah?
   c Ijma?
   d Qiyas?
   e Hadud and Al-Jynayaat crimes?

2 What punishment would you regard as appropriate in the following cases:
   a rape?
   b football hooliganism?
   c robbery with violence?
   d causing death by reckless driving?
   e kidnapping?
   f blackmail?
   g murder?
   h vandalism?
   i burglary?
   j arson?
   k not paying train fares?
   l manslaughter?

3 'The victim or the victim's family should have more say in the sentencing of the offender.' Do you agree? Give reasons for your answer showing that you have considered different points of view.

The ultimate punishment

A central principle of a just society is that every individual has a right to 'life, liberty and the pursuit of happiness'. It has been accepted for centuries that those individuals who violate this right must pay the ultimate penalty.

The debate about capital punishment for murder is dominated by two views. On the one hand, the murderers must be given the punishment that they deserve, which may be death. On the other hand, similar to the pacifist attitude to war, there is the view that under no circumstances is it possible to justify the use of the death penalty. While the rejection of the death penalty receives strong support from various religious groups, non-believers too propose strong reasons for its abolition.

Arguments for capital punishment

- Society must protect civilians and those who fight crime from individuals who are unable to control their violent impulses.

- Friends and relatives of the victims have a right to expect retribution. In this way, justice is clearly seen to be 'done'.

- Too often, 'life' prisoners are released after a much shorter sentence and can be regarded as a great risk to the community.

- The death penalty is the only sort of deterrent that certain criminals will understand.

- Some criminals would much prefer to be executed than to spend the rest of their lives in prison. In 1977, in the USA, Gary Gilmore opted for death by firing squad rather than face a life sentence in prison. He felt that death was preferable.

stop and think!

- The sanctity of life does not apply in warfare or in some aspects of medical ethics, so why should it apply in punishment?

Arguments against capital punishment

- There have been **miscarriages of justice**: people have been executed for crimes they did not commit, (for example, Timothy Evans and Derek Bentley (see page 216).

- The death penalty does not seem to work as a deterrent: many murders are committed on the spur of the moment, or because of mental illness.

- Certain violent criminals and terrorists, if executed, could be seen as martyrs, and this might provoke extreme action.

- A civilised state should defend life not take it – 'We cannot teach that killing is bad when we ourselves kill'.

- Some countries use the death penalty indiscriminately, to rid a government of its opponents.

- There is a certain lack of fairness seen in the judicial process: minority groups suffer most.

- Capital trials can be lengthy and very costly because of appeals. Juries are also less likely to convict if the death penalty is enforced.

Many countries throughout the world still have capital punishment. Despite the protests of groups such as Amnesty International many American states have the death penalty and others are considering re-introducing it.

 B This horrific photo of an execution by electric chair of a woman was secretly taken by a witness during the 1920s. Public reaction led to several US States banning the death penalty.

DAILY NEWS EXTRA EDITION

New York's Picture Newspaper

New York, Friday, January 13, 1928

DEAD!

Story on page 3

RUTH SNYDER'S DEATH PICTURED!—This is perhaps the most remarkable exclusive picture in the history of criminology. It shows the actual scene in the Sing Sing death house as the lethal current surged through Ruth Snyder's body 11:06 last night. Her helmeted head is stiffened in death, her face masked and an electrode strapped to her bare right leg. The autopsy table on which her body was removed is beside her. Judd Gray, mumbling a prayer, followed her down the narrow corridor at 11:11. "Father, forgive them, for they don't know what they are doing!" were Ruth's last words. The picture is the first Sing Sing execution picture and the first of a woman's electrocution.

 A Amnesty International's view

When the button is pressed, 2,400 volts surge into the body in a 2-minute burst. Doctors wait 10 minutes for the body to cool before examination. If still alive, another 2-minute burst is administered. The final cause of death is usually heart failure.

To make a person sit, day after day, night after night, waiting for the time when he will be led out of his cell to this death is cruel and barbaric... To be a mother or father and watch your child going through this living hell is a torment more painful than anyone can imagine.

 stop and think!

- Do you think that capital punishment has any place in a civilised society? Explain your answer.

215

The ultimate punishment

Until 1828 in Britain, death by hanging was the penalty for over 200 crimes, many of which would now be regarded as minor. People were hanged for trivial offences such as shooting a rabbit, picking pockets and even cutting down a tree in a park!

A number of well publicised cases in the 1950s led to the **abolition** of the death penalty for **murder** in December 1969, although technically it could still be used in cases of **treason** or **piracy**.

Timothy Evans (**C**) was given a full **posthumous** pardon when it was proved that he did not murder his wife. Evans was slightly mentally retarded and easily influenced by Dr John Reginald Christie who was a lodger in his house. Not realising how serious a 'confession' would be, Evans informed the police that he had murdered his wife. He believed he would be in trouble with the police because he had allowed his wife to undergo an abortion (then illegal) at the hands of Christie. Christie acted as the chief witness against Evans but he, in turn, later confessed to the murders of seven women, including Mrs Evans, and was found guilty and hanged.

C Timothy Evans, just after his arrest

Derek Bentley (**D**) was hanged for the shooting of a policeman by his 16-year-old accomplice, Christopher Craig. Bentley was already under arrest and was being led away by police officers when Craig opened fire and killed a police officer. Despite this, and the fact that Bentley had a low mental age, he was executed because in the eyes of the law he was of adult age and was an accomplice to murder. The jury recommended mercy but, in spite of a petition to the Queen, he was executed, Craig escaped the death penalty by being under age. After a long campaign, Bentley was granted a posthumous pardon. His trial and conviction was seen as 'a **travesty** of justice' even by the standards of 1953.

In November 1998 Britain joined the ranks of 'fully abolitionist' countries and on 20 May 1999 the Government made an international commitment to the permanent abolition of the death penalty when it accepted Protocol 6 of the European Convention on Human Rights. Protocol 6 is an international human rights treaty which commits a government to the permanent abolition of the death penalty.

D The grave of Derek Bentley

Islam

In Islamic law, there are at least three crimes which carry the death penalty: murder, adultery and apostasy (abandoning your faith). It is vital that the question of guilt is clear before a sentence is carried out, and only the proper authorities can implement the law prescribed by the Shari'ah (**E**).

With accusations of adultery, at least four witnesses to the actual act must be provided: this will rarely be possible. If the accuser fails to prove their case, he or she can be severely punished for slander. A freely given confession repeated four times in court would be acceptable proof in place of the witnesses.

It should be remembered that in an Islamic state, Islam *is* the state, and therefore any act of apostasy which leads to open rebellion against Islam, is an act of treason. Even in Britain, until 1999, it was still possible, technically, to be executed for high treason.

stop and think!

From 1931 to 1956 Alfert Pierrepoint was Britain's official executioner. No one could be better placed to comment on the use of the death penalty.

'Executions are only an antiquated relic of a primitive desire for revenge which takes the easy way and hands over the responsibility for revenge to other people.'

Alfred Pierrepoint, *The Independent*, 16 February 1991

- What does Pierrepoint mean by 'the easy way'?
- Would you ever send a mentally retarded person to prison?

Throughout all the teachings of the world religions there is an emphasis on the need for care to be taken when handing out punishment. Jesus pointed out to his followers how quick people are to criticise others while ignoring their own faults (**F**).

Similar sentiments can be found in the Qur'an (**E**).

Buddhists believe that punishment serves a purpose in protecting society from criminals but draws the line on harsh penalties, in particular, the death penalty. The teachings always emphasise the aim of reforming criminals (**G**).

E Muslim teaching

Take not life, which Allah hath made sacred, except by way of justice and law.

Surah 6:151

If Allah were to punish men for their wrongdoing, He would not leave, on the earth, a single living creature.

Surah 16:61

F Christian teaching

… Jesus said to them, 'If any one of you is without sin, let him be the first to throw a stone at her.'… Jesus straightened up and asked her, 'Woman, where are they? Has no one condemned you?'
'No one, sir,' she said.
'Then neither do I condemn you,' Jesus declared. 'Go now and leave your life of sin.'

John 8:7–11

G Buddhist teaching

No matter how evilly someone behaves they always have the possibility of correcting their behaviour. To deny that possibility of change by imposing the death penalty, for example, is to contradict the whole spirit of Buddhism.
Human Rights from a Buddhist Perspective,
James Belither

QUESTIONS

1 Are the Christian and Buddhist viewpoints (**F** and **G**) realistic in this day and age?

2 'A man reaps what he sows.' (Galatians 6:7)
   a In what way does this quote appear to contradict the Christian teaching in **F**?
   b Which religious teachings are more in line with this saying?

3 '…The avenger of blood shall put the murderer to death when he meets him.' (Numbers 35:21) Why must we take care when we use such quotes to support a case for or against the death penalty?

1 What are three possible views about war that a religion might adopt?

2 What does the word 'jihad' literally mean?

3 Which Christian denomination totally opposes war? Why?

4 What was the attitude of the early Christians towards war?

5 What are conscientious objectors?

6 Describe, explain and analyse:

a the differences between a holy war and a just war.

b Christian and Muslim attitudes to war and conflict.

7 **a** Can you think of any problems which a country might face in attempting to meet all seven conditions for a just war?

b Do you think these conditions can be applied to a modern day conflict?

c Could they be applied in the scenario of a nuclear war? Give reasons for your answer.

8 Choose one religious tradition. Outline teachings which might help a religious believer to decide whether fighting a war is right or wrong.

9 Why are religions often accused of creating divisions and encouraging prejudice and discrimination?

10 Choose two different religious traditions and outline the teachings of each about prejudice and discrimination.

11 'By sending their children to religious schools, some religious believers are encouraging their children to be prejudiced against others.'

Do you agree? Give reasons for your answer, showing that you have thought about more than one point of view.

12 Explain how members of ethnic minorities might experience prejudice.

13 Explain how religious teachings might be used to overcome racial prejudice.

14 Outline the six main aims of punishment.

15 In England and Wales, criminal responsibility begins at the age of 10 years old. Is it right that children under this age cannot be prosecuted for criminal acts?

16 What are the two key aims of punishment set out by all the main world religions?

17 What are the four key elements of Shari'ah Law?

18 What are the seven crimes regarded as the most serious under Islamic law?

19 What are Al-Ta'azir crimes?

20 List all the different arguments for and against capital punishment. In your opinion which arguments are the strongest? Explain your choices.

21 In Islamic law murderers can be executed. However, the relatives of the victim can sometimes choose compensation from the killer rather than demand their death. A victim's family can at times be asked by a Muslim court to decide the murderer's fate by choosing between execution, compensation or freedom.

a Do you think it is a good idea to give the family of a victim the choice of punishment?

b Write down what you see as the advantages and disadvantages of such a system.

22 What new teachings did Jesus add to those in the Old Testament about the law and the way the criminal should be treated?

Points to remember

This book has been written to help you think about some of the major issues facing our world and how religious beliefs and teachings influence these issues. Whether you are using *One World: Many Issues* as part of a GCSE RE/PSE course or as part of a general RE/PSE course, we hope you find the book interesting and helpful. In writing this book there are four specific things we want you to remember.

- What you think is important and matters. We want to encourage you to think for yourself and to consider the different viewpoints and arguments which exist in the various issues you are studying.

- *One World: Many Issues* is about the place of religion in today's world, especially what differing religions have to say about contemporary problems and concerns. Whether you think religion is a force for good or bad in the world, there is no doubt it remains an important presence (if you disagree with this, then just watch the news for a week; it will be very surprising if religion does not feature).

- *One World: Many Issues* is designed to help you think about moral decisions and how we make moral choices (morals are often spoken of as making choices between right and wrong). When we make a moral choice (for example, finding some money in the street gives us a moral choice of: a) leaving the money, b) picking it up and keeping it, and c) picking it up and handing it in), there are all kinds of factors which influence our thinking. These include our conscience, our reasoning (thinking about the consequences of our actions), our family and friends. Within the world of religion there are other important factors, such as relevant teachings from sacred texts, tradition, and teachings from leaders of the religion today. Many of the major problems facing our world today were unknown at the time that some sacred texts were written. For example, the Bible does not directly speak about nuclear warfare or the ozone layer, but many Christians would say it does provide guidance on how we should care for our world and treat one another as human beings.

- Not everyone within an individual religion believes exactly the same things or practises their beliefs in the same way. This is especially true when thinking about religion and modern problems. If you asked a hundred Christians about their views on abortion, you would probably get a range of responses ranging from those who would say it could be right in certain circumstances, for example, if the pregnancy was caused by rape, to those who would say it could never be right. It is helpful to avoid phrases like 'all Jews believe that…' and it is important to recognise that there is diversity of belief, practice and viewpoints within the religions you are studying.

Ten examination tips

1 Make sure that you understand the layout and structure of your exam paper and how many questions you have to do. Every year, there are some students who attempt every single question on the entire paper when they only had to do four questions. Doing too much means your answers will be rushed and will not have the depth you need.

2 Remember that your exam in RE, no matter how good your general knowledge, is about the issues your course has covered. You must know about the key beliefs, practices and teachings from the religions you have studied and how these can be applied to the issues you have discussed.

3 An important part of the examination is the evaluation element. This is where you have the opportunity to share your views and ideas on the issues you have studied. Often, students do badly in this part of the examination because they do not develop their ideas fully enough. For example, on capital punishment, a response might be that it is wrong because you can kill an innocent person. However, if that is the only reason given, it can only score 1 mark. The other main reason for students doing poorly is that they might only present points from one side of the argument. On euthanasia, for example, a student might produce several reasons why he or she is against it, but show no evidence of being aware of the reasons why some people are for it. The really good answer is where a student clearly supports his or her own view with a range of reasoned arguments, and also shows a good awareness of other people's points of view.

4 Look carefully at how much each part of a question is worth. Avoid writing a long paragraph for a question worth only 1 or 2 marks but be aware that a question worth 10 marks will need a lot more than two or three sentences.

5 Make sure you know exactly how long you can spend on each question. If the exam is $1\frac{1}{2}$ hours and you have to do five questions, then that is eighteen minutes maximum per question. If you spend five minutes longer on the first four questions, you will have no time to answer the fifth question at all (so losing all the marks for that question).

6 If you have a choice of questions then exercise your choice carefully. Some students see the first part of a question, think they can answer it and rush into their response. They then realise they cannot do the other part of the question, and wish they had chosen another question. A few minutes careful reading before selecting your questions is vital.

7 Have an effective revision plan and stick to it. With *One World: Many Issues* you might find it helpful to make your own notes at the end of each unit, so that you can recall these when you need to. Remember that you cannot recall what you have never learnt in the first place.

8 Try to extend your reading. Magazines, newspapers, libraries and CD-ROMs all contain valuable information which can help you in your learning. Writing to organisations can greatly help you with coursework (but always enclose an SAE).

9 Try to stay focused on your work. Examination times can be hectic and stressful, and it is unlikely that you will ever take so many exams again in such a short period of time! If you can sacrifice some of your social life for a while and commit yourself to your work, it will help you improve your performance.

10 With coursework, be realistic about how much you can do. If you have been told an assignment should be about 1,000 words, then try to stick to this. Make sure your assignment allows you to use both your knowledge and understanding of the religions you have studied, and your own views and ideas.

Glossary

AAT	'Alpha-1-antitrypsin' – used to treat people with emphysema (lung disease) and cystic fibrosis
abolition	The enforced ending of something
agnostic	An individual who believes that we cannot know for sure that God exists
AIDS	'Acquired Immune Deficiency Syndrome' – a medical condition
Allah	Muslim name for God in the Arabic language
annulment	Roman Catholic declaration that a marriage bond never existed
Apartheid	The name given to the system adopted by the South African government (between 1948 and 1994) of segregation or discrimination on grounds of race
Apostles' Creed	The oldest and most important statement of belief in the Christian Church
arranged/assisted marriage	The selection of marriage partners organised by the parents or relatives
atheist	An individual who does not believe that God exists
'backstreet'	The term used to describe an illegal act
banishment	A punishment where offenders were sent abroad for a certain amount of time
battery farming	Intensive breeding and rearing of animals
Buddha	Title meaning 'awakened'; applied to Siddharta Gautama, the founder of Buddhism
calligraphy	Beautiful writing; used as an art form, especially by Muslims
chador	Muslim term for a large piece of cloth, worn by women to leave only the face exposed
chaos	Total and utter confusion
chromosomes	Structures that carry the inherited genetic information that influences the growth and functioning of the entire body
civil	A legal marriage without a religious ceremony
conscience	An inner feeling which tells us what is right and wrong
conscientious objector	An individual who refuses to fight in a war because of his beliefs
contraception	Methods used by couples to avoid pregnancy
curative	Tending to cure, heal or make better
derogatory	Insulting or offensive
destabilise	Disrupt or upset
destitute	A person who is without shelter and poverty stricken

detrimental	Harmful or damaging
diabetes	A medical disorder caused by a lack of insulin
diminished responsibility	Legal defence term used in murder cases meaning a person was not responsible for their actions
discrimination	Prejudice in action – unfair treatment of an individual or group
DNA	'Deoxyribonucleic Acid' – carrier of all genetic information present in nearly all living organisms
dominant	One who controls or has power over another
Down's Syndrome	Medical abnormality which leads to mental handicap and a characteristic physical appearance
dukkha	First of the Four Noble Truths – Buddhist term relating to suffering
eternal	Always existing; with no beginning and no end
ethics	Moral principles; rules of conduct and behaviour
Evangelical	A group within Christianity that believes faith, studying the Bible and learning about the religion are more important than ceremonies
excommunicate	Exclude or refuse to be allowed as a member of the Church
extinct	No longer in existence
fertile	Able to have children
free range	Animals allowed to roam and graze freely
free will	The ability to choose for ourselves whether to perform good or evil acts
fundamentalist	Someone who holds extremely strictly to their beliefs
gene therapy	The attempt to replace defective/faulty genes in order to combat human diseases.
genetic engineering	The process of changing the make up of living organisms
geometry	Mathematical arrangement of objects or parts
gospel	Literally means 'good news' a. The name given to the first four books of the New Testament b. Refers also to the Christian 'message' of salvation
Gurdwara	Sikh place of worship. Literally the 'doorway to the Guru'.
Hebrew	A community that was to become Israel
hijab	Muslim term meaning modesty in dress

HIV	The abbreviation for Human Immunodeficiency Virus which gradually destroys the body's natural defence mechanisms and can develops into AIDS
Humanist	A non-religious person who believes in the importance of living life fully for the welfare of others
idolatry	The worship of idols
immanent	To be present in the world or the universe
impersonal	Distant, unknowable and mysterious
incest	Sexual intercourse between individuals who are too closely related to marry each other
infant mortality rate	The number of children dying before reaching the age of one year
infidels	People with no religious beliefs; in the past, a term used to describe any non-Christian
infinite	Not limited in any way; endless
Insulin	Hormone that regulates the amount of glucose in the blood; an imbalance of it causes diabetes
Jain	A member of an East Indian sect, established about the sixth century BCE, which is committed to never harming a living being
Judiciary	Court of law
karma	Literally 'actions'. Law followed by Buddhists, Hindus and Sikhs; the results of one's actions determines the nature of future rebirth
manslaughter	Legal term for the unlawful killing of a person – either unintended or where there is a reason which will be taken into account
martyr	Someone who dies for their faith or beliefs
materialistic	Preferring material possessions and physical comforts which are linked to financial success
miscarriage of justice	When someone has been unfairly accused and punished for a crime they did not commit
monogamy	The practice of being married to one person at a time
morality	Accepted rules and standards of behaviour
mourning	Expression of sorrow following the death of a person
murder	The illegal, deliberate killing of another person
nirvana	Buddhist term meaning state of secure, perfect peace
non-sentient	A being that is incapable of sensation and does not respond to stimulation

oestrogen	Hormone produced naturally in women, which, when taken daily in the contraceptive pill, prevents egg development
omnipotent	All powerful
omniscient	All knowing
Orthodox	a. Someone who accepts the established traditions of a particular religion b. Orthodox Church – one of the three main branches of the Christian Church
pagans	Those who do not belong to one of the main world religions
personal	Close, directly concerned with the feelings and needs of people
piracy	Robbery or hijacking of ships at sea
polygamy	The practice of having more than one husband or wife at the same time
population explosion	The sudden sharp increase in population in certain countries
pornography	The viewing/reading of explicit sexual matters
posthumous	Occurring after death
prejudice	'Pre-judging' a situation or a person; an unjustified dislike
progestogen	Reproductive hormone produced naturally in women, which, when taken daily in the contraceptive pill, prevents ovulation
Psalms	Book in the Old Testament containing sacred songs or hymns
qawwali	Religious poetry set to music, especially in Sufism
Rabbinic	Relating to the opinions and teachings of rabbis or to the Jewish law
reconciliation	A reunion between parties in disagreement; settling of an argument
Reform	Jews who do not accept a number of the traditional observances of Orthodox Judaism
reincarnation	The belief in the rebirth of the spirit/soul in a new body
repent	To feel sorry for having done something and willing to start again or change a past action
resurrection	The central Christian belief that Christ rose from the dead
sacred	Connected with religion or used for a religious purpose

sacrificial	Describing something valued that is given up for the sake of something else more important or worthy
sanctified	Someone or something that is set apart or regarded as holy
secular	Not religious
secularist	Not concerned with religion
sentient	A being that is conscious, capable of sensation, responsive to stimulation
Shari'ah	Islamic law – the 'way' of the Prophet
spiritual	Concerned and inspired by sacred or religious things
stereotype	An over-simplified or exaggerated picture of people or situations
steward	An individual appointed to keep order and look after another's property
stigma	A psychological mark, or sign of disgrace or discredit
subordinate	Someone who is lower in rank or under orders from another
Sufism	A Muslim mystical sect, differing in dress and customs
suicide	The intentional taking of one's own life
Sunnah	Model practices, customs and traditions of the Prophet Muhammad
surrogacy	When one woman bears a child on behalf of another woman
taboo	A forbidden subject
Tenakh	The collected 24 books of the Jewish Bible made up of three sections Torah, Neviim and Ketuvim (Te; Na; Kh)
terminal	Ending in death
theist	A believer in the existence of gods or a God
theory of evolution	The view, normally associated with the work of Charles Darwin, that the human race evolved developed from earlier, primitive forms of life
transcendent	Existing 'outside or beyond the created world or universe', not limited to space or time
transgenic	An animal/plant having genetic material introduced from another species
travesty	Something that is totally unfair or unjust
treason	Attempting to kill or overthrow the ruling body of a country

vagrancy	The state of having no place to live or regular work
vegan	An individual who refuses to eat or use any animal products
vegetarian	An individual who will not eat animal meat but may eat dairy products
Yemenite	Originating from the Republican of Yemen
Zakah	One of the Five Pillars of Islam – tax on income to provide money for the less fortunate